COUNCIL OF EUROPE

CONSEIL DE L'EUROPE

# DEVELOPMENT EDUCATION

WITHDRAWN

**Cassell Council of Europe series**

This series is the result of a collaboration between the Council of Europe and Cassell. It comprises books on a wide range of educational material, drawn largely from seminars and research which have been initiated and sponsored by the Council of Europe.

# DEVELOPMENT EDUCATION

## Global Perspectives
## in the Curriculum

*Edited by Audrey Osler*

CASSELL

Cassell
Villiers House
41/47 Strand
London WC2N 5JE

387 Park Avenue South
New York
NY 10016–8810

First published 1994

**British Library Cataloguing-in-Publication Data**
A catalogue record for this book is available from the British Library.

ISBN: 0–304–32567–8 (hardback)
     0–304–32565–1 (paperback)

Typeset by Litho Link Ltd, Welshpool, Powys.
Printed and bound in Great Britain by Redwood Books, Trowbridge, Wiltshire.

# Contents

CONTENTS

# List of Contributors

Ingrid Abrahams-Lyncook is a teacher of Religious Education at Holy Trinity School, Birmingham.

Adrian Blackledge is Senior Lecturer at Westhill College, Birmingham.

Fionnuala Brennan is Director of the Development Education Support Centre, Dublin.

Anne Helms is a teacher of English and Religion at Mulernes Legatskole, a Gymnasium-School in Odense.

John Hopkin is Senior Advisory Teacher for Geography, Birmingham.

Liisa Jääskeläinen is Senior Adviser in Environmental and International Education at the National Board of Education, Helsinki.

Chris Leach is Headteacher of Boulton Primary School, Birmingham.

Solveig Lindberg was formerly a teacher of English at Katedralskolan in Turku.

Catherine McFarlane is Projects Co-ordinator at Development Education Centre, Birmingham.

Catherine Midwinter leads curriculum development projects at Development Education Project, Manchester.

Alfred Ojwang is Co-ordinator of *Pied Crow* magazine, CARE-Kenya, Nairobi.

Martin O'Shaughnessy is Senior Lecturer in Modern Languages at Nottingham Trent University.

Audrey Osler is Lecturer in Education at the University of Birmingham.

Scott Sinclair is Director of Development Education Centre, Birmingham.

Hugh Starkey is Principal Lecturer at Westminster College, Oxford.

Maitland Stobart is Deputy Director of Education, Culture and Sport, Council of Europe.

Margaretha Thyr is a former elementary school teacher currently working for Save the Children (Sweden).

André Zweyacker is General Inspector at the Ministry of Education, Paris and President of the French Federation of Unesco Clubs.

# Foreword

'Our education systems should encourage all young Europeans to see themselves not only as citizens of their own regions and countries, but also as citizens of Europe and of the wider world.' This recommendation by the Council of Europe's Committee of Ministers summarizes our organization's approach to education for international understanding, and, to help schools and teachers to carry out this challenging task, we have examined how global problems and other parts of the world are presented in schools in Europe. This was done at a series of 20 teachers' seminars, which involved over 1,000 European teachers, representatives of other international institutions (in particular UNICEF and Unesco), specialists from non-governmental organizations, and educators from other continents. Audrey Osler, the editor of the present volume, was one of the experts who helped the Council of Europe to bring about this ambitious pooling of innovation and good practice, and we are grateful to her and the other contributors for sharing their experience and ideas with colleagues in other countries.

Our seminars pointed out that, in spite of its present economic problems, Europe is a privileged part of the world in terms of health, nutrition, education, social services and industrial development. They argued, therefore, that 'Europe has a moral duty to work for greater social justice in other regions and for a balanced sharing of the world's resources'. On the other hand, they recognized that Europe is dependent on other continents, and they stressed that, if Europe is to compete successfully in world markets, its citizens will need a global vision, sophisticated intercultural skills, and a knowledge of non-European languages.

Schools are, of course, not the only source of information and opinion on global issues and other cultures, and the mass media, in particular television, have increased the speed with which we learn about the world, as well as the scope of what we learn about it. Nevertheless, schools have a special role to play because they can provide young people with the intellectual tools to use information in a vigorous and responsible way, and help them to understand the complexity of global issues, accept cultural diversity, dispel stereotypes and avoid a 'headline mentality'.

In the time available in schools, it is clearly impossible for young people to learn about all countries and all world problems, and curriculum planners and teachers are thus faced with difficult questions of defining criteria for the selection of content. As this book shows, it may be necessary to use examples or case studies to illustrate such broad themes as industrialization, migration, urbanization, tourism, cultural diversity, regionalism and national identity. A set of key concepts can provide a helpful framework for the selection of these themes and topics. It should include: peace; justice; human rights and democracy; solidarity; sharing and co-operation; interdependence; development and change; continuity; conflict; resources; diversity and similarity; and cultural identity. Care should be taken to establish a proper balance between political and economic topics on the one hand and cultural, artistic and spiritual ones on the other. Teachers should also avoid an undue emphasis on disaster, suffering and poverty because such emphasis can leave young people with feelings of helplessness and pessimism.

Extra-curricular activities can reinforce, in a significant way, formal teaching about other countries and cultures, and many schools in Europe have established direct contacts with schools in other parts of the world through twinnings and correspondence by letter or audio-cassette. More recently, the new communication technologies have been used to open windows on the world with the help of electronic mail, faxes, tele-conferencing, and even satellite relays. Furthermore, non-governmental organizations like Oxfam, Médecins sans frontières and Brot für die Welt can provide examples of successful campaigns for North–South solidarity, while the idealism of young people can find a practical outlet in such activities as fund-raising for development projects or emergency appeals.

Many schools in Europe have become, in fact, 'international schools' because of immigration and migration, and in their classes are young people of different nationalities, cultures, religions and races.

In 1988, the Council of Europe and the European Communities organized the European Public Campaign for North–South Interdependence and Solidarity. This led the Council of Europe to set up, in Lisbon, a European Centre for Global Interdependence and Solidarity. Its main task is to raise public awareness in Europe of global interdependence, and it holds workshops and seminars on global education, North–South training courses and major international colloquies on global issues. In 1992, as a contribution to the United Nations 'Earth Summit' in Rio de Janeiro, the Centre organized a special campaign to increase public understanding of the relationship between development and the environment. In 1994, it will co-ordinate another project called 'People on the Move', which will focus on people, population and migration.

In the past few years, there have been disquieting cases of xenophobia and racism in most European countries, and the problem of intolerance was one of the main items on the agenda of the first Summit of the Heads of State and Government of the Council of Europe's member States, which was held in Vienna last October. The Summit expressed alarm at the development of a climate of intolerance in Europe and the increase in acts of violence against migrants and people of immigrant origin. To counter these manifestations of intolerance, which 'threaten democratic societies and their fundamental values', the Summit decided that the Council of Europe should launch a broad European campaign 'to mobilize the public in favour of a tolerant society based on the equal dignity of all its members and against manifestations of racism, xenophobia, anti-semitism and intolerance'. The campaign will culminate in 1995, which has been proclaimed the International Year of Tolerance by the United Nations. The present handbook is a practical contribution to this campaign because Audrey Osler and her colleagues show how development education can help young people to acquire the skills, attitudes and intercultural understanding which they will need as 'citizens of Europe and of the wider world'.

*Maitland Stobart*
*Deputy Director of Education, Culture and Sport*
*Council of Europe*

# Introduction: The Challenges of Development Education

*Audrey Osler*

> Development education is concerned with issues of human rights, dignity, self-reliance, and social justice in both developed and developing countries. It is concerned with the causes of underdevelopment and the promotion of an understanding of what is involved in development, of how different countries go about undertaking development, and of the reasons for and ways of achieving a new international economic and social order.
>
> (United Nations, 1975)

What is your definition of development education? A number of the writers in this book (quite properly) asked this question when they were first approached to make a contribution. My reluctance to give them a precise answer stemmed from the knowledge that definitions of development education vary so much from country to country, and that they continue to be revised as our understanding of development evolves. A narrow definition might have acted as a strait-jacket to individual creativity.

Nevertheless, the above 1975 UN definition (quoted in Hicks and Townley, 1982: 9 and referred to by a number of contributors) is useful in that it highlights human rights and social justice as the values upon which development education should be based. It also recognizes the importance of addressing development processes in both 'developed' and 'developing' countries. Development education can address these processes at local, national, regional and global levels. Such an approach should encourage North–South solidarity: a recognition that we live in an interdependent world, and that the future of our planet depends on co-operation between North and South to produce common action on common problems.

The UN definition does not exclude questions about the processes of education, since an education which focuses on issues of human rights, dignity, self-reliance and social justice must necessarily encourage students to reflect on these issues in their own lives. This clearly has implications for classroom methodology as the teacher seeks to develop in students the skills and attitudes which will encourage these values. Most importantly, development education encourages the linking of ideas with *action for change* and a radical approach to the issues we all face, working for 'a new international social and economic order'. Indeed it is educators from the South, such as Freire (1972) and Nyerere (1973), who, stressing the importance of educational processes, community participation and a forging of theory with practice, have inspired much of the learning methodology in development education.

Our understanding of development, and consequently the emphases in development education, have changed considerably over the last 20 years. International aid agencies working in the South now recognize the central role of women in development processes, and development educators in both North and South have given gender issues a more prominent place in their work. Similarly, we have, over the last decade, become aware of the close relationship between environment and development, with environmentalists and development educators working closely together.

In 1987 the Brundtland Commission published its report, *Our Common Future*, which called for 'sustainable development' – progress which meets the needs of the present while not compromising the ability of future generations to meet their needs. Questions of development were now firmly linked with questions of the environment, and environmental and development education became inextricable partners: environmental issues now feature in development education programmes, and environmental education has, of necessity, adopted a global perspective.

Gro Harlem Brundtland (1992) reminds us that

> one cannot 'save the environment' without profoundly changing some basic human activities: the way people govern themselves; the way these governments co-operate, the way people trade and do business; the ways in which energy, food and timber are produced; and the rates at which our species reproduces itself.

She further notes that prerequisites for such development include 'democracy and freedom of information, as people cannot change their ways without being involved in decisions over those changes'.

Any programme of education for development should clearly form part of a broad programme of political education. If we are to work for 'a new international economic and social order' it is important that we understand the social and economic power structures in our own communities, at national and regional as well as at global levels.

Political literacy and economic awareness are key areas in development education, and schools need to prepare their students with the necessary knowledge and skills to address social, economic and political questions within development processes at a appropriate level. Many of these issues have been built into the education agenda of a number of European countries. In 1985 the ministers of education of the member states of the Council of Europe adopted Recommendation R(85)7 acknowledging that

> throughout their school career, all young people should learn about human rights as part of their preparation for life in a pluralistic democracy.

While different governments have shown varying degrees of commitment in translating this recommendation into practice, none of them would dispute the principle that education in human rights and preparation for democracy are important educational goals. Similarly, they would acknowledge the continued importance of environmental education.

However, the Brundtland Commission also called for a redefinition of the concept of 'security' to include environmental security, noting that there can be 'no sustainable development in a world that spent $1,000 billion a year – and half of research and development budgets – on the military' (Brundtland, 1992).

While over 100 heads of state received *Our Common Future* and none of these seriously disagreed with its logic, the call for disarmament is low on the political agenda, and a discussion of the arms trade has not featured as a central issue for development educators in the 1980s and early 1990s. Peace education may have become unfashionable in many places, but the incidence of war and conflict has not declined and issues of security and development remain as pertinent as ever.

# THE CONTEXT OF DEVELOPMENT EDUCATION

The first part of this book is entitled 'The Changing Context of Development Education'. This part looks back over the history of the development education movement and identifies the broad challenges that face development educators today. In the first chapter Hugh Starkey reflects on the relationship between development education and human rights education. Tracing the history of development education, he argues that human rights values are international values which should form the basis of all education, but that they are especially valuable in development education as 'local, national and exclusive religious or secular formulations of values are inadequate when the topic is global responsibility and intercultural understanding'.

The second chapter discusses popular notions of citizenship in the context of a post-imperial Europe. It explores the relationship between multicultural, or more precisely intercultural and anti-racist, education and development education. Education for development needs a historical perspective, but it must, by its very nature, look to the future. Tragically, racism and inter-ethnic conflict remain acute problems for many societies in this last decade of the twentieth century. In an interdependent world, it is critical that we address these issues with young people in school. Development education has an important role to play in contributing to a new broader, more inclusive understanding of active citizenship, which acknowledges the global responsibilities of individuals and communities.

The success of development education has been largely dependent on the work of non-governmental organizations (NGOs). In the final chapter in Part I Scott Sinclair examines the role of NGOs in the UK and the contribution they have made to development education in schools. He raises questions about the relationship between NGOs and organizations in the formal sector of education and reviews various strategies that have been adopted, particularly the implications of NGOs working in partnership with teachers. He argues that NGOs, operating with limited resources, have tended to underestimate their own potential, but warns that continued effectiveness in a period of rapid educational change demands clarity of purpose and a willingness to review methods and styles of work.

# DESIGNING A GLOBAL CURRICULUM

In the second part four writers reflect on curriculum development and the meaning of a global curriculum. John Hopkin and Martin O'Shaughnessy look at the contribution of two traditional subject areas: geography, which for many people would seem to be the most obvious area in which to focus on development education; and modern language teaching, which has tremendous potential for creative work in this field. John Hopkin examines school geography textbooks and the ways in which they reflect changing models of development, looking particularly at recently published texts designed to meet the requirements of the new UK geography National Curriculum. Research in the late 1970s and early 1980s found that textbooks of that period frequently reinforced stereotyped and biased images of the peoples and countries of the South. Today's textbooks are compared with these earlier resources and an examination made of the current world-views presented to pupils in the lower secondary school.

Martin O'Shaughnessy also looks at resources, arguing that modern-language teachers have a unique contribution to make to development education, and that they have available to them some exciting materials; he offers practical strategies for adapting these to meet the needs of language learners and increase their motivation. Since the principal value of languages lies in the access they offer to other peoples and cultures, and since many of the languages most commonly studied in Europe are widely used in the South, they can deepen pupils' insights of distant places. He reminds us that: 'Development issues should never be considered in a way which is divorced from their human and cultural context; language teaching can help establish this context and permit a direct dialogue between individuals.'

In her chapter, Catherine Midwinter presents us with a media studies curriculum development project designed to encourage teachers and their pupils to examine ways in which the media creates, reaffirms or challenges images of the peoples and countries of the South and North. The chapter reviews the research into media portrayals of the South, and particularly of Africa, and the impact of these representations on children. She discusses Southern perspectives on these issues, noting that a number of Africans involved in development education felt that 'misinformation about Africa in Europe was essentially a European problem'. The findings of this research clearly have implications for development educators, and for all teachers concerned with equipping their students with the skills to actively participate in an interdependent world; most particularly they have implications for the education of teachers. The chapter analyses strategies for teaching about the media developed for an in-service course.

Media studies may be timetabled in some secondary schools; in a number it forms part of language studies, while others may have adopted a cross-curricular approach. Chris Leach, writing from the perspective of a deputy headteacher in a primary school, discusses how development education can be introduced across a whole school community to enhance the quality of education offered to children. The chapter outlines how development education, as an approach to learning and teaching, can provide a framework in which teachers can work together to bring about curriculum change, empowering both teachers and pupils. Recognizing that such an approach may challenge established views about teaching and learning, he describes how one school has set about creating a global curriculum while at the same time meeting the demands of a heavily prescriptive National Curriculum. The curriculum he advocates is global, not only in the sense that it examines global issues and relates them to the experiences of the children but also in that it encompasses all aspects of school life, including classroom practice, management approaches, school policy and ethos, and the formal curriculum.

# CASE STUDIES IN DEVELOPMENT EDUCATION

The case studies in the third part of ths book confirm that development education is perceived in a variety of ways in different countries while reaffirming that development education, in both its processes and themes, has strong common elements in diverse places.

These case studies are written from a variety of perspectives, those of classroom practitioners, development educators within NGOs and in governmental organizations. They describe curriculum initiatives in primary and secondary schools on a variety of scales; curriculum innovation led by individual teachers, by groups of teachers within one school or across several institutions, or at national and international levels. A number of these initiatives are ones which have been based on partnerships, partnerships between teachers and learners as well as partnerships between NGOs and the formal sector.

Margaretha Thyr, working as a class teacher in a Swedish middle school, and

5

Ingrid Abrahams-Lyncook, working as a teacher of religious education in a UK secondary school, describe two different approaches to organizing cross-curricular work. Both teachers draw on the immediate environment of their pupils to explore development processes, the UK project focusing on issues of social justice and the Swedish one on a broader range of issues relating to development processes as students traced the origins of their local stream, studying issues relating to local industry, the effects of development on the natural environment and issues of defence, arms and peace.

This is a theme developed by Anne Helms, a teacher of English and religion in a Danish gymnasium-school. Working initially on her own, and later with a network of teachers concerned about peace, she describes how she has developed this theme, and has sought to engage the interest of her students in issues that they often perceive to be either outdated or irrelevant. She raises a number of important points about teaching controversial issues.

Fionnuala Brennan and Alfred Ojwang both describe initiatives designed to introduce development education in primary schools. The Irish initiative was a relatively small-scale pilot study, funded and supported by the government, to encourage primary school teachers to introduce a global perspective in the curriculum, and where possible, adopt participatory teaching methods. Alfred Ojwang provides a contrasting case study of development education in Kenya: *Pied Crow* magazine is designed as curriculum support material for use in Kenyan primary schools, to raise awareness and encourage local action on a broad range of development and environmental issues. The project is an excellent example of partnership: partnership between a group of Kenyan educationalists and an international aid agency; between the project team and the Ministry of Education; and a developing partnership between the project and the schools, children and teachers which it seeks to support.

In her analysis of a study visit to Kenya and Tanzania by a group of UK primary teachers Catherine McFarlane also examines an example of partnership, this time between a small NGO and the participating teachers. She discusses some general issues concerning visits by people from the North to the South, and reflects on the contribution that such visits can make both in raising the awareness of teachers to development on a personal level and as preparation for teaching about such issues.

While the main focus of this book is on the contribution that development education can make to the formal curriculum of schools, it is clear that it can take place in a variety of settings. André Zweyacker discusses the work of Unesco Clubs in France, and shows how the engagement of young people in extra-curricular activities can be an effective way of establishing partnerships between North and South and advancing understanding of development issues.

Adrian Blackledge discusses the common aims and objectives of anti-racist education and development education. He reviews various policies developed in the UK designed to prepare students to live in a multicultural society; and presents a case study of practice in one primary classroom, to challenge racism through a study of local development issues. Pupils were given opportunities to develop a range of skills, to enable them to participate more effectively in their community, and to take action to influence development processes.

The final case studies are of two projects initiated in Finland. One is presented from the perspective of the project co-ordinator Liisa Jääskeläinen, based on the National Board of Education, the other from that of Solveig Lindberg, a teacher in a participating school. Both are curriculum initiatives supported directly by the national education authority, working in partnership with non-governmental agencies. Focusing on human rights and environmental issues, these projects reflect the high level of official support given to development education in Finland. The Baltic Sea Project is especially interesting as it has sought to establish co-operation between educators in each of the countries bordering the Baltic and has engaged the imagination of teachers from a variety of backgrounds, particularly that of science educators.

It can be seen from this broad range of case studies that development education has flourished in a variety of institutional and cultural contexts, and that to a large extent, local interests and concerns have determined the themes. Nevertheless, as one would expect, there are a number of common challenges facing development educators; issues of social justice and human rights, environment and development are a common thread running through the studies. So too is the commitment among teachers engaged in development education to classroom processes which engage students actively in the learning process and encourage the development of skills and attitudes which will enable them to be active citizens committed to social justice at community, national, regional and global levels.

Over the last 20 years or so development education has caught the imagination of a variety of teachers working in very different contexts in primary and secondary schools and across a broad range of subject areas. Some of these teachers have worked in what would appear to be enviable conditions: the initiatives which they have taken have had the active endorsement of national education policies and have sometimes been supported and resourced by official government agencies. However, as a number of the case studies show, other teachers have worked in difficult and even hostile contexts; these teachers share a commitment to development and a recognition that the issues that they are encouraging their pupils to examine and the skills they are encouraging them to acquire remain critical in a context of increasing global inequality.

In 1988 the Council of Europe held a public campaign on North–South interdependence and solidarity designed to raise public awareness of the complex relationship linking the peoples of Europe and of the South:

> The fate of the countries of the North is intimately bound up with the future of those in the South; they depend on each other in an intricate web of economic, social, cultural and ecological links.

However, North–South relations are still characterised by dramatic

7

inequality and injustice; trade surplus and overproduction in the North, debt crisis, food shortage and over-exploitation of natural resources in the South.

. . . This situation is not only morally unacceptable, but, in the long term, one which threatens the peaceful development and economic wellbeing of the whole world.

(Council of Europe, 1988)

Development education, in a variety of dynamic forms, continues to have an important role in preparing pupils to understand the complexities of North–South relations and development processes and to contribute to the achievement of a more equitable international community.

# REFERENCES

Brundtland, G. (1992), 'Rio's unnatural law of selection', *The Guardian*, 17 April 1992.

Council of Europe (1988), *North–South: One Future, a Common Task*, Strasbourg: Council of Europe.

Freire, P. (1972), *Pedagogy of the Oppressed*, Harmondsworth: Penguin.

Hicks, D. and Townley, C. (eds) (1982) *Teaching World Studies: An Introduction to Global Perspectives in the Curriculum*, Harlow: Longman.

Nyerere, J. (1973), *Freedom and Development/Uhuru na Maendeleo*, Dar es Salaam: Oxford University Press.

# PART 1

# THE CHANGING CONTEXT OF DEVELOPMENT EDUCATION

CHAPTER 1

# Development Education and Human Rights Education

*Hugh Starkey*

In the 1990s, development education and human rights education are inextricable partners, but this was not always the case. This chapter traces some of the history of the two education movements and shows why they remained separate strands in the early years of development education. It also explains why they are now in a reciprocal and complementary relationship based on the pedagogical insights of development education and the international legal status and the universal values of human rights education.

## THE UNIVERSAL DECLARATION OF HUMAN RIGHTS AND WORLD DEVELOPMENT

The Universal Declaration of Human Rights proclaimed by the General Assembly of the United Nations in Paris on 10 December 1948 is a manifesto for world development. Although it has nothing to say on specific economic, trade or environmental measures, it does outline those features of world society that are indispensable for progress towards 'justice and peace in the world'. The Declaration notes that

> the advent of a world in which human beings shall enjoy freedom of speech and belief and freedom from fear and want has been proclaimed as the highest aspiration of the common people . . . the peoples of the United Nations have in the Charter reaffirmed their faith in fundamental human rights, in the dignity and worth of the human person and in the equal rights of men and women and have determined to promote social progress and better standards of life in larger freedom.

It is unlikely that there is yet any better or more concise definition of the objectives of world development.

Even before the specific covenants on economic and social rights, United

Nations officials considered that civil and political rights would in themselves lead to economic development. Secretary-General U Thant stated in 1965:

> The establishment of human rights provides the foundation upon which rests the political structure of human freedom; the achievement of human freedom generates the will as well as the capacity for economic and social progress; the attainment of economic and social progress provides the basis for true peace.
>
> (Centre for Human Rights, 1989: 1)

If U Thant is right, a free society, respectful of human rights, is a requirement for economic development and ultimately for peace. Or to put it the other way round, repressive and undemocratic governments, whatever their rhetoric about progress, are unlikely to be able to create the conditions for sustained economic development. The argument is complex, because the internal structures of a state are only one part of the equation. Parameters such as size, natural resources and geo-strategic position also need to be taken into consideration. However, whereas in the 28, mostly democratic, developed countries identified by Sivard, GNP capita rose by about $7,500 over the past thirty years, that of the 113 developing countries crept up by a mere $350. Within the latter group of countries, military governments were an increasingly common phenomenon (Sivard, 1991). Whereas in 1960 about one-quarter of developing countries had military governments, by 1989 this had risen to over half. In general, therefore, it cannot be claimed that undemocratic governments bring economic progress, though there are exceptions, such as China and South Korea.

Human rights are only rights when people know about them and can therefore exercise them. Education has thus always been an important complementary activity to the drafting and implementation of human rights charters. The Universal Declaration of Human Rights sets out aims for education as follows:

> Education shall be directed to the full development of the human personality and to the strengthening of respect for human rights and fundamental freedoms. It shall promote understanding, tolerance and friendship among all nations, racial or religious groups, and shall further the activities of the United Nations for the maintenance of peace.
>
> (Article 26.2)

These aims correspond very closely to aims drafted by development educators.

## ORIGINS AND GROWTH OF DEVELOPMENT EDUCATION IN THE UK

In June 1991 about 100 people gathered in Oxford, England, to celebrate 25 years of development education. They traced the beginnings of the movement to the appointment, in 1966, by the overseas aid charity Oxfam of Og Thomas with a specific brief to develop an education programme. The Oxford Committee for Famine Relief, which became Oxfam, was founded in 1942 and in its early years was concerned with problems of refugees and displaced persons resulting from the conflict in Europe. By the mid–1960s, however, its focus had shifted to conditions in the newly independent countries of what was starting to be referred to as the 'Third World'. In fact the British Labour government elected in 1964 had recognized development as a major and priority issue by creating a new Ministry of Overseas Development with a seat in the cabinet. The first minister was Barbara Castle. Nonetheless, if the charity and the government were well aware of the immense scale of deprivation in the newly independent countries of Africa and Asia, the mass of the general public had little notion of the conditions of life for the poorest people of the world's poorest regions. It was therefore logical to attempt to educate both the public at large and the next generation, namely those at school. Whereas the government was largely concerned with academic questions of how aid can be effectively delivered, the charity set about educating its supporters and potential supporters.

Certain high-profile events in the 1960s helped create a climate which supported and encouraged development education. Perhaps the crucial event in stimulating the public imagination on development issues was the opening of the Second World Food Congress in Washington DC by President John F. Kennedy in 1963. The key passage of his speech proclaimed: 'We have the means, we have the capacity to wipe hunger and poverty from the face of the earth in our lifetime, we need only the will.' His ringing declaration gave a vision and objective. The impact of the speech was similar to that of the Universal Declaration of Human Rights of 15 years previously. It brought world development to prominence on the political agenda and set off the movement, both in Europe and in North America, to educate the public about the issues (Mooney, 1986).

The people most affected by the education were the activists themselves. During the 1960s their analysis became more and more radical. The decade is sometimes characterized as one of idealism about the possibilities of world economic and social progress. It was also, however, a period of ideological East–West armed conflict by proxy where the belligerents were often identified as North and South. The Vietnam war was one such dramatic representation of this. This first televised war aroused the consciences and the interest of many people in Europe and North America. The notions of imperialism and exploitation seemed to provide a global explanation for the events, and Che Guevara, the fighter against these twin evils, became an icon for many of the younger generation. At the same time many of their respectable elders were identifying with the demands of the Haslemere Declaration of 1968, launched by a group based in the affluent home counties of the UK. In Maggie Black's words:

Socialist analysis and a vision of the Third World in justifiable revolt against exploitative Western capitalism were beginning to characterize an ideology of development whose primary context was neither economic nor humanitarian, but political.

(Black, 1992: 156)

Development education was thus, in a sense, a political movement, though one not identified with particular parties. From the beginning development education received strong support from the churches. They led a coalition which started a major campaign for public awareness of world inequalities and demanded a significant response by government. The World Council of Churches Assembly in Uppsala, Sweden in 1968 heard speech after speech from churches in the Third World demanding justice. The churches of the North were swift to respond. In Britain a huge petition was organized in 1970, calling for increases in overseas aid. This provided the impetus for the formation of the pressure group the World Development Movement in 1971. Throughout northern Europe public awareness campaigns sprang up. In the Netherlands a Peace Week was organized. This inspired the Swedish Ecumenical Development Week which started in 1973 under the theme 'Justice Cannot Wait' (Wahlstrom, 1986: 89–98).

It was this climate of informed and concerned opinion that enabled development education to become established in the UK. Groups of teachers and world development activists, often with the support of local churches, started to create resource centres, initially known as Third World Centres following the pioneering example of Norwich. The aid charities reinforced their educational programme, appointing teachers to work with schools and develop appropriate materials. At a national level the Voluntary Committee on Overseas Aid and Development sought to provide a focus for development education. This body continued its activities as the Centre for World Development Education, now Worldaware.[1]

## DEVELOPMENT EDUCATION AND A HUMAN RIGHTS DISCOURSE

The radical analysis adopted by development activists in the 1960s and 1970s arguably made it difficult for them to consider respect for human rights and fundamental freedoms as a priority. This analysis saw Third World governments as the legitimate representatives of the poor, struggling against neo-imperialist oppressors. African states, for instance, only recently independent, were given the benefit of the doubt. One-party rule and even military governments were considered to be choices with which rich, formal colonial powers had no right to interfere; for example, the Vietnam war was interpreted as an attempt by the former colonial powers to impose a corrupt form of democracy. To mention human rights and democracy in the context of the

Third World could thus be construed as neo-colonialist and paternalistic. The issue was made all the more difficult as, simultaneously, an American discourse of human rights was used as a cold war device to justify high arms expenditure and military intervention against nationalist movements, where these expressed communist sympathies. Given that development educators often felt sympathy for nationalist struggles against what was perceived as (neo)imperialism, only a bold and independent-minded Third World activist would feel comfortable placing human rights on the agenda.

## THE WORLD STUDIES PROJECT AND NEW METHODOLOGIES

In 1973 the Parliamentary Group for World Government and the One World Trust set up a curriculum development project in London, the World Studies Project, under the direction of Robin Richardson. This project, which called on the insights of American as well as British educators, was enormously influential in developing a methodology for teaching about world issues and in defining content (One World Trust, 1976). In particular, the methodology encouraged active learning based on small-group discussion and investigation. Among the very first activists associated with the project were the education officers of the overseas aid charity Christian Aid. By the mid-1970s several Oxfam education workers were also closely involved in developing materials and methodologies in conjunction with the World Studies Project.

At this time, as indeed subsequently, there was little distinction to be made between world studies and development education. Development education was, and to a great extent still is, world studies or global education where this is supported by overseas aid NGOs through their education workers or their supporters in the community and in schools. An interesting example of this close connection between world studies and development education is the UNICEF publication from Switzerland entitled, in French, *Éducation pour le développement* (Comité suisse pour l'UNICEF, 1977). This is, in fact, a direct translation and adaptation of the World Studies Project's *Learning for Change in World Society* (One World Trust, 1976). The Swiss booklet was prepared with the full collaboration of the London-based project, but the change of name is interesting.

## OXFAM AND DEVELOPMENT EDUCATION IN THE 1970s

By 1974 Oxfam was starting to build up a team of education workers which grew rapidly over the next decade so that there were education and youth workers in some fifteen locations over the UK, in addition to many Oxfam-supported projects and centres elsewhere. At the beginning of this educational expansion the charity set out its objectives and with them a definition of development education:

> The objective of Oxfam's educational work is to deepen people's understanding of their commitment and active response to development . . . we believe that our work of changing attitudes and encouraging involvement should reflect Oxfam's experience that true development only takes place when people decide, for themselves, to help themselves and improve their own conditions . . . We are committed to help people in this country to change their attitudes to people overseas and to understand the basis and type of development with which Oxfam is associated.[2]

The key ideas here are changing attitudes to people overseas and the notion of development as people deciding for themselves to improve their conditions. The former concern led, in the 1980s, to an overt identification of development education with multi-cultural and anti-racist education. It was able to do this once development educators realized that the focus for their concerns could, logically, no longer be confined to 'overseas'. But in 1974, the focus was very much on overseas because of the impetus given to development education by aid charities whose own focus was predominantly abroad.

The emphasis on people deciding for themselves was a reflection of the considerable prestige and influence of Paulo Freire, Julius Nyerere and Ivan Illich, whose writings were being published in accessible editions in Europe at this time.

> A true revolutionary project, on the other hand, to which the utopian dimension is natural, is a process in which the people assume the role of subject in the precarious adventure of transforming and recreating the world.
>
> (Freire, 1972: 72)

> People cannot be developed, they can only develop themselves.
>
> (Nyerere, 1974: 27)

> The only way to reverse the disastrous trend to increasing underdevelopment, hard as it is, is to learn to laugh at accepted solutions in order to change the demands which make them necessary. Only free men can change their minds and be surprised; and while no men are completely free, some are freer than others.
>
> (Illich, 1973: 143)

Interestingly, in the 1990s, reference is still made to Freire, but Illich, perhaps too tainted with unfashionable de-schooling, and Nyerere, whose political achievements tend to be belittled, are rarely cited.

# THE 1974 UNESCO RECOMMENDATION

The year 1974 was in many ways a significant one. As well as the World Population Conference in Bucharest and the World Food Conference in Rome, it was the year in which the massive oil price rises triggered by the Yom Kippur war of October 1973 began to affect the world economy, creating a dramatic and totally unplanned slowing of economic growth in the richer northern countries. Although the Americans had officially left Vietnam in 1973, fighting between the North and the South was still continuing. In August, the disgraced Richard Nixon resigned. Issues of world development and relationships between North and South were at the top of the international political agenda and international agencies, particularly those of the United Nations, were extremely active. This, then, was the context for a very significant recommendation from Unesco.

The General Conference of Unesco, at its eighteenth session in Paris from 17 October to 23 November 1974, adopted, on 19 November, a Recommendation concerning Education for International Understanding, Co-operation and Peace, and Education relating to Human Rights and Fundamental Freedoms. The 45 articles promote the full range of what are generally known separately as development education, peace education, environmental education, global education, world studies, and human rights education. Unesco members and experts clearly saw these as interconnected areas.

The Recommendation spells out objectives which are to be 'major guiding principles of educational policy', namely:

(a) an international dimension and a global perspective in education at all levels and in all its forms;

(b) understanding and respect for all peoples, their cultures, civilizations, values and ways of life, including domestic ethnic cultures and cultures of other nations;

(c) awareness of the increasing global interdependence between peoples and nations;

(d) abilities to communicate with others;

(e) awareness not only of the rights but also of the duties incumbent upon individuals, social groups and nations towards each other;

(f) understanding of the necessity for international solidarity and co-operation;

(g) readiness on the part of the individual to participate in solving the problems of his [sic] community, his country, and the world at large.

This list corresponds very closely to an agenda for development education, both then and now. What is interesting is that, in 1974, Unesco was not using the term development education or education for development, preferring to stress the international and the human rights dimensions. Oxfam, on the other hand, with an education programme very much on the lines of that proposed by Unesco, did not refer to human rights in its objectives.

The Unesco Recommendation also sets out some of the elements of a syllabus for such education. It lists a number of 'problems' to be studied. Some of these have a 1970s ring, for example: 'equality of rights of peoples and the right of peoples to self-determination'. This relates to the United Nations' concern for decolonization, which was still in progress. This concern is taken up further down the list and specifically linked with questions (the Recommendation would say 'problems') of development:

> economic growth and social development and their relation to social justice; colonialism and decolonization; ways and means of assisting developing countries; the struggle against illiteracy; the campaign against disease and famine; the fight for a better quality of life and the highest attainable standard of health; population growth and related questions.

Absent from the list are the question of trade, which came to dominate development debates in the later 1970s in the context of UNCTAD and Lomé negotiations, and the question of debt, the major topic of concern in the 1980s and 1990s.

Also absent from this syllabus is any sense that these are, in fact, global questions, as much of concern to countries of the North as to the South. The syllabus reads like a list of problems of the Third World, and, indeed, this was probably how it was conceived and how these questions were perceived at this time. This also applies to the section on human rights:

> action to ensure the exercise and observance of human rights, including those of refugees; racialism and its eradication; the fight against discrimination in its various forms.

The wording possibly implies that human rights questions are also mainly the concern of countries outside the circle of the democratic North and the comunist block. At this time teachers would tend to associate refugees with Africa and South-East Asia, and racialism with South Africa. Issues of concern to the democracies, such as women's rights (which were a topic of lively concern in Europe at the time) and the rights of people with disabilities (which were not), are not explicitly referred to. Nor, of course, are the Soviet gulags given the active participation of the Russian representative in drafting this section.

# DEVELOPMENT EDUCATION AND HUMAN RIGHTS CONCEPTS

The challenge of the Unesco Recommendation for development education to teach about human rights was scarcely taken up in the 1970s. The classic text of the period, *The Development Puzzle* (Fyson, 1984), does not include the term 'human rights' in its index, even in its final 1984 edition. There is a similar lacuna in the influential academic study *Development Studies: A Handbook for Teachers* (Jones et al., 1977). The programme and publications of Birmingham Development Education Centre, founded in 1975, show a predominance of activities and materials on the general theme of teaching and learning about other people, but with little reference to human rights.

Among material produced specifically for teachers, the World Studies Project alone focused both on development issues and the concepts of human rights, but does not link the two. *Learning for Change in World Society* contains a section on human rights in its appendix listing vocabulary. There is, however, a separate section on development and the environment and there are no activities specifically designed to teach human rights vocabulary. This separation is perpetuated in a series of books produced by the project. One of the four titles, *Fighting for Freedom*, concentrates very largely and explicitly on human rights in a global context. The most development-orientated of the books, *Progress and Poverty*, does not refer to human rights.

The Universal Declaration of Human Rights is, as noted above, a statement of the key values of development. These include peace, justice, freedoms, dignity, equality of rights, and these are universal values, to be applied equally everywhere. Writing on development makes constant reference to these concepts. Barbara Ward, for example, set out her vision of development which tried to turn the debate away from merely material considerations:

> As a rough first definition we can start by recognizing that any valid concept of dignity and equality includes a number of nonmaterial 'goods' – responsibility, security, participation, the free exchange of thought and experience, a degree of human respect that is independent of monetary rewards of bureaucratic hierarchies, and a realization that this respect is lacking where rewards and hierarchies are too restrictive or too skewed. All these goods of culture, of man's mind and spirit, need not be costly in terms of material resources. Indeed, they belong to the sphere of life where growth is truly exponential – in knowledge, in beauty, in neighborliness and human concern.
>
> (Ward, 1976: 6)

Nyerere set out his objectives thus:

> The building of a society in which all members have equal rights, and equal opportunities; in which all can live at peace with his neighbours without suffering or imposing injustice . . .
>
> (Nyerere, 1973)

19

The Cocoyoc Declaration of 1974 makes the same point, but negatively:

And at the local as at the international level the evils of material poverty are compounded by the people's lack of participation and human dignity, by their lack of power to determine their own fate.

(One World Trust, 1976)

In the context of development education, as opposed to writing on development economics, another important international resolution was that of the World Conference of Teaching Professions (WCOTP), at its 1976 conference 'Education for a Global Community'. This called on teachers to

encourage open discussion which allows students to develop a respect for all human beings; champion the cause of social justice for all students in their classes, schools and communities; promote the concept of a global community.

It can be concluded from the examples above that development education in the 1970s was based on a discourse informed by the Universal Declaration of Human Rights, even if few development educators acknowledged this fact. It was in the 1980s that development educators started to make specific reference to international human rights texts, and, indeed, to make these texts themselves more widely known.

## UNESCO, HUMAN RIGHTS EDUCATION AND DEVELOPMENT

The 1974 Unesco Recommendation gave an impetus to human rights education. In particular, a number of distinguished lawyers contributed to debates about the content of human rights education. Leah Levin was commissioned to write the still classic *Human Rights: Questions and Answers*, a shortened version of which appeared in the *Unesco Courier* of October 1978. The following year Unesco launched a journal *Human Rights Teaching* whose aim was: 'to serve as a means of liaison and co-ordination between teachers and institutions specializing in human rights and to contribute to all forms of research and reflection, essential to the teaching of human rights'. The content and focus of *Human Rights Teaching* is academic; the teaching is at university level and is essentially the concern of law schools.

As a global international organization, the majority of whose member states are in the South, many directly concerned with issues of food and dire poverty, Unesco is in a unique position to bring together human rights and development issues. Alston (1982), in an article in *Human Rights Teaching*, made an important contribution to this synthesis, noting the emergence within the United Nations of the concept of a 'right to development', finally legitimized in the resolution 32/130 of the General Assembly in 1977. This resolution maintains that social and economic rights are indivisible from civil and political rights and considers a new international economic order to be an essential element in effectively promoting human rights. Alston observes that development discourse had often seemed to suggest that economic goals were of greater importance than human rights goals; human rights abuses were tacitly condoned where governments could claim the need for authoritarian measures in order to help in the promotion of the conditions for economic growth. He quotes Sir Shridath Ramphal, himself a champion of human rights, who nonetheless maintained:

> It does the cause of human rights no good to inveigh against civil and political rights deviations while helping to perpetuate illiteracy, malnutrition, disease, infant mortality, and a low life expectancy among millions of human beings.
>
> (Alston, 1982)

Alston rightly points out that such simple either/or dichotomies are essentially false: 'One is offered bread or freedom, but never both.' Development is, he argues, more complex than this. The challenge 'is to find the best possible balance between competing goals'. Conflicts in values and of goals are inevitable, but these should be openly acknowledged and resolved by democratic means.

The 'right to development' is a way for the United Nations to reconcile its commitment both to human rights and to its member states. It is not, however, a new right, rather an idea well supported by classic human rights texts, or, as Alston puts it, 'a new formulation of existing rights'. If the right to development is not in itself a problematic concept in the abstract, there is considerable debate as to who can claim the right. For individuals to claim the right is nothing more than for them to claim their universal human rights. There is, however, a strong current arguing that the right to development is a collective right that should be vested in states. States could thereby demand aid and favourable economic conditions from other richer states. Such an interpretation has not yet achieved a consensus.

## HUMAN RIGHTS EDUCATION: FROM THEORY TO PRACTICE

Unesco's important work in the 1970s served to prepare the ground for a curriculum development process that had some real impact in schools. Early advocates of human rights education were rarely schoolteachers; indeed, they were often literally advocates in the sense of lawyers. To have any effect, human rights education needed to take root in the curriculum of schools and find teachers interested in taking it on. One important source of such teachers was the development education and world studies movement.

In Britain an important step was taken on International Human Rights Day in 1981, when a coalition of non-governmental organizations, including the

United Nations Association, the British Council of Churches and the biggest teachers' union, convened a one-day conference at the Institute of Education in London. The conference concluded that British teachers were scarcely aware of human rights issues and agreed to set up working parties to cover all types of formal education and explore ways of promoting awareness of human rights.

# THE COUNCIL OF EUROPE AND HUMAN RIGHTS EDUCATION

The Council of Europe is the international body responsible for the European Court of Human Rights; it was set up following the signing in 1950 of the European Convention on Human Rights. The Council also has an important role in encouraging co-operation in educational development between its member states. By 1992, some 40 European states were participating in some aspect of the programme of the Council of Europe, notably its Council for Cultural Co-operation.

In 1978 the Committee of Ministers of the Council of Europe passed a recommendation asking member states to include teaching about human rights in the curricula of their education systems. Five years later, in May 1983, the Council, with the support of the Austrian authorities, organized a symposium in Vienna under the title 'Human Rights Education in Schools in Western Europe'. The symposium brought together official representatives of member states, delegates from teachers' unions and other NGOs as well as some experts from universities.

One of the most important and subsequently influential contributions to the symposium was that of Ian Lister. Professor Lister has worked extensively in promoting political and social education, and his department at the University of York also included the Centre for Global Education. He situated human rights education in a cluster of educational movements, each with their own networks, newsletters, style and content, and which are characterized by their links with non-governmental organizations. The cluster includes world studies, development education and peace education. He observed that human rights education, while strong on official approbation, had no serious research, little financial backing, few examples of classroom materials or even evidence that it occurred at all. However, he concluded that the strong level of support for human rights education in official discourse should protect teachers from accusations of ideological bias or indoctrination to which those in the peace and development education movements, for instance, had been subjected (Lister, 1984).

The Vienna symposium concluded by making a series of recommendations, which broke new ground in spelling out in some detail how human rights education could and should be integrated into school curricula. It included specific reference to world development:

Human rights education is part of the curriculum which helps young people to live in a democratic and multicultural society. It includes international and intercultural understanding, world development and preparing for the future.

(Starkey, 1984)

To many observers, the contribution of the Council of Europe to promoting human rights education, particularly since 1983, has been highly significant (see, for example, Shafer, 1987; Starkey, 1991). This achievement undoubtedly owes much to the personal commitment of the former head of the School Education Division, subsequently Deputy Director of Education, Culture and Sport, Maitland Stobart. The Council was, and is, able to raise the profile of human rights education with governments, to bring together experts from many countries to share experience and approaches and also to involve teachers and NGOs in developing methods and materials for use in the classroom.

The main vehicle for defining and disseminating the Council of Europe's approach to human rights education is the recommendation of the Committee of Ministers 'on teaching and learning about human rights in schools' adopted on 14 May 1985. This recommendation, formally known as Recommendation R(85)7, was a redrafting of the conclusions of the 1983 Vienna symposium after these had been circulated to all member governments for comment and emendation. The adopted text consists of the recommendation itself and an appendix.

The recommendation sets the context, particularly:

the need to reaffirm democratic values in the face of:

- intolerance, acts of violence and terrorism;
- the re-emergence of the public expression of racist and xenophobic attitudes;

before concluding:

Believing, therefore, that, throughout their school career, all young people should learn about human rights as part of their preparation for life in a pluralistic democracy;

Convinced that schools are communities which can, and should, be an example of respect for the dignity of the individual and for difference, for tolerance and for equality of opportunity;

Recommends that the governments of member states, having regard to their national education systems and to the legislative basis for them, [should]:

(a) encourage teaching and learning about human rights in schools in line with the suggestions contained in the appendix hereto;
(b) draw the attention of persons and bodies concerned with school education to the text of this recommendation.

23

The appendix consists of six sections as follows:

1 Human rights in the school curriculum
2 Skills
3 Knowledge to be acquired in the study of human rights
4 The climate of the school
5 Teacher training
6 International Human Rights Day

Many governments took the opportunity of this Recommendation to ensure that the text was circulated widely. Each school in France, for instance, received a copy with a warm letter of endorsement from the minister. As well as the usual English and French versions, the text has been translated by a number of education ministries into their national language.

One important role of the Council of Europe was, and still is, to facilitate the sharing of educational ideas and practice by granting bursaries to teachers to enable them to participate in training courses in other member states. The Council has also supported international training sessions run by the International Institute of Human Rights in Strasbourg and by CIFEDHOP (Centre for Human Rights and Peace Teaching) in Geneva. Such courses also recruit from outside Europe, and the development concerns of delegates from African and Asian countries ensure that human rights education and development education are considered together.

## DEVELOPMENT EDUCATION AND HUMAN RIGHTS EDUCATION SINCE 1983

Lister's Vienna challenge to governments and the educational community to turn human rights education rhetoric into classroom reality struck a chord. Whereas elements of the political right in Europe and North America were deeply suspicious of the growing peace education movement, education for human rights can be linked to international treaty obligations and thus potentially command a broad consensus. The Vienna symposium provided the impetus for groups all over Europe to start developing new approaches to teaching about human rights. From 1983 the Council of Europe sponsored or provided bursaries for teachers' seminars on human rights education in Paris, Copenhagen, Donaueschingen, Geneva, Lisbon and other venues. Simultaneously countries with a centralized curriculum, particularly France and Sweden, set up national curriculum development projects.

### France

Interestingly, in the case of the French project, it was a problem thrown up by an earlier project on development education that provided further stimulus.

The French National Educational Research Institute, INRP, had conducted a five-year project on integrating development education into the history and geography curriculum (INRP, 1984). From 1977 to 1982 the team, under M. and Mme Margairaz, had followed the progress of students in eight secondary schools, four in Paris and four in the provinces, as they moved through from year 7 (6e) to year 10 (3e). The team of teachers involved developed their own teaching materials for use within the official syllabus. The problem encountered was that as student in multicultural urban classrooms learned about questions of underdevelopment they made explicit links with their own classroom. They became aware of the links between the situation in certain Third World countries and the presence in their class of students whose families came from the countries they were studying. This doubtless potentially beneficial realization became in reality a cause of friction as 'underdeveloped' became a term of abuse used personally and hurtfully against students from ethnic minority families.

The research report concludes that development education needs an element of human rights education if it is not to serve merely to reinforce inequalities and feelings of racial superiority. Fortunately, it notes, a human rights education think-tank was set up in 1982 under the director of the national institute, Francine Best, and this led to a full-scale project on human rights education from 1984 to 1989 under the direction of François Audigier and Guy Lagelee (INRP, 1987).

This research project was extremely influential in helping to formulate the non-statutory guidelines for the new civic education course that became compulsory in secondary schools from 1986. The ministerial guidelines (Ministère de l'éducation nationale, 1990) contain a special section on human rights education which, among other things, demonstrates that the notion of human rights or the text of the Universal Declaration can provide the link between the six official cross-curricular themes of the French National Curriculum. These are: safety; environment and heritage; information; development; health; and home economics.

## Sweden

With Sweden's long tradition of neutrality and support for international peace organizations, it is not surprising that the unifying concept for cross-curricular themes, which for the French is human rights, for the Swedes is peace. Non-statutory guidance, or 'service material' as it is referred to, on peace education was issued in 1985, to support the National Curriculum of 1980. The English-language version of this, issued in 1986, is entitled *Peace Education: Peace – Liberty – Development – Human Rights*. The author, Bengt Thelin, then Director of Education at the Swedish National Board of Education, clearly is also of the opinion that development education and human rights education are complementary, both being essential areas of study. In his evaluation report for the

Swedish National Board of Education (Thelin, 1991), he refers both to the Unesco Recommendation of 1974 and the Council of Europe Recommendation of 1985 as examples of international organizations influencing national curriculum thinking. In fact the Swedish National Board of Education initiated in 1989 an action programme for the internationalization of education, which in spite of a change of government was still in force in 1992.

# United Kingdom

Until 1988, there was no central control or even direction to the curriculum in the UK. Individual schools, local education authorities and non-governmental organizations, as well as national, ministry-funded bodies, were all active in producing new courses and materials. The pioneer in producing classroom materials on human rights in a development education context was a Scottish project based at Jordanhill College in Glasgow. The project's director, Jim Dunlop, had successfully applied to the Ministry of Overseas Development for a grant to produce materials to support the implementation of the 1974 Unesco Recommendation. The first unit, published for 12–14-year-olds, was entitled *Food* and the second, which came out in 1981, *Human Rights* (Jordanhill Project in International Understanding, 1981). However, with the change of government in 1979, this source of curriculum development funding dried up, and it was left to NGOs, and, interestingly, the European Community to fund development education.

Although, by 1983, influential academics were linking human rights and development education, it took another five years for this link to be reflected in the output of development education centres. In a paper linking racial justice, global development and peace, David Hicks stressed that development education 'must be rooted in action'. He quotes a 1975 FAO definition of development education:

> Development education is concerned with issues of human rights, dignity, self-reliance and social justice in both developed and developing countries.

> (Hicks, 1983)

Although no direct reference was made to human rights education as such, another paper published the same year included both development education and human rights education under the umbrella term 'world studies' (Selby, 1983).

Around this time some human-rights-focused NGOs produced new materials specifically based on human rights issues. In 1984 Amnesty International produced a teachers' pack with the same title as Lister's Council of Europe pamphlet, namely *Teaching and Learning about Human Rights*. The following year the Minority Rights Group published *Profile on Prejudice* (Gerlach and van der Gaag, 1985). Materials funded by overseas development agencies, however, still scarcely mentioned human rights.[3]

Among the events that served to promote an awareness of the importance of a human rights perspective for those involved in development education was a one-day conference sponsored by Amnesty International in May 1985. This attracted some 200 teachers to the World Studies Teacher Training Centre (subsequently renamed Centre for Global Education) at the University of York. Another landmark was the setting up of the Education in Human Rights Network in 1987. This Network arose from the experience of a group of educationalists who had worked with the Council of Europe on human rights education but who saw frustratingly little response to the Recommendation of 1985 in the UK. They called together all those who recognized themselves in the phrase 'human rights education'. This included teacher trainers from university departments, teachers and inspectors, and those involved with a range of NGOs. Of the major sponsors of development education – the aid agencies – only Oxfam was represented at the initial meeting. As its first activity, the Network organized a Human Rights Education Forum and Fair to coincide with the celebration of the 40th anniversary of the Universal Declaration in 1988 (Bobbett, 1991). Development education was very significantly represented at this event, which brought together some 60 groups and organizations.

The 40th anniversary of the Universal Declaration also saw the publication of the first specifically human rights education material from a development education source. Birmingham Development Education Centre brought out two related publications: *Do It Justice!* (Osler, 1988) and *40 Years On* (Bridle et al., 1989). Further impetus was given to a human rights dimension within development education with publications from UNICEF (UK) and Save the Children based on the 1989 UN Convention on the Rights of the Child (Jarvis et al., 1990 a–c).

With the phased introduction of a prescriptive national curriculum from 1988 onwards, both human rights education and development education made strenuous representations to ensure their concerns were included. The development education lobby is relatively well funded and certainly well organized. It was able, with some success, to push for a global perspective in all subject areas. The more recent human rights education lobby concentrated on the cross-curricular theme of citizenship. Its approaches were strengthened by the publication of the report of the all-party Speaker's Commission on Citizenship ('Speaker' here refers to the Member of Parliament elected to perform the traditionally neutral role of chairing debates in the House of Commons) which quoted at length the Council of Europe Recommendation of 1985 (The Speaker's Commission, 1990). The guidance document on Citizenship produced by the National Curriculum Council does, in fact, give space to the consideration of human rights (National Curriculum Council, 1990: 4).

The increasingly close co-operation of development education and human rights education was demonstrated in the summer of 1992, when the Commonwealth Institute in London, well known for its development education activities, organized a major one-day conference entitled 'Human Rights Education Materials for the National Curriculum'. Another important and symbolic initiative was the launch by the World Studies Trust of a teacher training programme, on Teaching Democracy, Social Justice, Global Responsibility and Respect for Human Rights. The project is funded both by the European Community's ERASMUS programme and by a consortium of the major aid agencies.

# CONCLUSION

As the French experience quoted above demonstrates, development education needs human rights education to complement it. John Fien, an Australian academic, summarizes the case:

> The whole purpose of development education is to promote social justice, to change the world, through understanding, empathy and solidarity with the patterns of life experienced by societies different from our own. In particular it is concerned with the lives and future well-being of the oppressed, the people who live in the Third World countries of the 'South' or under Third World conditions in the 'North'.

and so:

> in relation to values, the role of development education is a pro-active one which involves planning learning experiences which promote the adoption of core democratic values conducive to a sense of justice and a commitment to human rights and dignity.

(Fien, 1991)

Local, national and exclusive religious or secular formulations of values are inadequate when the topic is global responsibility and intercultural international understanding. These perspectives demand the universal values which are cogently expressed in human rights texts adopted by the whole international community.

The last decade of the twentieth century is a time when education for democracy is firmly back on the international agenda. Human rights, as democratic values, are central to this concern. Any focus on democracy that fails to include a global perspective will be inadequate. Development education and human rights education are now consequently inseparable.

# NOTES

1 Worldaware, 1 Catton Street, London WC1R 4AB.
2 Oxfam, November 1974, quoted in an internal working party report, October 1985.
3 To take one example, the major series of six workbooks Teaching Development

Issues, published by the Development Education Project in Manchester in 1985 as the result of a three-year project funded by Christian Aid and the EC, do not include human rights in the glossary nor in the map of the contents of the project.

# REFERENCES

Alston, P. (1982), 'Human rights and development' in *Human Rights Teaching,* Vol. III, Division of Human Rights and Peace, Paris: Unesco.

Black, M. (1992), *A Cause for Our Times: Oxfam, the First 50 Years*, Oxford: Oxfam.

Bobbett, P. (1991), 'Human rights education and non–governmental organizations: a variety of approaches', in Starkey, H. (ed.) *The Challenge of Human Rights Education*, London: Cassell.

Bridle, M. et al. (1989), *40 Years On*, Birmingham: Development Education Centre.

Centre for Human Rights, Geneva (1989), *ABC Teaching Human Rights*, New York: United Nations.

Comité suisse pour l'UNICEF (1977), *Éducation pour le développement*, 8021 Zurich.

Fien, J. (1991), 'Commitment to justice: a defence of a rationale for development education', in *Peace, Environment and Education*, 2 (4), Sweden: Peace Education Commission, School of Education, Box 23501, S–200 45 Malmo.

Freire, P. (1972), *Cultural Action for Freedom*, Harmondsworth: Penguin.

Fyson, N. L. (1984), *The Development Puzzle*, Sevenoaks: Hodder & Stoughton.

Gerlach, L. and van der Gaag, N. (1985), *Profile on Prejudice*, London: Minority Rights Group.

Hicks, D.(1983), *Racial Justice, Global Development or Peace: Which Shall We Choose in School?*, World Studies Document Service 6, Centre for Global Education, University of York.

Illich, I. (1973), *Celebration of Awareness*, Harmondsworth: Penguin.

Institut National de Recherches Pédagogiques (1984), 'Rencontres pédagogiques No. 2', *Éducation au Développement*, INRP, 29 rue d'Ulm, 75230 Paris cedex 05.

Institut National de Recherches Pédagogiques (1987), 'Collection rapports de recherches 1987 No. 13', *Éducation aux Droits de l'Homme*, Paris: INRP.

Jarvis, H. et al. (1990a), *It's Our Right*, London: UNICEF (UK) and Save the Children.

Jarvis, H. et al. (1990b), *Keep Us Safe*, London: UNICEF (UK) and Save the Children.

Jarvis, H. et al. (1990c), *The Whole Child*, London: UNICEF (UK) and Save the Children.

Jones, P. et al. (1977), *Development Studies: A Handbook for Teachers*, London: School of Oriental and African Studies, University of London.

Jordanhill Project in International Understanding (1981), *Human Rights*, JPIU, Jordanhill College, Glasgow G13 1PP.

Lister, I. (1984), *Teaching and Learning about Human Rights*, Strasbourg: Council of Europe.

Ministère de l'éducation nationale (1990), *Éducation Civique. Éducation aux Droits de l'Homme. Classes des Collèges. Horaires/Objectifs/Programmes/Instructions*, CRDP, 29 rue d'Ulm, 75230 Paris cedex 05.

Mooney, P. (1986), 'A development education agenda on North–South food issues', in NGLS/Geneva, *Development Education: The State of the Art*, Geneva: UN Non-Governmental Liaison Service, pp. 19–30.

National Curriculum Council (1990), *Curriculum Guidance 6: Citizenship*, York: NCC.

Nyerere, Julius K. (1973) *Socialism and Rural Development*, Dar es Salaam: Oxford University Press.

Nyerere, J. (1974), *Man and Development*, Dar es Salaam: Oxford University Press.

One World Trust (1976), *Learning for Change in World Society*, London: One World Trust.

Osler, A. (1988), *Do It Justice! Resources and Activities for Introducing Education in Human Rights*, Birmingham: Development Education Centre.

Selby, D. (1983), *World Studies, The Participant Classroom, The Open School*, World Studies Document Service 10, Centre for Global Education, University of York.

Shafer, S. M. (1987), 'Human rights education in schools', in Tarrow, N. (ed.), *Human Rights and Education*, Oxford: Pergamon.

Sivard, R.L. (1991, 14th edition), *World Military and Social Expenditures 1991*, Washington, DC: World Priorities.

The Speaker's Commission (1990), *Encouraging Citizenship*, London: HMSO.

Starkey, H. (1984), *Human Rights Education in Schools in Western Europe*, Strasbourg: Council of Europe.

Starkey, H. (ed.) (1991), *Socialisation of School Children and Their Education for Democratic Values and Human Rights*, Amsterdam: Swets & Zeitlinger.

Thelin, B. (1991), 'Peace education – a tentative introduction', *R 91:11 Reports – Planning, Follow-up, Evaluation*, Stockholm: Swedish National Board of Education.

Wahlstrom, Per-Ake (1986), 'Development education and the churches', in *Development Education: The State of the Art*, Geneva: UN Non-Governmental Liaison Service.

Ward, B. (1976), *The Home of Man*, Harmondsworth: Penguin.

# CHAPTER 2

# Education for Development: Redefining Citizenship in a Pluralist Society

*Audrey Osler*

Development education is concerned with North–South solidarity and interdependence, and with development issues at all levels – local, national and regional, and global. This chapter considers the contribution that development education and an understanding of development issues might make towards promoting racial equality and social justice, and the part it might play in establishing a reconstructed understanding of the concept of citizenship.

It begins by reflecting on Europe's colonial past, and on aspects of racism today, before addressing racism and anti-racism in education. European education systems have tended to remain largely monocultural and have failed to keep pace with changes in the population of Europe. Similarly, citizenship education has emphasized the rights and duties of the national citizen, and perhaps latterly the European citizen, without examining popular understandings of national identity and European identity. Just as development education is concerned with local, national, regional and global issues, so education for active participation in society should address all these levels. It will be argued that development education has an important contribution to make in encouraging young people to become active members of their communities, and to develop a new understanding of national and global citizenship. The chapter ends by considering how teachers and development education workers might build upon the initiatives that have been taken to promote a curriculum which is anti-racist, global, and relevant, and which helps towards a redefinition of our understanding of citizenship.

## EUROPE'S IMPERIAL PAST AND IDEOLOGIES OF RACISM

Development education in the North has largely concerned itself with questions of global interdependence and with challenging negative images of the South and of peoples and cultures of the South. If we are to understand why such views of the South are held and propagated in Europe today, it is necessary to look back into Europe's imperial past and explore the relationship between racism and imperialism.

A commonly held view is that racism was developed as an ideology to justify the power relationships which existed between the European imperialists and their colonial subjects during the nineteenth century. Ideologies of racism and cultural superiority were clearly convenient rationalizations of colonial rule used to justify the actions of traders, armies, administrators and missionaries in the colonies. However, the link may be a more complex one; these ideologies seem to have been formulated in advance of colonial rule, and were there in place ready to be developed to justify the exploitation of subject peoples by the colonists.

Long before European powers had established their empires, they were dividing up the world as their God-given inheritance. Birth and breeding were used by royalty and aristocracy alike to justify their right to rule. A number of writers (for example Anderson, 1983; Cohen, 1988) make links between the ideologies of racism and class. In a study which examines the origins of various forms of racism in modern Britain, Cohen argues that racism developed out of certain traditions in English class society where the assumption of the superiority of the upper classes was justified. This belief system was then reapplied in new contexts, first by slave traders and plantation owners to justify their trade and treatment of black people, then by imperial governments and later to black communities in Britain. He highlights 'the "civilising mission" through which the English governing class sought to conform both the native proletariat and its colonial subjects to its own highly racist models of "culture"' (1988: 26). A way of defining the lower classes within both Britain and Ireland as inferior was transferred first to slaves, then to colonial peoples in distant parts of the world and to black settlers in Britain.

At the same time 'race' took on a new meaning: originally it denoted dynastic descent, but it later came to be part of an ideology of inheritance. The European aristocracy were able to justify their right to govern through hereditary entitlement, establishing a form of racism centred on what Cohen (1988: 64) calls a 'code of breeding': social and moral superiority were assumed through aristocratic lineage, granting those in power certain rights over their social inferiors. Racism had at base an economic function, permitting conquest and exploitation of resources within the colonies. Before the establishment of empire, the European aristocracy assumed a superior status: they were born to rule. After the initial conquest of imperial territories, large numbers of soldiers and administrators were needed to maintain colonial rule. At this stage the notion of superiority of the European over the newly colonized was extended and no longer remained the exclusive property of the ruling class.

The precise origins of racism may be open to debate but that European nineteenth-century imperialism was racist in character is evident. Before considering how development education might contribute to greater North-

South solidarity and co-operation, it is important to reflect on present-day relationships between Europe and the South and on the impact of racism in Europe today.

# PRESENT-DAY RELATIONSHIPS BETWEEN EUROPE AND THE SOUTH

Economic structures set up to exploit the resources of the European colonies to the benefit of the colonial powers have continued to function after formal independence. Transport links between and within the newly independent African states of the mid–twentieth century, for example, were usually inadequate to support regional trade, and so these newly independent states had no real alternative but to continue trading with the former colonial powers. This situation was reinforced by another colonial legacy, that of language; regional communication in West Africa, for example, continues to be influenced by individual states' use of either English or French as an official language, as a medium of instruction in schools and as the language which provides access to higher education.

While many states have sought to become self-sufficient, a number have encountered extreme difficulties, sometimes struggling to grow enough to feed their own populations, particularly where the best and most fertile land is planted with cash crops such as coffee or tea which in turn are subject to variations in world commodity prices. Furthermore, these prices are fixed by transnational corporations, whose first concern is profit rather than the welfare of the producers.

Similarly, aid and development programmes, set up ostensibly to support and benefit the recipient countries, have all too often effectively brought their greatest benefit to investors. With the ending of the cold war, developing countries have been freed from the pressure to become involved in East–West conflict that was often a consequence of accepting foreign 'aid'. However, the ending of this conflict may lead to a new set of difficulties if much of this investment is transferred to eastern Europe. Nevertheless, as many states currently move towards more democratic systems of government, there remains a continued pressure to adopt particular models of democracy, imposed from without, with little regard as to whether they are the most appropriate, but with the continued assumption that we in the North know what is best. Although it is encouraging that more widespread concern is being shown for human rights, there remains the danger that the human rights discourse is used as a cover to maintain a degree of political and economic control over the countries of the South.

Racist ideology continues to justify and perpetuate unequal relationships at a global level, and to support the exploitation of the countries of the South to the advantage and profit of the North. The next section will examine ways in which racism operates to reinforce many of the social and economic inequalities that exist today at local, national and regional levels within Europe.

# RACE AND RACISM IN EUROPE TODAY

A front-page headline in a national newspaper declared, 'Even whites think Britain is still racist' (Kellner and Cohen, 1991). The paper, reporting on a survey carried out in association with the Runnymede Trust, found that there is a widespread perception in Britain that black people experience discrimination in employment, in the criminal justice system and in local government services. Over half those of South Asian descent, two thirds of white people and almost 8 in 10 of African Caribbean people find Britain to be either fairly racist or very racist. These perceptions are based firmly in reality; a government-sponsored survey of the access of various ethnic groups to a broad range of services, the Policy Studies Institute (PSI) study of 1982, found widespread disadvantage among black people in a number of areas (Brown, 1984). The PSI survey findings are supported by a number of more recent studies focusing specifically on employment (Brown and Gay, 1985), housing (CRE, 1987), and education (CRE, 1988).

In Germany, which recently has seen the worst industrial and social unrest since World War II, and a growth in support for far right and neo-fascist parties, there has been a dramatic rise in racist attacks, with over 600 attacks reported to the police in a three-month period, a five-fold increase on the previous year (Bradshaw, 1992). Germany has no race discrimination laws protecting the rights of ethnic minorities, since officially it is not a multicultural society, but it has had the most generous asylum laws in Europe, which have permitted anyone arriving in Germany and claiming asylum the right to remain until his or her case is considered.

Paradoxically, there is no official immigration, and the need for labour during a period of economic growth has been met by allowing foreigners entry and the right to work while denying them citizenship rights. Seven per cent of the population is classed as foreign, and although many of these people were born in Germany and pay taxes, they lack the right to vote and take up certain jobs such as teaching and the police. Germany's citizenship laws, drawn up in 1913, are based on ethnicity, literally on 'blood', and not on birth or residency; many 'ethnic Germans' born outside the country, whose families may have left the country generations ago and who no longer have ties with the country, have the right of citizenship whereas others, born and brought up in the country, do not.

The situation in France is somewhat different, where over the past decade 1.2 million foreigners, most of them from North Africa, have become citizens. As Michael Ignatieff (1991) writes:

> Their *travail dur* – running public transport, assembling the cars, digging the ditches and harvesting the melons – is a key reason for France's economic success. The statistics tell a story of their steadily rising educational attainment and income, mastery of the French language and culture and gradual insertion into French life.

He goes on to argue that despite this apparent integration into French society a myth has been created of a white population threatened by alien Arabs in their midst. As the media persist in presenting France's ethnic minorities as a social problem, so politicians have sought votes among those who are anti-immigration. A myth has been created of a nation, culture and national identity which is being subjected to a new threat. Although France has been a nation of immigration for hundreds of years, this fact is forgotten as anxieties emerge out of this myth of national identity.

This is a theme developed by Gill (1992) in an examination of the societal myth relating to British identity and national characteristics. Addressing the issue of multicultural education, he argues that its opponents, in failing to address the facts of the actual experiences of black people in Britain, contribute to a situation 'where myths alluding to an imperial past have to be clung to like straws as the nation struggles to assert an identity in the face of changes wrought by time'. He argues that these narratives must alter to bring them closer in line with people's real histories, and suggests the need for a new myth to be created which incorporates values and qualities to which the whole of society can relate. Since education cannot avoid being part of the process of myth-making, this process will take place either by design or default; the challenge to educationalists is to address the questions of self- and national identity, and to contribute towards the creation of a non-racist society.

Development education has an important role to play in this process since it invites students and teachers to examine a variety of perspectives and to look beyond national boundaries. As students reassess concepts of national identity to include all communities within a pluralist society, they will be engaged in redefining citizenship.

# MULTICULTURAL EUROPE

In a report, 'Action to Combat Intolerance and Xenophobia in the Activities of the Council of Europe's Council for Cultural Cooperation' (Perotti, 1991), the author declares:

> No multicultural society – and all European societies are compelled to acknowledge their *de facto* multicultural nature – can recognise its multiculturalism in law and in spirit, without at the same time engaging in activities on all fronts, be they socio–economic, legal, educational or cultural. It would be futile to expect that a shortfall in one sector, say education, could be meaningfully offset by progress involving only one of the other factors.
>
> (Perotti, 1991: 5)

Perotti suggests that the multicultural nature of Europe has developed in three distinct ways. First there are those multi-ethnic and multilingual communities which have arisen as the result of the formation of nation states (there are 48 European minority language groups representing 30 million people). Secondly, in the post-colonial period there are communities made up of those who have migrated from former colonies and their descendants who have either retained the citizenship of one of the former colonial powers or who have claimed a European nationality (about 17.5 million people). Thirdly there exists a group of about 15 million people who have the status of foreigners and who are living in Europe as the result of a variety of social, economic and political factors, including those who arrived as refugees.

In reality, those in the two latter categories may well overlap: many members of minority ethnic communities who can take their histories back to Europe's former colonies are also living in Europe as a result of a variety of interrelated social, economic and political factors. For example, many migrants from former Caribbean colonies first came to Britain in response to employers' direct appeals for labour in the post-war period; a number of Asian settlers from East Africa arrived in the UK as refugees in the 1970s but they were also British passport holders whose very presence in East Africa was directly related to the British government's colonial policies and rule. The 'foreign' status of a number of other communities living in Europe may owe more to certain European governments' willingness to accept and exploit migrant labour while denying these workers and their families effective citizenship and political rights.

The opening up of the European Community in 1992 has been heralded as a great new economic opportunity for the peoples of the twelve member states, with the opening of internal borders and the free movement of workers and goods. Much attention has been given to the economic and social implications of the Single European Act (SEA) for the citizens of the European community but less thought has been given to questions of race equality in the new Europe or to the ways in which the citizenship rights of minorities might be secured and guaranteed. Black and migrant communities across Europe are placed in a vulnerable position as governments seek to clarify rules and procedures concerning immigration, free travel of citizens, and border controls.

Ethnic minorities in Britain, although subject to continued widespread discrimination, do have recourse to justice through the 1976 Race Relations Act which takes into account indirect as well as direct discrimination in employment, housing, education, the provision of services and advertisements, and the publication or distribution of material likely to encourage racial hatred. Regrettably, Britain is the only member state of the European Community with such wide-ranging legislation on racial discrimination. Thus black British citizens cannot be guaranteed the same rights elsewhere in Europe, where ethnic minorities are offered less protection by national laws (Birmingham City Council, 1991).

Minority ethnic communities in Europe that trace their descent from the countries of the South are likely to be subject to stereotyping linked to Europe's imperialist past, with all the connotations of superiority of culture and 'race' which have been inherited from this past age. This is likely to be the case whether or not they are living in a territory which is a former colonial power or whether or not they are in any way related to a former colony.

Similarly they also carry the stereotype of 'immigrant', a term which has come to be so closely related to skin colour that it is rarely if ever applied to an English person settled in France or Spain, or an Irish national living in Britain, but is regularly used to describe any black person living in Europe, regardless of nationality or legal status. This is true even in the official terminology of the European Community where, for example, funds are made available to disadvantaged minorities, who must nevertheless apply for them as 'migrants' or 'migrant workers'. For many communities the notion of a multicultural Europe, where minority rights are protected, discrimination outlawed, and freedom to live without the threat of violence guaranteed, remains as little more than an ideal. The notion of multiculturalism disguises the limited citizenship rights of many minority ethnic communities and the real inequalities of power which continue to exist.

# RACISM AND ANTI-RACISM IN EDUCATION

Existent racism in European society and restrictive notions of national and European identity clearly raise a number of questions about the content and focus of education most appropriate to meet the needs of young Europeans now. This education must recognize the rights of all the peoples of Europe and acknowledge the multicultural nature of contemporary European society. If all communities are to participate on the basis of equality then such an education must contribute to the creation of a non-racist society and the abandonment of the myths of an old imperialist past; it also needs to replace them with a new sense of European identity and a reconstructed understanding of European citizenship which is inclusive rather than exclusive of minority rights, identities and cultures.

Policies developed in response to the presence of black pupils in Britain have been well documented (see for example Mullard, 1982; Troyna and Williams, 1986). Mullard traces the changes in response from the assimilationist model of the 1950s and early 1960s through the integrationist model adopted in the mid-1960s, to the cultural pluralism of the 1970s. It was the clear failure of the earlier policies to assimilate black students into white middle-class values and behaviours which led to the policy of cultural pluralism, expressed in the form of multicultural education.

Difficulties with the cultural pluralist model began to be apparent from the late 1970s. Learning about each other's cultures (or arguably learning about a static, white liberal representation of black communities and their cultures) does not ensure that children will value or respect these cultures or unlearn the hierarchy into which they have previously placed them. As Cohen reminds us: 'the multicultural illusion is that dominant and subordinate can somehow swap places and learn how the other half lives, whilst leaving the structures of power intact' (1988: 13).

Moreover, many black parents and communities were rightly suspicious of an education which in practice often presented a differentiated package to their children, purporting to give them a sense of identity and self-pride, while effectively denying them access to examinations, to certain types of employment and to higher education (Stone, 1981). Within the black communities there is widespread recognition of the ways in which education generally has failed black children and communities; rather than tackling racism and injustice operating within society, it continues to reproduce and reinforce social injustice:

> The education system's success can be measured directly in terms of Black children's failure within it. By institutionalising the prejudices and the undermining assumptions we face in our everyday lives, the schools have kept our children at the very bottom of the ladder of employability and laid the blame on us. The schools' ability to churn out cheap, unskilled factory fodder . . . may have served the economic needs of this society; it has not met the aspirations of a community which has always equated education with liberation from poverty.
>
> (Bryan et al., 1985)

During the 1970s concerns within the black community about the failure of the school system to serve its children led to a government inquiry into the educational attainments of black pupils and ways in which resources might be best used to keep educational performance under review. The interim report of the Committee of Inquiry into the Education of Children from Ethnic Minority Groups (1981) acknowledged racism as the major factor contributing to their children's underachievement.

In 1985 the Committee of Inquiry published its final report, known as the Swann Report, which to the anger of many within the black communities seemed to play down the factor of racism, but which nevertheless appeared to give multicultural education credence and offered support for the promotion of cultural diversity and racial equality. This major United Kingdom government-sponsored report, 'recognizing the contribution of schools in preparing all pupils for life in a society which is both multi–racial and culturally diverse', defined a good education as one which gave every individual 'the knowledge, understanding and skills to function effectively as an individual, as citizen of the wider national society in which he [*sic*] lives and in the interdependent world comunity of which he is also a member' (Committee of Inquiry, 1985: vii and 319).

The report highlights other features of a 'good education' for all pupils: the use of teaching materials which are multicultural in content and global in perspective; the provision of opportunities for pupils to identify and challenge racism; the inclusion of effective political education, with scope for pupils to consider how power is exercised and by whom in society; and the identification and removal of practices and procedures which directly or indirectly work against pupils from any ethnic group. The report stresses that these issues should be addressed in all contexts, and should be given particular emphasis in predominantly white or all-white areas (Committee of Inquiry, 1985: 318–40).

In identifying the need to prepare students to be both citizens of the wider national society in which they live and citizens of the interdependent world community, the Swann report advocates what would appear to be two of the essential ingredients of an appropriate education for the people of Europe as we enter the twenty-first century: one which focuses first on citizenship at different levels and which encourages the development of an inclusive rather than exclusive understanding of national identity and citizenship. This revitalized view of education would promote an understanding of the rights and responsibilities of democratic citizenship not dependent on ethnic affiliation or identification but recognizing and supporting diversity both within and between societies. This view of education for active, participative citizenship might therefore acknowledge diversity, interdependence and differences in perception, and might approach areas of study from a variety of cultural perspectives, encouraging students to recognize shared values. It follows therefore that the rights of British citizens, for example, will depend not on skin colour, physical appearance or culture but on a new broader and more inclusive understanding of what it means to be British and on an exploration within society, for example within the media, of a shared system of values.

Secondly, students would be encouraged to look beyond their national boundaries in order to understand something of current global interdependence and its historical roots. Schools working to achieve these goals would encourage all pupils, including those from ethnic minorities, to recognize and claim their rights as citizens, while at the same time maintaining their rights to a self-identity which allows individuals and groups to maintain their distinctive cultural heritage. The national heritage would, in turn, acknowledge this rich variety of contributions.

In advocating a curriculum which is multicultural in content and global in perspective as key features in challenging racism, the Swann Report is proposing education for development; it recognizes that such an education must include the development of political awareness, the analysis of how power is exercised and by whom. This remains a key issue in the preparation of students for citizenship within a democratic framework.

Recent education reforms have distracted many teachers and other education-alists from the goal of promoting racial equality and from implementing many of the recommendations of the Swann Report. Despite the reference in the 1988 Education Reform Act to entitlement for all children and the stress on breadth, balance, continuity and progression, the National Curriculum, put together largely as a collection of separate subject documents, is already proving itself to be unwieldy, overladen and content heavy. The DES document *National Curriculum: From Policy to Practice* (1989: 3.8) stated that:

> The whole curriculum for all pupils will certainly need to include at appropriate (and in some cases all) stages: career education and guidance; health education; other aspects of personal and social education; and a coverage across the curriculum of gender and multi-cultural issues.

There is, as yet, little evidence that the National Curriculum is providing this cross-curricular coverage of gender and multicultural issues. Teachers are faced with the task of trying to implement the reforms while the curriculum becomes increasingly assessment driven. Curriculum areas such as English and history have become the sites of fierce debate, seen as they are by government advisers and the political right as important vehicles for promoting and sustaining British culture, interpreted in a way which is exclusive and élitist. Curriculum reform imposed upon teachers without thorough consultation is unlikely to be successful; all such reforms depend on the co-operation of teachers who control the process of implementation. If teachers do not understand the underlying philosophy or do not subscribe to it then it is likely to be bypassed or subverted.

Nevertheless, although citizenship remains one of the cross-curricular themes, it is difficult to see how the recommendations of the Swann Report can be put into practice, in a context where the curriculum appears to be assessment driven and where teachers are faced with a choice between providing what they perceive to be a good education for their pupils and enabling those pupils to meet the requirements of imposed assessment procedures. Media education, for example, has been excluded from the revised English curriculum, although it is an area which is critical for the development of political awareness and for preparation for citizenship within a democratic framework.

# A EUROPEAN RESPONSE TO RACISM THROUGH EDUCATION

The work of the Council for Cultural Co-operation (CDCC) of the Council of Europe in challenging racism and xenophobia in school systems has largely been through programmes focusing on the revision of history teaching, media education, intercultural education and education in human rights and democratic values (Perotti, 1991). Concerns identified by the CDCC, such as the bias of history textbooks and the Eurocentric focus of many history courses, the contribution of history to teaching young people about the ways in which human rights were won and defended in hard-fought struggles, and the new rights emerging as societies develop, all relate closely to the key concerns of development educators.

Equally, development education places considerable emphasis on a pedagogy of involvement and responsibility, and on the political environment of learning and the importance of teaching students from a very early age to decipher photographic and audio-visual material. The recognition that cultures do not exist in a state of isolation, that they intercommunicate and interact through exchanges or conflicts, and that equality is seldom a feature of intercultural relationships is also an important dimension of both anti-racist and development education.

Sadly, European education systems have tended to remain largely mono-cultural (ethnocentric) and have failed to keep pace with new realities within Europe, such as those of the settlement of large communities of 'foreign origin' (Perotti, 1991: 8). Reform of these education systems, to bring them in line with Europe's current realities, would seem to be an urgent priority, particularly when it is also recognized that new media and technologies are bringing the various communities of Europe into closer daily contact both with each other and with communities in other parts of the world. A clearer understanding of North–South relationships and global interdependence would seem to demand a re-evaluation of the concept of citizenship and citizenship education, including education for global citizenship.

# CITIZENSHIP IN A PLURALIST SOCIETY

The concept of citizenship has changed considerably through time and the citizen has enjoyed a variety of rights and responsibilities at different points in history. The concept is not clear-cut today, and this presents a number of difficulties in any discussion of citizenship and citizenship education. Citizenship is often used in a legal sense to mean national citizenship, and Lynch (1992) reminds us that much of what might be classified as citizenship education has in fact been teaching about national citizenship.

The concept of citizenship has been linked in political discourse to notions of cultural and national identity. A notorious example of this was the 'cricket test' of April 1990 when a former British cabinet minister alleged that the patriotism and political allegiance of British Asians could be assessed according to whether they supported England or Pakistan in test match cricket. It might seem absurd to many that a particular sporting allegiance be equated with a person's patriotism but in the resulting controversy the citizenship rights of the black British communities came under question as sections of the media chose to equate national identity and 'Britishness' with a narrowly defined, white cultural identity.

In Europe, relaxtion of internal border controls and freedom of movement of individuals between states, following the implementation of the Single European Act (1992), depend largely on the individual's citizenship status. Non-EC nationals (known as Third Country Nationals) resident in Europe are likely to be subject to increased surveillance, with the opening up of internal borders leading to a tightening up of external borders and the creation of

Fortress Europe. At the Luxembourg Summit in June 1991 the British Prime Minister restated a popular European demand for stronger external border controls by demanding 'a strong, tight perimeter fence around Europe', adding that 'We must not be wide open to all comers simply because Paris, Rome and London seem more attractive than Algiers and Bombay' (John Major, quoted in Birmingham City Council, 1991).

Calls for Fortress Europe and a control on immigration are likely to have a considerable impact on the citizenship rights of members of black and minority ethnic communities within Europe, whether or not they hold EC nationality. In the United Kingdom, media discussion of the 1991 Asylum Bill made explicit connections between refugees seeking asylum, the need for tight immigration laws and the position of black British citizens. Justifying the need for the government bill, designed to impose restrictions on the rights of those seeking entry to Britain as refugees, Foreign Secretary Douglas Hurd told Amnesty International that although the government 'understood and shared Amnesty's concern', ensuring that 'Britain respects its obligations to the refugee' had to be reconciled 'with a truth dinned into me through the years when I was Home Secretary, namely that the good relations between communities in this country depend to a very large extent on a firm and fair system of immigration control' (*The Guardian*, 26 November 1991). In other words, the position of minority ethnic communities and the maintenance of citizenship rights are dependent on the control of numbers. The implication is that the rest of the population has a limited tolerance of minorities.

Sally Tomlinson reminds us that formal citizenship rights may not in practice guarantee equality between citizens, and that British minorities

> have faced a forty-year struggle to acquire and to exercise their political, civil and social citizenship rights. They have also faced a white majority seemingly determined to reject non-white groups as equal citizens within the British nation.
>
> (Tomlinson, 1992: 35)

Tomlinson shows how these same minorities have, particularly during the 1980s, been blamed for many of society's problems which in turn has strengthened a particular type of nationalism providing 'encouragement to the white majority to consider the demands made by minorities so unreasonable as to preclude them from claims to equal citizenship rights' (Tomlinson, 1992: 44). If, as Tomlinson asserts, 'Britain is a nation state resisting the idea that it is a multicultural society' (1992: 47), and the racism in British society is also reflected in a number of other European nation states, this raises a number of questions about the nature and focus of education for citizenship.

## EDUCATION FOR CITIZENSHIP

Despite the struggles of minority ethnic communities within Europe, their citizenship rights, often based on nationality, and sometimes on an exclusive understanding of national identity, have not always been secured. Teachers seeking to promote education for active citizenship at local, national and regional and global levels may well be looking for legitimization of their efforts. This may well be a particular concern at a time when messages in the media and from some politicians may seem antagonistic to their goals; the popular political messages relating to refugees, asylum seekers, and particularly the peoples of the South may well be at odds with the aims of development education to promote greater North–South solidarity and an understanding of global interdependence.

At the same time the need to promote social justice and global responsibility in education would appear to be more urgent than ever as we become more acutely aware of the limited nature of the world's natural resources and the need for sustainable development. This growing awareness has led to a greater understanding of the relationship between environmental, development and human rights issues, and a recognition of our inability to find solutions to a number of development issues at local or national levels. As Lynch expresses it:

> at a time of surging competition for the world's scarce and non-renewable economic resources and of growing cross-national radioactive and other pollution, there can be no redemption or rectification in single-nation initiatives. In an age when conflicts are increasingly supranational, deriving from age-old ideologies such as religions, when major conflict between haves and have-nots is growing, no one nation, not even one of the superpowers, is competent to resolve the ideological, economic and environmental pressures facing all travellers on spaceship earth.
>
> (Lynch, 1992: 16)

This realization demands not only a re-evaluation of citizenship and citizenship education to meet the new demands of global society but also raises questions about the values upon which such an education might be based.

Starkey (1986) argues that the appropriate values for world studies, the related area of development education, and multicultural anti-racist education must be those of human rights; he asserts that 'Human rights are the explicit values on which all education should be based.' Tracing the development of the European Convention for the Protection of Human Rights and Fundamental Freedoms (1950) and examining its implications for educators in Europe, he reminds us that the Convention is, at European rather than national level, the main legal instrument guaranteeing human rights. Human rights instruments provide us with internationally agreed statements which might form the basis upon which conflicts and development issues are negotiated.

Moreover, since human rights values, as expressed in the Universal Declaration of Human Rights 1948, are internationally agreed values which apply to all human beings, they can be used as the basis for reassessing education for citizenship. These values, based on the concepts of justice and peace, equality and dignity, democracy and freedom, solidarity and reciprocity, universality and indivisibility, together with their implications for education, are discussed in some detail by Starkey (1986). It is, however, important to note that in 1985 the Committee of Ministers of the Council of Europe adopted a recommendation on 'Teaching and Learning about Human Rights in Schools' (Council of Europe, 1991: 256–9) which expresses agreed positions on what schools in member states might do to promote knowledge and awareness of human rights issues and values (Starkey, 1991: 20–38). Teachers seeking official justification for their work and a set of values upon which they might base their work in education for development and racial equality will find it in this text.

Human rights values are a sound basis which will allow us to look beyond old notions of national citizenship with all their attendant problems towards a new concept of citizenship education at local, national and regional and global levels.

# THE CONTRIBUTION OF DEVELOPMENT EDUCATION

Development education contributes a global perspective to the school curriculum and explores development issues at local, national, regional and global levels. A recognition of global interdependence provides a framework in which students may explore economic and power relationships, allowing them to understand and challenge racism and injustice.

Geography has often been seen as the subject which most easily lends itself to the teaching of development issues, but any study of such issues which lacks a historical perspective may arguably provide an inadequate explanation of the inequalities which currently exist both within multicultural Europe and in North–South relationships. Analysis of the current inequalities between North and South set outside of any historical context may reinforce rather than challenge the racist assumptions which have traditionally underpined the curriculum. A study of colonialism would therefore seem to be an essential part of any curriculum designed to promote a greater understanding of North–South interdependence.

Development education workers in partnership with teachers have developed a pedagogy which is student-centred and which stresses the active participation of the learner, drawing particularly on the ideas and practice of the influential Brazilian educator, Paulo Freire. This pedagogy has an important contribution to make towards education for active citizenship since it is designed to provide students with the skills they are likely to need in participating in their communities; these include enquiry skills and the ability to interpret and assess information from a variety of sources, including printed and audio-visual sources; the ability to understand and test concepts relating to world society; and particularly the political skills which will enable them to influence and participate in decision-making at local, national and international levels.

Many teachers would seem to have been attracted to development education both by its emphasis on an active approach to learning and by the desire to broaden the curriculum to include a variety of cultural perspectives. Development education materials frequently focus on the methodology of teaching and learning and on practical ways of enabling children to understand development issues. These materials are often of a very high quality and have been influential in encouraging teachers to introduce development education into their schools and classrooms.

There is, however, a danger in this approach if teachers fail to address the questions of development at an adult level; the question remains as to whether teachers can be effective development educators if they have not studied and explored these issues for themselves. A focus on active learning and on cultural pluralism may be the necessary first steps in challenging a traditionally biased and Eurocentric curriculum, but they will not effectively challenge the societal myths which have emerged concerning national and European identity, and furthermore they are unlikely to be effective in challenging the gross inequalities which exist both in our own society and at a global level. Such an approach may achieve little more than many of the multicultural approaches first adopted in the 1970s.

A focus on active learning and the use of materials from a variety of cultures are unlikely to reassure those within the minority ethnic communities who demand an equal chance for their children and who are seeking an education which will challenge rather than reinforce the inequalities and injustices that they experience in their everyday lives. Nor is it likely to be of great long-term value in promoting values of social justice among those children educated in predominantly white or all-white schools.

It might be argued that a type of development education which focuses strongly on classroom practices but which fails to engage teachers as adult learners remains a soft option for those in the North whose own education has left them inadequately prepared to understand the power relationships and structures which operate within society. Culture and power are closely related, and any examination of other cultures or societies whether here in Europe or in the South which ignores the dynamic and complex nature of culture or which neglects structural inequalities is likely to be inadequate. It may, by default, present an explanation of the subordination of black and migrant communities which focuses on their alleged cultural deficiencies rather than on racist designations which allege cultural inferiority. Development education must address the existing divisions, conflicts, discrimination and inequalities within society and teachers must be encouraged to examine their own values as part of the process of preparation and training. Development education workers and teachers need to recognize that the deficiencies of our own education are a more serious problem than has perhaps hitherto been acknowledged and that these deficiencies continue to undermine our efforts to become effective development educators.

One of the strengths of multicultural and anti-racist education is the alliances that have been forged between educators from minority ethnic communities and white educators also committed to racial equality; these alliances have sometimes been extended to include the local community. Within the development education movement, which has different origins and different sources of funding, such alliances have developed less frequently. One of the challenges facing development educators in Europe is that of establishing genuine and purposeful partnerships with those communities from the South that are resident in Europe and that share similar concerns, and with those groups and organizations in the South that are also involved in development education. Such alliances will permit participants to engage in debate and should promote a deeper understanding of universal human rights values. It is through such alliances and debates that perspectives may be broadened and we may develop the concept of global citizenship.

# CONCLUSION

It has been argued that development education has a critical role to play in education for a pluralist society and in challenging the racism which remains prevalent in Europe today. Such an education might play a part in challenging attitudes which work to hinder social justice; it will also provide opportunities for students to develop skills which will enable them to actively participate as citizens at all levels.

The development of a new concept of citizenship and citizenship education which overrides old notions of national citizenship and is not dependent on ethnic or cultural affiliation will make a significant contribution towards a new understanding of national and European identity and towards a non-racist society. This goal will not be achieved through education alone, but nevertheless education and schooling play an important part in either reinforcing or challenging inequality and injustice and therefore need to be exploited to the full.

# REFERENCES

Anderson, B. (1983), *Imagined Communities: Reflections on the Origin and Spread of Nationalism*, London: Verso.

Birmingham City Council (1991), *1992 and Race Equality Fact Pack*, Birmingham: Birmingham City Council Race Relations Unit.

Bradshaw, B. (1992), 'Report from Berlin', *The World This Weekend*, BBC Radio 4, 17 May 1992.

Brown, C. (1984), *Black and White Britain: 3rd PSI Survey*, Oxford: Heinemann.

Brown, C. and Gay, P. (1985), *Racial Discrimination: 17 Years After the Act*, London: PSI.

Bryan, B., Dadzie, S. and Scafe, S. (1985), *The Heart of the Race: Black Women's Lives in Britain*, London: Virago.

Cohen, P. (1988), 'The perversions of inheritance: studies in the making of multi-racist Britain', in Cohen, P. and Bains, H. (eds), *Multi-racist Britain*, London: Macmillan.

Commission for Racial Equality (1987), *Living in Terror*, London: CRE.

Commission for Racial Equality (1988), *Learning in Terror*, London: CRE.

Committee of Inquiry into the Education of Children from Ethnic Minority Groups (Rampton Committee) (1981), *West Indian Children in Our Schools*, London: HMSO.

Committee of Inquiry into the Education of Children from Ethnic Minority Groups (Swann Committee) (1985), *Education for All*, London: HMSO.

Council of Europe (1991), 'Recommendation No. R(85)7 of the Committee of Ministers to member states on teaching and learning about human rights in schools', in Starkey, H., *The Challenge of Human Rights Education*, London: Cassell.

Department of Education and Science (1989), *National Curriculum: From Policy to Practice*, London: HMSO.

Gill, B. (1992), 'Moral dilemmas of societal myth making', in Leicester, M. and Taylor, M. (eds), *Ethics, Ethnicity and Education*, London: Kogan Page.

Ignatieff, M. (1991), 'The tricolour seen in whiter shades of pale', *The Observer*, 21 July 1991.

Kellner, P. and Cohen, N. (1991), 'Even whites think Britain is still racist', *The Independent on Sunday*, 7 July 1991.

Lynch, J. (1992), *Education for Citizenship in a Multicultural Society*, London: Cassell.

Mullard, C. (1982), 'Multiracial education in Britain: from assimilation to cultural pluralism', in Tierney, J. (ed.), *Race, Migration and Schooling*, London: Holt, Rinehart & Winston.

Perotti, A. (1991), *Action to Combat Intolerance and Xenophobia in the Activities of the Council of Europe's Council for Cultural Co-operation 1969–1989*, Strasbourg: Council of Europe.

Starkey, H. (1986), 'Human rights: the values for world studies and multicultural education', *Westminster Studies in Education*, **9**, 57–66.

Starkey, H. (1991), 'The Council of Europe recommendation on the teaching and learning of human rights in schools', in Starkey, H. (ed.), *The Challenge of Human Rights Education*, London: Cassell.

Stone, M. (1981), *The Education of the Black Child in Britain: The Myth of Multicultural Education*, London: Fontana.

Tomlinson, S. (1992), 'Citizenship and minorities', in Jones, N. and Baglin Jones, E. (eds), *Education for Citizenship*, London: Kogan Page.

Troyna, B. and Williams, J. (1986), *Racism, Education and the State*, Beckenham: Croom Helm.

# CHAPTER 3

# Introducing Development Education to Schools: The Role of Non-governmental Organizations in the United Kingdom

*Scott Sinclair*

Non-governmental organizations (NGOs) have played a major role in introducing development education content and approaches to the school system in the UK. This chapter takes stock of some of that experience and explores issues about effective strategies for this work.

The implications of defining development education are considered and reviewed in terms of different approaches to NGOs' work with schools.

The nature of the 'development education system' is explored and reviewed in the context of the role of the voluntary sector and the potential for developing long-term strategies. Particular attention is given to the strategy of working in partnership with teachers and their schools.

The chapter concludes by reflecting on the need for NGOs to review their role.

## NGOs AND DEVELOPMENT EDUCATION

Despite limited resources much has been achieved over the past twenty years of development education initiatives. A range of experimental work involving different subject areas and age groups has led to the evolution of teaching approaches and case studies that have been widely disseminated.

A range of styles of work have been employed to back up the introduction of development education to schools. These include offering basic resource services in the form of resource shops, catalogues and small libraries; introductory in-service work and in-service work targeted at particular areas of the curriculum; team teaching, involving the co-planning and input to a scheme of work; curriculum development projects involving teachers meeting to develop ideas about the potential for a development education approach within their particular area of responsibility; the production of a wide range of teaching material, some of which has been produced in partnership with teachers; contributions in response to the proposals for the National Curriculum; and research and development of background materials on contemporary issues.

Much of this work has grown out of organizations which collectively make up what Arnold (1987) described as the 'development education system'. He observed that the lack of government support for development education in the 1980s had resulted in the responsibility for this work being left with NGOs.

The address list in the Oxfam Education catalogue (Oxfam) and the National Association of Development Education Centres' membership list (NADEC) introduce the wide range of organizations involved in development education. They include the major aid and development charities; solidarity groups which typically have a link with a particular country or region; groups with special interest in environmental issues or human rights issues; and groups with development education as their main brief. The latter category include a national network of local organizations known as Development Education Centres.

## DEFINITIONS AND THEIR IMPLICATIONS

The definition of development education which is most often used was produced by the United Nations in 1975. It states that development education seeks

> to enable people to participate in the development of their community, their nation and the world as a whole. Such participation implies a critical awareness of local, national and international situations based on an understanding of the social, economic and political processes.
>
> (Quoted in Hicks and Townley, 1982: 9)

The UN definition then outlines development education content as

> concerned with issues of human rights, dignity, self-reliance and social justice in both developed and developing countries. It is concerned with the causes of underdevelopment and the promotion of an understanding of what is involved in development, of how different countries go about undertaking development, and of the reasons for and ways of achieving a new international economic and social order.
>
> (Quoted in Hicks and Townley, 1982: 9)

This definition reflected a growing awareness of the need to question assumptions about the processes of development and to move away from the notion that such processes are about simple models of the South catching up or following the priorities set by the North.

51

In the long term, NGOs involved in introducing development education to the curriculum and to the schools system are centrally concerned with the need to equip future generations with skills which will enable them to function in what is increasingly a global society and to play an effective part in development processes.

Economically the world has become more integrated than ever before. The growth of transnational companies, the influence of stock markets and the technology of communications enable economic decisions to affect many parts of the globe at the same time. The evolution of the European Community, the growing role of the UN, the collapse of the Soviet Union and the importance of strategic resources such as oil all require us to build up a political literacy which extends beyond the local setting of national politics. Events which take place thousands of miles away can have an immediate political, economic and environmental impact on us.

Strategically we all have a growing awareness of the implications of the arms race. As a result of television we are more aware of the realities of conflicts in other parts of the world and of the extent to which we are implicated in them.

Morally there is an increasing awareness of the need to respond to widespread injustice, inequality and poverty. There is increasing awareness that this needs to be seen in its global political context.

These economic, political, strategic and moral contexts underline the need for a long-term approach to introducing a development perspective and a global dimension. They also highlight the ongoing dynamic of the issues involved and the need for opportunities for teachers to explore their own understanding of those issues.

Some groups have seen development education as a way of focusing on poverty and hunger, and our responses to them in isolation from other factors. There is a danger that this view of development education is linked to a traditional view of development, itself centred on Western concepts of progress. From that perspective development involves the transfer of Western technology, knowledge, finance and institutional structures. The belief is, despite the rhetoric, that we have the answer. This view of development is an ethnocentric and partial view, and usually leads to an educational response which centres on information, knowledge and transmission models of learning. Much of the work of development education NGOs has increasingly challenged this approach.

Development is seen as a common experience – one which links us to other apparently quite different situations. Development education is about introducing a global dimension and a development perspective. This has a role to play in many aspects of the taught curriculum as well as having implications for the ethos of the school and the hidden curriculum. This approach focuses on fundamental similarities between the experiences of people in different parts of the world. It suggests that there are common questions which can be asked about the influences on particular developments in those locations. It also highlights the fact that those local situations are directly linked to situations in other places as a result of the social, political, economic and natural systems which function at a global level.

This approach would therefore highlight the need to study many issues which may be basically seen as local, in their global context. It would, for example, be inappropriate to make a study of local employment/unemployment without reviewing the influences of international economic systems, the ownership and decision-making of companies, and the international nature of the marketplace.

It is also important that education related to issues such as race, gender, culture, peace, human rights and environment complements and is complemented by education relating to development. There is a real danger that each of these domains can become 'a cause' with a resultant collective effect which is like so many 'spears' targeting young people, competing for the agenda and contributing to a growing sense of powerlessness. There is need to be concerned, for example, that the cumulative effect of such initiatives does not de–skill young people and leave them in despair. Indeed, it might be argued that development education should contribute to building up people's confidence and their optimism about the possibilities of change.

The different organizations which have a particular focus on each of these domains have, therefore, to seek out a common ground and a shared educational agenda which takes account of the needs of young people. The issues need to be dealt with in a way which offers them a positive experience and one which gives them confidence to relate to those issues in the real world.

Development education aspires to avoid ethnocentric and gender bias and to contribute to an awareness of the role of such bias in our everyday thinking. It is not simply a question of eradicating bias; it is one of building into learning processes opportunities for students to re-evaluate for themselves the nature and origins of their attitudes and assumptions relating to any particular theme or issue.

Working definitions of development education have evolved over the last twenty years as experience has been gained. It became clear that a focus on Third World problems did little to help our understanding of them; such a focus meant that these 'problems' were seen in isolation from their local context, from global economic and political factors; and the ways in which we ourselves were connected with them were not acknowledged. Development education needed to focus more on injustice and the causes of poverty, and to recognize the limitations of dividing the world into first, second and third.

While being aware of the limitations of the term 'Third World' we should also recognize that the term 'South' does not necessarily provide us with a more accurate collective description. It is also useful to recall the positive use of 'Third World' reflecting the notion of the 'third way' or 'third estate'. Alternative approaches offered by many innovatory thinkers from the South challenge particular models of development and their application, not only in their own countries, but also in countries in the North. To listen to questions about development and change which stem from the South makes it increasingly clear that the greatest need for change was often in the North.

Many of the strategies used for introducing development education, as well as the inspiration for learning methodology, also came from educationalists such as Freire, who were working on conscientization programmes in the South. These ideas, reapplied in the context of our own society, continue to be central in creating effective strategies for engaging a wider interest in development education.

A definition of development education by the Birmingham Development Education Centre (DEC) offers a framework in which some of the central challenges in curriculum innovation can be addressed:

> Development education is about developing the skills necessary for effective participation in the world:
>
> - skills of recognising one's own values and the influences on these;
> - skills of empathy with people in different situations and with different cultures;
> - skills of acquiring information and of critical analysis of such information;
> - skills of recognising the validity of different points of view;
> - skills of forming one's own conclusions;
> - skills of recognising the way one relates to the world;
> - skills of recognising possibilities for future action.
>
> Development education is, also, about developing attitudes which are consistent with living in an interdependent world. Clearly, this cannot be achieved by simply telling people what to think. It involves creating opportunities for developing skills which enable people to respond to and question situations as they arise.
>
> Finally development education is also about knowledge – about our involvement in world affairs, and our potential for influencing them, and thus about concepts fundamental to an understanding of development.
>
> (DEC, 1981)

Since its publication, this definition has served as a focal point for a strategy involving a wide range of curriculum projects involving teachers working with early years, primary and secondary pupils. More than ten years later a project on the geography curriculum (DEC, 1992) was able to make a close correlation between this definition and what have been described as the common characteristics of the National Curriculum cross-curricular themes.

In the final analysis, fine tuning of the definitions of development education by NGOs within the 'development education system' is of little consequence unless they are also owned and implemented by those working in schools. This has implications not only for the strategies used by voluntary organizations but also for how development education is seen to relate to other aspects of the educational agenda.

# APPROACHES TO SCHOOLS

Many factors influence the approach an organization adopts to working with schools including their attitudes and assumptions about teachers. The unchecked influence of these is particularly significant if development education is only a secondary objective of the organization.

At one extreme, some organizations see the main objective of their work in schools as a form of public relations for *their* organization or a way of getting over *their* message and analysis about a particular issue, whether the issue be famine, South Africa, Central America, or trade. This approach is, in some instances, directly related to fund–raising in schools. Even organizations which make educational objectives their first priority can have an underlying rationale about fund-raising and may, for example, have a long–term goal of 'building a new donor base'. There is as a result, in many larger organizations, often a divergence in outlook between those making decisions about the availability of resources for development education and those who are developing strategies for implementing development education in schools.

In terms of the day-to-day relationship with schools and teachers it is useful to identify three different kinds of approach.

1 Organizations make an *input* into schools' curriculum activities by offering speakers or special simulation events. These may also be supported by materials promoting aspects of the organization's work.

Clearly there are limits to the potential impact of this work. At best it provides an opportunity for bringing people into the school who have a commitment to justice issues and who can share something of their commitment and enthusiasm. At worst, such sessions may be a form of indoctrination and/or may make extensive use of very negative stereotypes of people from the South. In such cases the approach would clearly be counter to the aims of development education as described in this chapter.

2 Organizations offer special events which are *extra-curricular* and which may in some cases relate to specific campaigns or even fund-raising.

At best such events may enhance student involvement and experience and may encourage the development of a range of skills relating to decision-making and action. At worst this approach provides a basis for exploiting young people as an accessible source of funding.

There have been a number of initiatives linking schools with other schools and communities in the South. Some of this work has run counter to the strategies advocated in this chapter for introducing development education; but at best such links may provide inspiration and opportunity for a wide range of development education work.

3 Organizations offer opportunities for teachers to resource and *develop the curriculum* for which those teachers have responsibility.

This approach involves designing work which embraces both the development education agenda and other teacher agendas relating, for example, to a particular curriculum area or age group. It gives priority to projects which teachers can initiate and builds teacher confidence to do so; it is important that such initiatives have an educational rationale to which the teacher is able to subscribe.

Schools can gain from each of these approaches in quite different ways. They are each distinctive but do not have to be mutually exclusive. However, development education organizations need to make priorities which reflect their objectives and apply suitable approaches rather than assume that all work in schools, and with teachers, is essentially the same.

# THE POTENTIAL OF THE VOLUNTARY SECTOR

In his discussion of NGOs and their contribution to development education, Arnold (1987) made it clear that he was not suggesting that the 'development education system' was highly organized or clearly identifiable. He did, however, like others, locate the core of such a system with NGOs in the voluntary sector.

Arnold collected his data during visits to Britain from the United States of America. It is arguable that his analysis reflects the dominant views that the 'development education system' had of itself. His papers were then used by those debating plans for the future of development education to give credibility to certain myths about the Charity Commissioners and funding.

The Charity Commissioners (the legal body responsible for NGOs which are registered as charities) were seen by Arnold as a key limiting factor on the ability of the voluntary sector to effectively introduce development education. Charities in the UK are not allowed to use the money they raise for what are described as political purposes. There is much to debate about what this means in practice; however, there is no evidence whatsoever to suggest that development education work is a problem for the Charity Commissioners. The problem arises when NGOs see education simply as a way of getting their own views across, particularly if such views are perceived as politically controversial.

Arnold also highlighted finance as a key constraint in strategic planning. While there is clearly a need for more substantial funding, limited budgets can sometimes provide a creative influence on the strategies adopted by some organizations. On the other hand, organizations may allow limited funding to act as a blinker which hinders any review of long-term objectives or strategic issues relating to effectiveness and relationships with the 'education system'. There is in particular a need to review the ways in which NGOs work in partnership with schools and teachers. Additional funds would not solve these strategic issues; indeed, they would add to them.

There is a lack of collective confidence within the 'development education system' which has made it difficult for collective strategies to emerge. Little priority has been given to the identification and debate of basic strategic principles applicable to the planning of development education projects. There is a sense of vulnerability within an under-resourced system which is defensive about its effectiveness and divided by the apparent success of some within the system. At the same time these organizations are brought closer together by the threat of superficial 'evaluation' by those who may have influence on the availability of funds; these include some key staff in the aid/development agencies and government advisers on Overseas Development Administration policy.

This situation has been compounded by the fact that some of the key actors proposing greater 'co-ordination' of the 'development education system' have tended to see such co-ordination in terms of management objectives and the need to develop centrally controlled programmes of work prioritized within a national plan. There is also a tendency to justify this management approach in terms of the limited funding 'cake' which has to be divided; in this way limited funding becomes an institutionalized constraint.

An alternative enabling approach would support both the need for growth in local initiative and also exponential growth involving partners in development education. This enabling approach to co-ordination would recognize that partnerships and genuinely shared agendas would also enable other sources to contribute finance to the 'development education system'. Such an approach would also acknowledge the massive potential for other systems, such as the education system, to use their own resources to further development education. It is the uptake of development education by people, such as teachers, for themselves that must provide the measure for the strategies used by NGOs.

Questions about the role of development education NGOs are reflected in debates within the wider voluntary sector, which was described by former Home Secretary Douglas Hurd as 'a third force alongside the public and private sectors of the economy'. There are over 150,000 charities operating in Britain; the sector also includes organizations such as campaign groups, solidarity groups and small unincorporated associations.

This spectrum of organizations reflects a wide range of work, political outlooks and viewpoints about the role of voluntary organizations. It is therefore very difficult to generalize about them or about the complex interrelationship between the voluntary sector and the private and public sectors. There are difficulties in viewing the voluntary sector as distinctly separate from the other two. First, government money, either from central government or via local authorities is an important source of finance for the voluntary sector, as is money from the private sector. Secondly, government policies at local and national level have a considerable effect on the work of voluntary organizations which either have to work to compensate for the effects of such policies or respond to the opportunities they provide.

The move towards greater privatization in the education system, for example, has created a dilemma within the voluntary sector about the nature of its role. In what ways, for example, are voluntary sector organizations different from a commercial company if they are competing for the provision of services? They may be in a strong position to offer an effective bid but they also have to consider the extent to which success in the 'market' might move them away from their central function.

As development education NGOs become more efficient, build up a reputation in their field and shed the image of amateurism, it remains important, but increasingly difficult, that they do not lose sight of their central function. A successful voluntary organization as it becomes more established will have bigger financial headaches, but at the same time an increasing range of potential work opportunities. In this context there is a particular need for clarity about functions and a need to review them within a long-term perspective.

Development education NGOs have tended to underestimate their potential for long-term planning as uncertainties about finance and status have encouraged a sense of vulnerability. However, the experiences of the last twenty years, working with the education system, would suggest that the voluntary sector can, if it chooses, maintain consistent policies and priorities over a long period of time. In many ways it has more potential to do this than the better-resourced curriculum initiatives inside the education system, which can be 'cut'. The extent to which development education organizations are often 'idea led' rather than 'finance led' may bring uncertainty, but can also increase the potential for longer-term strategies. NGOs tend to stress the weakness of their assets in terms of finance rather than the strength of assets in terms of 'people involvement' and motivation.

## WORKING IN PARTNERSHIP WITH TEACHERS

If an organization's objectives are about long-term curriculum change then priority has to be given to approaches which engage teachers in working on those processes for themselves and which enable the education system to take on a development education agenda.

Much of the subject matter of development relates to complex interrelationships between social, economic, political and natural systems. Within that context any one issue attracts a variety of viewpoints from the different people involved as well as different frameworks for analysing what is happening. Development education sets out to make these complex interrelationships more accessible to students. This clearly has implications not only for what is taught but for *how* it is taught. Similarly, there is a need to offer opportunities for teachers to learn about these issues and to develop their own perspectives on them.

Development education is not a clearly defined curriculum package which can be handed over to each school to try out. The emphasis is on adopting approaches and asking questions which will lead to individual schools developing their own plans within the context of the school's own agenda. Development education therefore takes on many forms in practice and can realistically contribute to all aspects of the curriculum, at all ages, as well as enabling work on the influence of the hidden curriculum.

To undertake this work, NGOs have to maintain a close relationship with the education system and an awareness of the debates taking place within it. At the same time it is important for them to maintain clarity about their own role in order that they are not simply subsumed within the education system. There is always the danger that they may be adopted as a wing of official policy; indeed, they may provide the education system with a cheap alternative!

One of the barriers to working in partnership with teachers is the deficit model of teachers which has an influence on NGOs. Widely used metaphors like 'targeting' and 'points of entry' suggest a sense of isolation and imply an approach which is not about shared agendas. Such an approach may obstruct a real potential for partnership and for using resources in a way that unlocks the considerable energy that exists within the teaching profession. The introduction (in England and Wales) of a National Curriculum renewed an existent danger, that of engaging the education system without interacting with it. It was possible simply to respond to curriculum documents and to opportunities perceived within them; this strategy could be adopted as an alternative to working with the teachers who have to implement the curriculum.

NGOs are likely to be most effective when working in close partnership with those people inside the system who are open to sharing the development education agenda. These 'volunteers' are then a significant asset in contributing towards change. For example, by designing focused curriculum projects it is possible to offer an appropriate opportunity for teachers to be involved in creative work to help meet their own curriculum needs; these creative processes can then be developed to share with other teachers.

This is a long-term approach. There are of course as many limitations to such an approach as there are limitations to the education system itself. There is far more evidence that schools replicate and reproduce patterns in society than that they change them. Those who think that they can develop a formula with a simple correlation between input to schools and particular changes in society are going to have a frustrating time. It would in any case not be desirable to find such a formula because if it existed, there are far more powerful vested interests that would wish to make use of it!

## REVIEWING THE ROLE

The changes that are taking place in the education system also have an impact on NGO planning. The introduction of local management of schools (LMS), the changing role of local education authorities (LEAs) and the increasing role of central government including the evolution of a National Curriculum all add up to fundamental change.

NGOs need to review continually what is happening in schools in order to identify new opportunities for involving teachers and schools in development education. Whenever changes are being made because of political policy, the implementation always provides the opportunity for introducing a development perspective and a global dimension to the plan. The potential (in terms of ideas and possible partners, if not funding) is therefore considerable even at times when frustration is high and morale low within schools. Indeed, NGOs can at such times have a vital role in contributing hope and helping to maintain a long-term perspective towards further, more positive change.

This increases the need for NGOs to be clear about what it is they are attempting to achieve and to review the strategies that might best serve those purposes. It is a question of identifying which of all the opportunities should be taken up and recognizing that it is not possible to respond to them all.

There are many parallels about such choices to be found in the models of change adopted and developed by agencies working in the South. In that context the pattern of placing the resources of the NGOs so that they are most accessible to change potential within the system, without being in the control of the system, is a familiar one. A Birmingham Development Education Centre project involved a group of advisory teachers in a study visit to The Gambia and Senegal. They produced a chart (*Elephant Times*, 1989) to share some of their work, which highlights observations about the promotion of development in The Gambia. Alongside this they reflected on experiences of promoting development in the British education system. They found that each gave insight into the strengths and weaknesses of the other. It was very much a two-way process which highlighted a number of the issues that were being overlooked in the British context.

Much of the funding for development education still comes from the aid agencies, yet the popular ideas of charity and the images that have been used in fund-raising have contributed to a sanitized compassion which fogs awareness of many global political and economic realities. The advertising success in the past has been so great that now a wider range of more positive and accurate images are used; despite this, what large sectors of the public actually 'see' are the negative stereotypes. The aid agencies are also facing challenges about their central functions and the extent to which they should give priority to building up awareness of the political dimensions of the issues they are dealing with. Development education has a role to play in contributing to this awareness but there is a need to convince the agencies about the importance of long-term investment in political literacy rather than the packaging of agency analysis as simple messages for public consumption.

As development education NGOs evolve, they have to take stock of their role; part of this process involves reviewing how they relate to both the private and public sectors. They also need to consider what can be learned from the styles of work and methods that are used in those sectors. Planning processes can be stimulated by outside practices; however, NGOs need to consider these in the context of what they are trying to achieve.

So, for example, a publisher's prime reason for producing a book is to generate income and publishers will therefore use a pricing structure which gives an effective return. A development education organization's priority, however, is dissemination of resources – selling as many publications as possible and, what's more, getting them used. This may be less profitable but in terms of the organization's objectives it is more effective. However, if the NGO goes to the other extreme, by making things too cheap or free, it loses the access to an infrastructure which helps the dissemination and evaluation of its work.

An LEA teachers' centre or a private business offering courses will identify demand from teachers and schools and will plan its programme accordingly. A development education NGO may wish to do this in part; however, it would also wish to include a development education perspective in any course, even if that made it less attractive in the 'marketplace'. It would, for example, be very easy for an organization to spend all its efforts on running successful in-service courses relating to the National Curriculum, which might be very worthwhile, but could well be a diversion from its main aims; in the medium term it might also limit future options for work to those dictated by the demands of the marketplace.

As a longer-term strategy, an NGO might wish to offer courses which attract a sector of the market, made up of teachers, that could be described as potential change agents. An NGO would therefore, unlike an LEA, probably not wish to cover all aspects of the curriculum or all schools but would prefer to build on the areas and people where there is most interest and potential. NGOs may also have a particular role in providing those teachers with the opportunity to work more creatively, on perspectives which are above and beyond current restraints and pressures such as the delivery of the National Curriculum.

# CONCLUSION

Much has been achieved in introducing development education to British schools; there has been a wide variety of innovatory work and numerous strategies adopted (not always consciously). The changes in the education system have brought new challenges as well as opportunities for development education. NGOs concerned with development education have to review these changes, take stock of their collective experiences and develop new long-term plans to maximize the opportunities for the education system to take on the development education agenda. In the current climate teachers and others in the system are overwhelmed by the implementation of change over and above their normal work. NGOs therefore have a specific role and responsibility to support long-term thinking and awareness of the potential for future change. The central challenge is, however, one of making good use of the creative work that has been done and building up confidence among a wide range of teachers about effective use of a global dimension and development perspective in their work with young people of all ages.

There is a need for NGOs to maximize the involvement of teachers and others within the education system in all aspects of their work with a view to more and more initiatives evolving from within the system, using its own resources. This work needs to be backed up by research, strategic documents and academic papers exploring the central, rather than peripheral, role that development education might play in meeting young people's needs as 'world citizens' in the twenty-first century.

# REFERENCES

Arnold, S. (1987), 'Constrained crusaders – NGOs and development education in the UK', Occasional Paper, Institute of Education, University of London.

DEC (1992), *Developing Geography: A Development Education Approach at Key Stage 3, A Teacher's Handbook*, Development Education Centre, 998 Bristol Road, Birmingham B29 6LE.

DEC (1981), 'What is development education?', Occasional Paper. Birmingham: Development Education Centre.

*Elephant Times* (1989), DEC newsletter, Birmingham: Development Education Centre.

Hicks, D. and Townley, C. (eds) (1982), *Teaching World Studies: An Introduction to Global Perspectives in the Curriculum*, Harlow: Longman.

NADEC, National Association of Development Education Centre, 29–31 Cowper Street, London EC2A 4AP.

Oxfam Education catalogue, Oxfam Education Department, 274 Banbury Road, Oxford OX2 7DZ.

# PART 2

# DESIGNING A GLOBAL CURRICULUM

# CHAPTER 4

# Geography and Development Education

*John Hopkin*

The world we know and attempt to understand is shaped by our own individual experiences of places, by what we hear from others, and by the images, maps and text provided by books and the media. When pupils of any age learn geography in school they are extending their world picture and reshaping it.

(Roberts, 1992: 46)

This chapter links changes in the world-view adopted by school geography curricula and textbooks with changing paradigms of development and asks whether recently published geography textbooks reflect a different view of development, and a different world-view, from those found in books analysed in the 1970s and 1980s.

## GEOGRAPHY AND MODELS OF DEVELOPMENT

Geography has always had a world-view, though necessarily a changing one. Europeans' conceptualization of the world, and in particular those regions we might today call the countries of the South, is one which geographers and geography teachers reinforce, reflecting as well as helping to shape current ideas in Western society. However, it is apparent that Europeans' world-view has not always been an acceptable or useful one on which to construct their interactions with the wider world.

### Determinist and modernization paradigms

In the nineteenth and early twentieth centuries the European colonial powers referred to the South as being 'underdeveloped'. In the popular (and scientific) mind a form of social Darwinism linked with environmental determinism helped to explain why 'backwardness' was a natural state of affairs for these regions and for their peoples. This determinist paradigm provided a convenient justification for the social, economic and political imperatives of the colonial era; it was widely accepted that it was the duty of Europeans to look after and develop the backward colonies and their people; the 'white man's burden'.

This was an era when many British classrooms and geography lessons were dominated by pink-shaded world maps showing the extent of the imperial dominions. As Marsden (1976) points out, Victorian England had no doubts about the superiority of the English over all other races, a view prominent in the geography textbooks of the period; he quoted from *The Fireside Traveller through Many Lands*, published in 1840 (see Figure 1):

ENGLISH.

THE dress and manners of the English are plain and simple. They are distinguished by a love of their country, and generosity is a particular trait in their character. The manners and conversation of true Englishmen mark their sincerity and upright intentions. Although there are many exceptions, the generality of the inhabitants are good and honest, and probably in this respect superior to those of every other nation. Their attention to commerce, literature, and the arts, has raised them to the greatest eminence.

NEGROES.

NEGROLAND is in Africa. The inhabitants are of a black complexion, and idolaters. The men are generally tall and well-made, and of a cheerful disposition: the women are short and robust, performing the most laborious work. Their food consists chiefly of roots, herbs, fruits, cockles, and oysters; and their common drink is water. Their weapons are swords, daggers, darts, and bows and arrows. They are very fond of dancing, and often spend their evenings in that diversion.

**Figure 1** From *The Fireside Traveller through Many Lands* (1840)

After the Second World War and the subsequent anti-colonial struggles, modernization theories became the dominant paradigm for viewing development in what by then had become known as the 'Third World'. Development was assumed to involve a process of catching up with the 'First' and, to some extent, the 'Second World'. Rostow's (1960) model of economic development, with its linear progression from traditional society, through 'take-off' to 'maturity' and 'the age of high mass-consumption', was particularly influential. As Toh (1986: 117) points out, modernization theory 'has dominated mainstream academic analysis, and the policies of advanced industrialized governments, most Third World governments, and large official aid agencies'. It gained renewed vigour in some quarters in the 1980s, the decade of monetarism and trickle-down economics.

The modernization paradigm, and specifically Rostow's model, appeared frequently in British geography textbooks of the 1970s and 1980s. Their message seemed to be that traditional societies are merely the starting point for development along a path to the affluent Western life style with its consumerist values, being hindered only by their own internal deficiencies – a view little different from the determinist, ethnocentric world-view of the past.

The modernization paradigm is closely allied to geography's positivist tradition, with its emphasis on empirical models and the primacy of rational, 'economic man' as the basis for the economic development and the spatial organization of capitalist societies. Gilbert (1984, 1986) asserts that these characteristics impart geography with a conservative bias in which geography syllabus writers, textbook authors and teachers have become complicit and that, as a result, students fail to learn anything of the nature of social power or the social processes that create spatial patterns. This issue will be returned to when geography textbooks are considered.

## Alternative paradigms

Although in the 1960s modernization theorists predicted that infrastructure and industrial investment would rapidly close the 'development gap' between rich and poor countries, by the late 1960s it had become apparent that the reverse was happening and that the optimism of the post-war years was misplaced. For some theorists, such as A. G. Frank, it was apparent that high living standards in the core regions of the West were related to a process of underdevelopment and exploitation of the periphery; control of international flows of capital and goods ensured the prosperity of the former at the expense of the latter. This theory of underdevelopment implied that radical change in the world order was a precondition of advancement in the 'developing world'.

A liberal interpretation of the underdevelopment paradigm and of the essential links between the industrialized West and the South can be found in the Brandt Report (1980, 1983), with its reconceptualization of the world as North and South within a global economic system. In turn, ideas about development have moved on to embrace the diversity of peoples and economies within the South and to emphasize the small-scale, basic needs approach currently favoured in the West by the aid agencies. To this can be added two new themes, gender and development, and sustainable development, the latter gaining particular impetus from renewed concern about global environmental issues in the 1980s, and increasing consciousness of the links between environment and development reflected in the aspirations of the Earth Summit in Rio in June 1992.

These alternative paradigms, whose various strands Toh (1986) characterizes as an alternative, radical PEACE paradigm (Participatory, Equitable, Appropriate, Conscientization and Ecodevelopmental), are more closely connected with humanistic and radical geography, and with emancipatory ideas about education, in particular about methodology, such as those propounded by Freire (1972).

The collapse of the Eastern bloc in the late 1980s reinforced the message that the First, Second and Third Worlds are no longer an appropriate framework for viewing the world. Taylor (1989, 1992) argues strongly against developmentalism as a model for viewing the world and points out that such formal constructs as 'The Third World' or 'The South', while probably preferable to terms like 'developing' or 'developed' countries, clearly are inadequate because of the sheer diversity of the region, a region which is in any case defined in terms of its relative poverty. Instead Taylor proposes a core–periphery framework as a way of organizing our ideas about development: 'the beauty of this construct is that it is interactive and functional: a core cannot exist without a periphery and vice versa. This is the language of world-systems analysis.' The advantages of such a world-view is that it is a dynamic, rather than a static, model, and it provides an opportunity to focus on and begin to understand global inequalities within a single world economy.

This chapter considers whether UK geography curricula and textbooks published in the early 1990s have kept pace with these changing ideas about development in the wider community. As a starting point it considers the relationship between geography in UK secondary schools and development education in the 1970s and 1980s.

# DEVELOPMENT EDUCATION AND GEOGRAPHY IN UK SECONDARY SCHOOLS IN THE 1970s AND 1980s

The term 'development education' is often used to describe those parts of the curriculum concerned with the development process; perhaps one of the most useful definitions is that of the United Nations, quoted in Hicks and Townley (1982: 9):

Development education is concerned with issues of human rights, dignity, self-reliance, and social justice in both developed and developing countries. It is concerned with the causes of underdevelopment and the promotion of an understanding of what is involved in development, of how different countries go about undertaking development, and of the reasons for and ways of achieving a new international economic and social order.

Learning about distant places has always been an important part of school geography and, since for many teachers development education has largely been, at least initially, identified with learning about developing countries, in many UK secondary schools it has thus taken place largely or wholly within geography lessons. Learning about the South has featured prominently in both UK geography curricula and textbooks for secondary schools.

During the 1970s and 1980s curriculum changes in geography at secondary school level developed a view of learning which began to acknowledge the importance of process as well as content. New perspectives in geography, such as welfare and humanistic geography, promoted the study of issues relevant to children and their future, emphasized the role of people's attitudes in the development and analysis of spatial patterns, sought to engage pupils' own values and beliefs, and focused on the importance of critical enquiry in finding out about the world.

At the same time the focus of development education broadened out from its early focus on the study of developing countries to include a greater emphasis on classroom methodology and in particular learner-centred approaches:

Development education is about developing the skills necessary for effective participation in the world . . . in addition, about developing attitudes which are consistent with living in an interdependent world. The challenge for geography teachers . . . is to help pupils to use their own awareness of situations as a basis for increased knowledge and understanding.

(Daniels and Sinclair, 1985: 7)

Development education in UK schools has been promoted largely by the voluntary sector – through bodies such as the aid agencies and Development Education Centres – but also in the past through such quasi-governmental agencies as the Schools Council, a curriculum development body now disbanded, and through some local education authorities (LEAs). However, the extent and quality of permeation of development education ideas and practice have been arguably patchy. The UK's tradition of schools' curricular autonomy led to considerable variations between LEAs, between schools and even within schools; development education in the UK has prospered particularly through the efforts of Development Education Centres – especially through in-service training and publication – in partnership with a minority of enthusiastic teachers.

In many secondary school curricula the focus of development education in the 1970s and 1980s stressed the study of individual localities and countries, or the South as a whole, an approach which did not always guarantee that children learned about these distant places in an appropriate or accurate way. As Robinson (1988) points out, the approach taken by school curricula, textbooks or teachers is related to the framework within which their world-view is constructed:

One of the most exciting aspects of geography is finding out about far away people and places that are very different from those around you. Over the last thirty years this aspect of school geography has been largely subsumed within the study of the Developing World. Within this framework the world has been presented almost exclusively as a 'problem'. From most school geography courses you would hardly believe that the world is full of interesting, happy people, splendid natural environments and endless possibilities and potential.

# DEVELOPMENT EDUCATION AND GEOGRAPHY IN THE 1990s

In 1988 the UK government introduced the National Curriculum as part of its Education Reform Act, implementing for the first time in England and Wales extensive central control over the curriculum in state schools. It is widely considered to embody a conservative view of the curriculum, enacted at a time when schools were felt by government to be underperforming and teachers not to be trusted with curriculum design; indeed, considerable political control was exercised in determining, and in some cases subsequently revising, the content of a number of the subject areas.

As the then Secretary of State for Education Kenneth Clarke made clear, geography is seen by the government and its advisers as the main area of the curriculum through which children will find out about the wider world:

> Geography has a fundamental relevance to young people because it relates to many aspects of their lives and the environment in which they are growing up . . . study at regional, national, international and global level is required as well, all are vital for pupils' understanding of the increasingly complex and interdependent global village in which we live.
>
> (Clarke, 1992)

Although the rather restrictive framework of the whole curriculum and narrow view of appropriate content for other National Curriculum subjects is likely to restrict opportunities for development education approaches to geography in many schools, the new statutory framework will bring some gains in this field. It will ensure that all children from the earliest age are entitled to be taught something about the wider world. For example at ages 11–14 (Key Stage 3), the main opportunities will occur through the study of a selected economically developing country (see Figure 2), and for more able pupils, of international trade. While in human geography pupils will consider migration issues and 'indicators of development', in environmental geography they will learn about environmental management and global environmental change.

However, in many respects the National Curriculum framework is limiting; as Roberts (1992) points out, in spite of Kenneth Clarke's aspirations to enhance pupils' understanding of the global village, the view of the wider world pupils in this age group develop will be at best partial; she notes that, although no geography course could attempt to study everywhere in the world, the economically developing world is under-represented in National

**Economically Developing Country**

Pupils should be taught:

• the geographical features and conditions of an economically developing country selected from Bangladesh, Brazil, China, Egypt, Ghana, India, Kenya, Mexico, Nigeria, Pakistan, Peru or Venezuela;

• to describe the features and occupations of a locality in the country selected and compare them with those of the local area; how the locality has changed as a result of human actions; and to investigate recent or proposed changes in the locality;

• to examine the impact of landscape, weather and wealth on the lives of people in a locality of the country selected;

• how the occupations, land–use and settlement patterns of a locality in the country selected are related to the locality's environment and location;

• to outline the distribution of population in the country selected and how this is influenced by the features of and conditions of the country.

Pupils working towards level 7 should be taught to:

• evaluate the extent to which the country displays the characteristics of development.

**Figure 2** Excerpt from Programme of Study, Key Stage 3

Curriculum geography, and most of the very poorest countries are excluded (see Figure 3).

The focus on detailed study of people and environments within a real locality, set in the context of an 'economically developing' country as a whole, potentially represents a significant advance for development education in those schools where the 'developing world' in general was the focus of study. However, when considering the requirements at the international and global scale it is difficult to feel so optimistic. For example, at level 6 pupils will be taught to 'compare levels of economic development and welfare in different parts of the world using appropriate indicators; for example: compare Gross Domestic Product, literacy rate, people per doctor, secondary school enrolments' (DES, 1991). The National Curriculum's world-view is set within the modernization paradigm: 'economically developing' countries, although worthy of study in their own right, are, when considered in an international context, still measured as behind, and trying to catch up with, the West.

At levels of attainment 7 and 8 pupils will have opportunities to study the patterns of trade and economic interdependence between countries. At level 9, the most able pupils will be taught to 'analyse the role of inward investment on the economic development of an economically developing country', a change made by Secretary of State Clarke himself; his advisers had earlier suggested

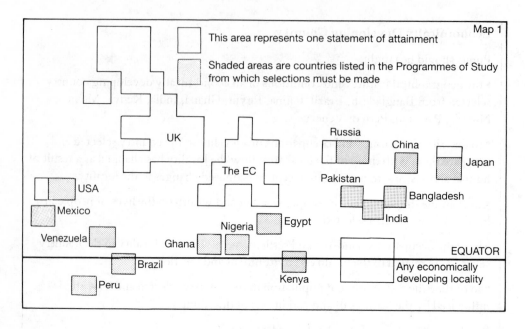

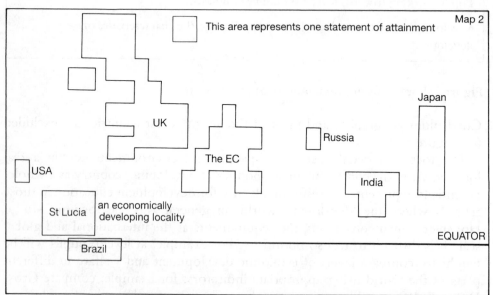

**Figure 3** Map 1 The world of the National Curriculum, AT2. The areas of places are drawn in proportion to the number of statements of attainment in AT2 on them.

Map 2 The world a pupil might study from AT2 during 11 years of National Curriculum geography.

*Source: Times Educational Supplement*, 10 April 1992. © Times Supplement Limited, 1992. The maps were originated by Margaret Roberts.

that pupils should be taught to 'assess the role of transnational companies on the economic development of an economically developing country' (DES, 1990).

The wording . . . has been changed to create a geographical education designed almost exclusively for information storage and retrieval. The pupils are to be passive receivers. This is poor preparation for life in a rapidly changing world . . . these changes create a sterile geography far from reality and little help in understanding or coping with the world now or in adult life.

(Elephant Times DEC, 1990)

In relation to the wider view of learning implied by 'development education', the geography National Curriculum appears to marginalize the developments in school curricula of humanistic and welfare perspectives; Dowgill and Lambert (1992) point out that the geography National Curriculum was evidently intended to break with these grass-roots developments. They suggest that its emphasis on place knowledge and factual content links with 'back to basics' movements and with the potentially insular 'cultural literacy' ideas of Hirsch (1987), who argues that there is a fund of essential knowledge which everyone must acquire to function effectively and progress in (Western) society.

The National Curriculum represents a return to the positivist tradition of the earlier 'new geography', Fien and Gerber's 'diet of geographic learnings that clutter the mind with facts, concepts, models and theories which serve to disguise the nature and impact of social processes' (1986: 7). It is clearly a more functional, and to some commentators regressive, view of the subject, in which enquiry, issue-based and learner-centred approaches fit uneasily. If the National Curriculum is founded in this limiting framework of ideas, it is unlikely to be open to changing ways of looking at the world.

The National Curriculum will clearly be a very significant influence on the organization and content of school geography in the 1990s; however, it remains to be seen to what extent it represents an advance or a set-back for development education. The emphasis on factual knowledge might imply that there is less room for innovative ideas; however, some aspects are open to fairly wide interpretation and there remain some openings through which development education may continue to be promoted: for example, the National Curriculum does not specify classroom methodology.

One force to be reckoned with is the same group of committed teachers, who, in partnership with the voluntary sector, will seek to interpret and build on the National Curriculum framework to ensure a continuation and development of good practice in this field. An example of such co-operation is to be found in *Developing Geography* (Serf and Sinclair, 1992), a collection of teaching ideas, case studies and planning frameworks which aims to

> highlight the ways in which development education can contribute to a relevant and stimulating geography that also encompasses the requirements of the National Curriculum . . . the challenge is to place teachers at the centre of curriculum development and their students at the centre of the learning experience.

73

The framework within which geography textbooks and other sources of information are constructed and the way teachers interpret these are likely to be highly significant in determining the extent to which geography lessons make the most of these opportunities in the National Curriculum and ensure that their pupils understand and experience development issues in the South in an accurate and appropriate way.

## LEARNING ABOUT DEVELOPMENT FROM UK GEOGRAPHY TEXTBOOKS

Research in the late 1970s and early 1980s, particularly that by David Hicks and David Wright, found evidence that British geography textbooks for secondary age (11–16) pupils frequently offered stereotyped and biased images and information about countries and peoples of the South. Of particular concern was the compelling evidence of the links between perceptions of the countries and peoples of the South, derived from textbooks, television and other media, and racist attitudes towards minority groups in the UK. Indeed, it was clear that many classroom resources promoted a Eurocentric view of the world which was demeaning to the countries of the South and by implication, if not overtly, to minority groups living in the UK:

> There is a direct link between the presence of minority groups in the UK and our colonial past. Attitudes towards such minority groups are closely related to British perceptions of the Third World peoples. Racist attitudes . . . tend to be the norm in Britain. If geographers are concerned with fostering international understanding and tolerant attitudes then it is important to consider how the portrayal of minorities in Britain may affect black self-image and also white prejudice.

> (Hicks, 1981b)

Wright (1979), for example, concentrating on visual images of Africa in textbooks, concluded that they greatly emphasized traditional agricultural work at the expense of manufacturing or tertiary activities, and thus presented a stereotyped 'backward' image of the continent with no opportunities to consider development of any kind. He found little difference in the images of Africa presented between textbooks written in the 1950s and those written in the 1970s.

Wright followed this work up (1983, 1985) with a more detailed examination of the explicit and implicit attitudes to race shown in the treatment of Australia and West and South Africa in three common textbooks, and discussed their effects on the attitudes of children in multiracial classrooms in the UK. He found the books conveyed an overwhelmingly negative impression of Africa through their photographs, text and activities, while virtually ignoring the Aboriginal experience in Australia. Asking whether geography textbooks are racist, Wright concluded that the problem is an unconscious ethnocentrism derived from the wider values current in society as a whole, particularly through teachers' own education:

> The fundamental problem is not 'this book' and it is certainly not this publisher . . . The problem is that we – the teachers of geography – are the products of a society which has not yet adequately examined its own values and assumptions, and we are not yet skilled in spotting racism and bias.
>
> (1983: 14)

Hicks (1981a) analysed how geography textbooks on the Third World addressed a series of key issues, including the explanations they offered of poverty and underdevelopment, and how they dealt with population, food and farming, interdependence, colonialism and minority rights. He also analysed the portrayal of minority groups in the UK in textbooks on the British Isles. Hicks considered that the majority of texts focused on the Third World were ethnocentric in approach, while those focused on the UK contributed little to multicultural understanding. He found that the textbooks were most unlikely to analyse the causes of underdevelopment, whereas they often saw Third World countries and their people as the problem; on the other hand they were likely to present images of Third World people as victims, as backward and ignorant.

Hicks classified the books according to their world-view, ranging from 'status quo' (conservative) through 'liberal' to 'radical', and then related this to the degree of perceived bias, ranging from racist, through non-racist to antiracist. Unsurprisingly perhaps, he found a tendency for those books with a conservative outlook which focused on problems to be most biased, and those focusing on development issues to be least biased.

Robinson (1987b) devised a similar classificaton based on the textbooks used by the teachers he interviewed. He found that 'traditionalist' teachers largely used 'world problems' textbooks, while 'radical' teachers used little other than 'modern development' books.

Robinson's research into teaching and learning about the South suggests that pupils' conceptualization and understanding of development in the South are closely linked with their own personal geographies, frameworks through which they unconsciously interpret and assimilate images and information from sources as diverse as family and friends, school textbooks and teachers. He suggests that learning in many geography lessons makes little impact on these personal geographies because of inadequate pedagogy, and that in order to restructure pupils' often wildly inaccurate versions of reality, geography lessons must acknowledge the knowledge and experiences they bring to the classroom, and engage and develop them through active learning methods:

> Students' responses to issues in the developing world are conceptualised in their own version of reality. Too often this reality has been created through crude stereotypes and highly generalised public knowledge and

may be simplistic, biased and overwhelmingly ethnocentric as a result. When experiential or regenerative knowledge has not been legitimated in the classroom, most of the students' images are found in their experiences of media and interaction outside.

(1987a: 48)

Robinson asserts that in order to develop and change students' personal geographies, teachers need to pay attention to developing their skills in thinking, valuing and decision-making; especially through student–centred experiential methods. He concludes that the characteristics and values held by individual teachers may well be most influential in effecting a change in pupils' understanding of development.

> Firstly it is who teaches you, rather than what or how they teach, that makes a discernible difference. Secondly, in spite of the high quality of both the teachers and the students, the understanding of development in the developing world is at best rudimentary.

(1987b: 368)

## Textbooks for the geography National Curriculum

Teaching about development is now a statutory part of the geography curriculum in UK schools and, as has been shown above, previous research suggests that textbooks are a key point of reference in teaching about the South. Textbooks represent an important source of information for both pupils and teachers, particularly as they deal with areas of the world of which the majority in either group are unlikely to have had extensive first-hand experience.

One effect of the National Curriculum has been for publishers to commission large numbers of new textbooks to support all subject areas. Since UK textbooks are not subject to any form of government control there is considerable diversity in approach, although clearly the National Curriculum imposes a degree of commonality in subject material.

In geography, ten different series were produced for Key Stage 3. Of these, textbooks published for years 7 and 8 (age 11–13) in 1991 and 1992 were studied to analyse their approach to development and to the South and to determine what understanding about these issues pupils would gain in their first two years at secondary school. Year 9 textbooks had not been published at the time of survey. Two questions were formulated:

- Within which framework of ideas – which world-view – were the textbooks constructed?
- Since the earlier research, had curriculum development and discussion within geography led to improvements in the way the South and its people were represented?

Nine series were studied, a total of eighteen books; one series, *Exploring Geography* (Longman, 1991), was withdrawn from the survey when it became clear that its year 7 and 8 books contained no material at all on the South. The subject material, photographs and activities of the remainder were analysed.

## Text

The analysis of the subject material of the books was based on Hicks's survey (1980, 1981a). Hicks identified a number of areas of concern which, he suggested, led to misinformation and bias about the South in many of the textbooks he analysed. Hicks classified the books in his sample according to the world-view evident in their approach to development issues, which he characterized as 'status quo', 'liberal' or 'radical'. Hicks did not explain in detail his criteria for sorting his sample, so in the current survey his areas of concern were used to suggest a checklist of features likely to be found in those textbooks written with a view of development founded in modernization theory ('status quo'), compared with those written within a framework of ideas based on alternative views of development ('radical'):

| Status Quo | Radical |
|---|---|
| **1 Images of Underdevelopment/Development** | |
| development as catching up | development as self–help |
| poverty as a general condition | inequality; diversity |
| symptoms | explanations, causes |
| large–scale, external | small–scale, indigenous |
| **2 Images of Population** | |
| Population as a problem *per se* | explanations of population growth |
| **3 Images of Food and Farming** | |
| as a problem | as a resource |
| deficiencies | farmers' skill |
| **4 Images of Interdependence** | |
| 'us' helping 'them' | local contributions |
| paternalism | underdevelopment |
| **5 Images of Colonialism** | |
| | explanations of colonialism |
| **6 Images of Minorities** | |
| concern for the 'primitive' | validity of life styles |
| [In addition, the following were considered to be good indicators:] | |

**7 Indicators of Development**

descriptive                                critical; quality of life

**8 Women**

                                           as an issue in development

**9 Environment**

                                           as an issue in development

**10 Disasters**

people as victims

The proportion of space devoted to development issues in each series was also established; it seemed likely that those series putting a higher priority on material on development and the South would also be more thoughtfully written in this respect and thus display more 'radical' characteristics.

The results (see Figure 4) revealed that, of the eight series analysed, *Cambridge Geography Project*, *Geography Today* and, to a lesser extent, *Enquiry Geography* contained material with a number of 'radical' features. For example, *Cambridge Geography* and particularly *Geography Today* contained material on farming in India, stressing farmers' decisions and local farming development projects; *Geography Today*'s chapter on development choices in the Narmada valley is a model of its kind. Both series also contained chapters on the issue of deforestation in Amazonia, linked with the life style of forest peoples and their fight to defend the forest. These two series also devoted most space to development and the South. *Enquiry Geography* is alone in including substantial material on women and development, based on a development scheme in rural South India, although unlike the other two series it has no material on urban India for comparison.

The other series proved more difficult to categorize, as they included some 'status quo' and some 'radical' characteristics. *Worldview*, for example, emphasizes the skill of Indian farmers in making a living from the land and includes material on India's technological and industrial base; however, population growth in the South is defined simply as a problem, rather than explained as people's response to poverty.

*Key Geography* contains more 'status quo' characteristics; for example, the chapter on developing countries contains descriptive and stereotyped accounts of traditional Maasai and Kikuyu rural life in Kenya, while the material on Nairobi mentions urban inequalities but is dominated by the problems of its shanty towns. Some chapters are more adventurous; for example, a section on migration from Mexico, based on personal accounts, encourage pupils to consider some of the processes and issues involved. One rather worrying feature is that at times the authors use the same text and activities in material on both Kenya and Egypt; for example, we learn that:

**Figure 4** Analysis of text: Development Issues

| Series | % of pages on the South | Development/Undevelopment | | Population | | Farming | | Interdependence | | Minorities | | | Indices of development | | | | |
|---|---|---|---|---|---|---|---|---|---|---|---|---|---|---|---|---|---|
| | | Poverty, problems | Self-help projects/solutions | As a problem | Explanations | As a problem | As a resource | Us helping them | Their contributions linkages | Colonialism: explanations | 'Primitive' | Validity of life style | Generalization | Critical, quality of life | Women and development | Environment and development | Disasters |
| Cambridge Geography Project | 26% | ✓ | ✓ | | | | ✓ | | ✓ | ✓ | | ✓ | | ✓ | | ✓ | |
| Geography Today | 17% | | ✓ | | | | ✓ | | ✓ | ✓ | | ✓ | | ✓ | | ✓ | |
| Worldview | 17% | | | ✓ | | | ✓ | | ✓ | | | | | | | ✓ | ✓ |
| Key Geography | 17% | ✓ | | ✓ | | | | | | | | | | | | | ✓ |
| Access to Geography | 16% | | | | | | | | ✓ | | | | | ✓ | | | ✓ |
| Enquiry Geography | 14% | | ✓ | | ✓ | | | | | | | | | | ✓ | ✓ | |
| Folens Series | 12% | | ✓ | | | | | | | | | | | | ✓ | ✓ | ✓ |
| Geothermes | 10% | | | | | | | | | | | | | | | ✓ | |

79

In Kenya it is mainly the Kikuyu who move. Their traditional home is in area 2 on map B. When driving through rural Kikuyu countryside it is hard to see why they want to move. It is one of the few parts of Kenya with roads [sic]; it has the best farmland and water supply in the country and the environment appears clean and pleasant. To those living there, especially those at school or just starting a family, it is less attractive.

In Egypt, it is mainly the people who live in the Nile Delta who move. To a visitor, the Delta appears to be a good place to live. It is one of the few parts of Egypt with roads. It has the best farmland and water supply in the country and the environment seems clean and pleasant compared to urban areas. To those living there, especially those still at school or just starting a family, it is less attractive.

(Waugh and Bushell, 1992: 83)

The clear implication is that people experience these very different places in exactly the same way, and since these are the only two studies in any detail of 'economically developing countries' the reader might conclude that others are very similar too. As Robinson points out:

> Negative stereotypes are widely held by British people, adults and children alike . . . the developing world is (already) too often just 'one place' to a student and narrow generalisations are freely applied.
>
> (1987a: 51)

## Images

Photographs are a good source of evidence, and particularly important in helping to form pupils' perceptions of the South. Analysis of the photographs of the South showed that nearly one-quarter of these were of unpopulated landscapes. A system of classification, based on Wright's analyses (1979, 1983), was used to categorize the remainder into those types of image likely to convey positive and negative impressions (see Figure 5).

1 Jobs: primary, secondary, tertiary. Wright noted that primary occupations dominated at the expense of a more balanced view of occupational structures. In these series, 63 per cent of images of people working are of primary occupations (largely farming).

2 Images of rural life. In total, images of traditional farming and village life outnumber images of self-help and development by two to one. In some books, for example Key Geography and Enquiry Geography, there is a marked discrepancy, whereas Geography Today has a near balance.

3 Images of urban life. All books contained some images of urban shanty towns and urban problems. However, out of all the urban scenes, these were considerably outnumbered by street scenes showing everyday activities and

**Figure 5** Images of the South

| Series | Landscapes, vegetation, wildlife | Jobs | | | Rural | | Urban | | | | Family, school, community | Other people | Total photographs |
|---|---|---|---|---|---|---|---|---|---|---|---|---|---|
| | | Primary | Secondary | Tertiary | Traditional and village life | Self-help and development | Shanty towns; urban problems | Wealth, street scenes | Disasters: victims | Speaking out | | | |
| Cambridge Geography Project | 30% | 14% | 0% | 0% | 12% | 7% | 4% | 9% | 4% | 11% | 2% | 7% | 56 |
| Geography Today | 17% | 10% | 5% | 2% | 13% | 15% | 2% | 8% | 0% | 24% | 2% | 2% | 86 |
| World-view | 22% | 9% | 4% | 4% | 20% | 6% | 10% | 16% | 7% | 0% | 2% | 0% | 101 |
| Key Geography | 21% | 12% | 0% | 4% | 28% | 3% | 9% | 9% | 7% | 7% | 0% | 0% | 57 |
| Access to Geography | 6% | 0% | 6% | 6% | 6% | 0% | 23% | 23% | 18% | 12% | 0% | 0% | 17 |
| Enquiry Geography | 13% | 10% | 8% | 5% | 36% | 8% | 3% | 5% | 0% | 5% | 5% | 2% | 39 |
| Folens Series | 45% | 11% | 0% | 0% | 11% | 11% | 0% | 0% | 22% | 0% | 0% | 0% | 18 |
| Geothemes | 50% | 13% | 0% | 6% | 0% | 0% | 6% | 6% | 0% | 0% | 0% | 19% | 16 |
| Totals | 23% | 10% | 3% | 3% | 19% | 8% | 6% | 10% | 5% | 9% | 2% | 2% | 390 |
| | | | | | 27% | | 16% | | | | | | |

images of wealth. Two series, *Worldview* and *Access to Geography*, included images of homelessness or poverty in the North in an attempt to make a more general point about inequalities.

4 Images of disasters. Images of natural disasters such as famine, flood and earthquake dominate media images of the South (see Chapter 6). Such images reinforce an impression of Third World people as passive victims, often linked with the provision of Western aid. Taken as a whole, these books do not greatly emphasize such images, although they play less part in some (*Geography Today, Cambridge Geography*) than in others: for example, half the images of developing countries in *Key Geography* Book 1 are of flooding in Bangladesh. Indeed one image, of Bangladeshi women in a home surrounded by flood waters, occurs in several series.

5 Images of people speaking out. Some books selected images which showed people from the South speaking for themselves, sometimes as 'talking heads', a device used successfully by *Geography Today* and *Cambridge Geography*, and sometimes in situations such as meetings or demonstrations. Such images convey impressions of real people with valid concerns, often asserting some control over their own lives; the very opposite of images of disaster victims.

6 Images of family, school and community. These occurred infrequently but were assumed to convey an idea of valid life styles to which pupils might relate.

The survey showed considerable variation in approaches taken by different textbook series to the selection of images of the South. Taken as a whole these textbooks achieve a rough balance of photographs with more positive characteristics, such as everyday street scenes and urban wealth, people speaking for themselves and images of development, with those considered to reinforce Eurocentric prejudices about the South, such as images of disasters. Classifying images into positive and negative can be rather problematic; for example, images of shanty towns might be used in a very positive way to show self-help and community development. Images of traditional life can present a positive and dynamic image of the people and locality concerned, although Wright considered such images to convey a negative view. However, it can certainly be argued that where such images dominate, or where few which stress development have been selected, the effect may well be to convey a static and one-sided view of the country as a whole.

## *Activities*

The activities which authors plan for children to interpret and engage with the text and images they present is arguably as important as the resources themselves. Indeed, Robinson (1987b), in the light of his findings about the importance of methodology, heavily criticized the textbooks he surveyed for their failure to involve students in open responses or to solicit their own views. Two series, *Geography Today* and *Key Geography*, were analysed to see whether the variation in approach to content, to photographic images and to the space devoted to the South extended to differences in the type of activity suggested for pupils (see Figure 6). Although both series contained a similar proportion of comprehension activities using text, tables and diagrams, *Key Geography* contained a far higher proportion of activities involving manipulating text, for example cloze procedure, selecting, sorting and ranking. *Key Geography* contained rather more activities based on skills such as map and graph work, while *Geography Today* contained a much higher proportion of activities which involved pupils in an open response, such as asking their own views and pair or group discussions.

For example, in *Key Geography 2: Connections* (Waugh and Bushell, 1992: 79), at the end of a section on 'Kenya – what is the Maasai way of life?', pupils are invited to:

---

1 (a) Give two facts about (what is meant by) a developing country.
  (b) What is meant by 'an ethnic group'?
  (c) Kenya is found in which continent?
2 (a) Give two reasons why cattle are important to the Maasai.
  (b) Write a paragraph to describe the Maasai way of farming. Include these words: *cattle and goats, flat land, grass, rain, nomadic*.
3    Sketch E shows a Maasai hut and several questions. Draw the hut and add several labels by answering the questions.
4    How do photo A and your Maasai hut suggest that the weather is
  (a) usually warm
  (b) not very wet

---

The clear difference in approach taken by the series to activities are shown by this extract from *Geography Today Book 2* (Brookes et al., 1992: 93) at the end of a section on development choices in India, comparing the costs and benefits of small and large-scale projects;

---

5    What are the main differences between the Narmada Project and the scheme at Ralegaon Siddhi?
6 (a) Explain why Ralegaon Siddhi is an example of development.
  (b) Suggest reasons why some people believe that big projects like the one at Narmada are necessary for development.
7    Think about these two ways of development. In pairs, discuss the advantages and disadvantages of both projects. Now on your own, write down which project you would choose. Give reasons.

---

**Figure 6** Activities related to material on Development

| Series | Comprehension | Sorting/defining | Tables/diagrams | Graphs | Activities Map work | Photo interpretation | Interpretation | Pair/group discussions | Synthesis/ summary |
|---|---|---|---|---|---|---|---|---|---|
| | from text, tables, diagrams | cloze procedure, complete/select sentences, true/ false, ranking | Complete a table/diagram label sketch | draw a graph, interpret graphs | interpret maps/atlases | | suggest reasons, what would happen, why do you think, imagine | make a list, brainstorm, role-play | |
| Key Geography | 22% | 28% | 18% | 3% | 6% | 11% | 7% | 2% | 3% |
| Geography Today | 24% | 9% | 4% | 11% | 8% | 3% | 27% | 11% | 3% |

8 (a) In the same pairs decide why we call a country 'economically developed' or 'economically developing'.

(b) Britain is an economically developed country. Look at your own area and decide if there is anything in your area which needs to be improved. Write a plan to say how help is needed, and what can be done about it. Will it include help from the government? Does your plan involve help from local people?

Why not investigate? From an aid agency, find out all you can about a development project in an economically developing country. Write about the project and what it is trying to do. How is the aid agency involved in the project? Is an economically developing country helping with the project? . . . Describe any other links that exist between the economically developed country and the economically developing country.

---

Waugh and Bushell's activities are little more than a comprehension exercise, based on somewhat dubious textual material; pupils' understanding of development in this context is likely to be very limited. Those more fortunate pupils studying from *Geography Today* are likely to gain a much better understanding of development issues because they are encouraged to study the evidence, think for themselves, report back, apply their findings to their local area, and engage in further research. It is also clear that, as material for combating stereotyped and racist ideas about people in the South, the latter activities are likely to prove far more effective.

## Summary

The geography textbook series published to support National Curriculum geography approach issues of development in developing countries from a range of perspectives. The analysis of text shows that some series, notably *Cambridge Geography Project* and *Geography Today*, contain material with, in Hicks's terms, many 'radical' characteristics. Indeed, some textbooks have moved on to address concerns of the 1980s and 1990s, such as environment and development and women and development. (It is notable that neither of these issues, which have had a high profile within geography as well as the wider arena in recent years, feature prominently in any of the series.) Other series proved more difficult to classify, containing a number of 'status quo' characteristics as well as some 'radical' ones. Returning to Hicks, these can be classified as 'liberal'.

Analysis of textbook images suggests that textbook authors and publishers also adopt a range of policies in selecting images. Some, again notably *Geography Today* and *Cambridge Geography* together with Heinemann's *Worldview* and *Enquiry Geography*, clearly attempt to select positive images of the South and are unlikely to present negative images.

Although there is some relationship between the amount of space devoted to development and the South and the perspective adopted by each series, this is not as close as expected, so teachers using this as one criterion for selecting textbooks need to look at other factors as well. If, as seems likely, teachers select textbooks which are congruent with their own values and perspective of the world, we can conclude that although the National Curriculum might appear to suggest a degree of uniformity in teaching about the wider world, this is unlikely to be the case and in fact this survey suggests that pupils in different schools will continue to experience development issues and the South in quite different ways.

# CONCLUSION

The degree of correlation in findings between the analysis of text and images presented by UK textbook series written for National Curriculum geography suggests that the framework of ideas or paradigm of development within which the books were written and produced is strongly represented in the world-view of the books themselves. Thus some books present a view of the world, and of development, founded in radical/alternative paradigms. Others have some basis in modernization theory, as well as elements of alternative, less Eurocentric perspectives. The latter probably fairly accurately reflect the spirit of National Curriculum geography, whereas we may speculate that the former may have attempted to go beyond, and improve upon, National Curriculum requirements and to maintain some of the principles of earlier humanistic and radical perspectives in curriculum development.

It is also clear that curriculum development and debate within geography which preceded the National Curriculum led to improvements by authors and publishers in comparison with surveys of textbooks made in the early 1980s. The new textbooks are presenting a less Eurocentric, more appropriate and probably more accurate view of the South. However, although overtly racist material in geography textbooks appears to be largely a thing of the past, there remain areas of concern where at times stereotyped and damaging ideas about the South and its people are presented, and there remain issues such as women and development which have as yet hardly appeared on the agenda.

Although there are clear deficiencies in the geography curriculum adopted by the UK to educate its young people, in many classrooms at least they will be studying the South and its peoples using better resources than in previous decades. There are cogent moral, as well as instrumental, reasons why, in a plural society and increasingly interdependent world, development issues should continue to play an important role in young people's geographical education – and that therefore the curricula and materials they use should be founded in a world-view appropriate to the final years of the twentieth century.

Note: International comparisons between the approaches taken by geography textbooks to development issues would be an interesting extension to this research. Correspondence on this issue would be welcomed.

# APPENDIX: LIST OF TEXTBOOKS

Beckwith, A. and Sutcliffe, A. (1992), *Exploring Geography 2: The UK within Europe*, Harlow: Longman.

Brookes, G. et al. (1992), *Geography Today Book 1 (National Curriculum Edition)*, London: Collins Educational.

Brookes, G. et al. (1992), *Geography Today Book 2 (National Curriculum Edition)*, London: Collins Educational.

Greasley, B. et al. (1991), *Enquiry Geography Book 1*, Sevenoaks: Hodder & Stoughton.

Greasley, B. et al. (1992), *Enquiry Geography Book 2*, Sevenoaks: Hodder & Stoughton.

Kemp, R. and Carvin, P. (1991), *Access to Geography 1*, Oxford: Oxford University Press.

Kemp, R., Mason, R. and Sims, T. (1991), *Access to Geography 2*, Oxford: Oxford University Press.

Lambert, D. (1992), *Cambridge Geography Project: Jigsaw Pieces*, Cambridge: Cambridge University Press.

Lambert, D. (1992), *Cambridge Geography Project: Green Pieces*, Cambridge: Cambridge University Press.

Martin, F. and Whittle, A. (1991), *Worldview 1*, Oxford: Heinemann Educational.

Martin, F. and Whittle, A. (1992), *Worldview 2*, Oxford: Heinemann Educational.

Murray, S., Punnett, N. and Webber, P. (1991), *Geothemes 1*, Hemel Hempstead: Simon & Schuster.

Murray, S., Punnett, N. and Webber, P. (1992), *Geothemes 2*, Hemel Hempstead: Simon & Schuster.

Rickerby, S. (1990), *People and Places*, Dunstable: Folens.

Rickerby, S. (1991), *Environments*, Dunstable: Folens.

Ross, S. and Eyre, P. (1991), *Exploring Geography 1: The Local Environment and the UK*, Harlow: Longman.

Waugh, D. and Bushell, A. (1991), *Key Geography 1: Foundations*, Cheltenham: Stanley Thornes.

Waugh, D. and Bushell, A. (1991), *Key Geography 2: Connections*, Cheltenham: Stanley Thornes.

# REFERENCES

Brandt, W. (1980), *North–South – A Programme for Survival*, London: Pan World Affairs.

Brandt, W. (1983), *Common Crisis North–South: Cooperation for World Recovery*, London: Pan World Affairs.

Brookes, G. et al. (1992), *Geography Today Book 2 (National Curriculum Edition)*, London: Collins Educational.

Clarke, K. (1992), 'Geography in the National Curriculum', speech delivered at the Royal Geographical Society on 24 September 1991, *Teaching Geography*, **17** (1), 28–30.

Daniels, A. and Sinclair, S. (eds) (1985), *People before Places*, Birmingham: Development Education Centre.

Department of Education and Science (1990), *Geography for Ages 5–16*, London: HMSO.

Department of Education and Science (1991), *Geography in the National Curriculum*, London: HMSO.

Dowgill, P. and Lambert, D. (1992), 'Cultural literacy and school geography', *Geography*, No. 335, **77** (2), 143–51.

*Elephant Times* (1990), Birmingham: Development Education Centre.

Fien, J. and Gerber, R. (1986), Introduction, in Fien, J. and Gerber, R. (eds), *Teaching Geography for a Better World*, Brisbane: Australian Geographical Association with Jacaranda Wiley.

Freire, P. (1972), *Pedagogy of the Oppressed*, London: Penguin.

Gilbert, R. (1984), *The Impotent Image: Reflections of Ideology in the Secondary School Curriculum*, Lewes: Falmer Press.

Gilbert, R. (1986), 'That's where they have to go; the challenge of ideology in geography', *Geographical Education*, **5** (2), 43–6.

Hicks, D. (1980), *Images of the World: An Introduction to Bias in Teaching Materials*, Occasional Paper No. 2, University of London Institute of Education, p.2.

Hicks, D. (1981a), *Bias in Geography Textbooks: Images of the Third World and Multi-ethnic Britain*, Working Paper No. 1, Centre for Multicultural Education, University of London Institute of Education.

Hicks, D. (1981b), 'The contribution of geography to multicultural misunderstanding', *Teaching Geography*, **17** (2), 64–7.

Hicks, D. and Townley, C. (eds) (1982), 'The need for global literacy', in *Teaching World Studies: An Introduction to Global Perspectives in the Curriculum*, Harlow: Longman.

Hirsch, E. D. (1987), *Cultural Literacy*, Boston: Houghton Mifflin.

Marsden, W. E. (1976), 'Stereotyping and Third World geography', *Teaching Geography*, **1** (5), 228–31.

Roberts, M. (1992), 'Squaring the circle', *Times Educational Supplement*, 10 April.

Robinson, R. (1987a), 'Exploring students' images of the developing world', *Geographical Education*, **5** (3), 48–52.

Robinson, R. (1987b) 'Teaching and learning about development in the developing world', Ph.D. thesis, Department of Curriculum Studies, School of Education, University of Birmingham.

Robinson, R. (1988), 'Teaching development issues', *Teaching Geography*, **13** (1), January, 7.

Rostow, W. W. (1960), *The Stages of Economic Growth: A Non-communist Manifesto*, Cambridge: Cambridge University Press.

Serf, J. and Sinclair, S. (eds) (1992), *Developing Geography: A Development Education Approach to Key Stage 3*, Birmingham: Development Education Centre.

Taylor, P. J. (1989), 'The error of developmentalism in human geography', in Gregory, D. and Walford, R. (eds), *Horizons in Human Geography*, London: Macmillan, 303–19.

Taylor, P. J. (1992), 'Understanding global inequalities: a world systems approach', *Geography*, No. 334, **77**, (1), 10–21.

Toh Swee-Hin (1986), 'Third World studies: conscientisation in the classroom', in Fien, J. and Gerber, R. (eds), *Teaching Geography for a Better World*, Brisbane: Australian Geographical Association with Jacaranda Wiley.

Waugh, D. and Bushell, A. (1992), *Key Geography: Connections*, Cheltenham: Stanley Thornes.

Wright, D. (1979), 'Visual images in geography texts', *Geography*, **64** (3), 205–10.

Wright, D. (1983), 'They have no need of transport . . . a study of attitudes to black people in three geography textbooks', *Contemporary Issues in Geography and Education*, **1** (1), 11–15.

Wright, D. (1985), 'In black and white: racist bias in textbooks', *Geographical Education*, **5** (1), 13–17.

# CHAPTER 5

# Development Education and the Teaching of Modern Languages

*Martin O'Shaughnessy*

Modern language teaching's contribution to development education may not seem at all obvious, yet it has an essential role to play, a role that no other area of the curriculum can duplicate. This chapter will consider why languages have an important part to play in development education, what precisely we might teach and, finally, how we should go about it.

## THE CONTRIBUTION OF MODERN LANGUAGES

Current talk in language circles is about 1992 (or 1993), the single European market and its implications. As language teachers, we assume that there will be more trade, more travel, increased opportunities for working abroad, increased communication through all forms of media; and as a result a greater demand for modern language learning and a greater need for our services. At the same time we feel a greater prestige and respect being accorded to our subject.

While we may welcome the enhanced prestige of language learning and the accompanying openness towards other European cultures, we must be wary of the danger of replacing an old narrow nationalism with a new, respectable 'European nationalism'. We must not allow ourselves to be agents of a vision of Europe that is seen solely in terms of a white, Graeco–Roman and Christian heritage – a vision that excludes minorities and which denies both age-old contact with other parts of the globe and a true understanding of the complex, interdependent nature of the contemporary world. Development education aims to increase our awareness both of the complexity and diversity of our own locality and our own society, and of Europe and of Europe's connections with a wider world; such an education is essential and languages have a vital part to play.

Languages, by their nature, are supposed to broaden minds. Yet they can also be used to shut the doors that they should open. Ideally languages are the perfect vehicle for understanding other cultures and countries, for hearing other voices, for seeing other viewpoints, for realizing the relativity of culture and of language itself. However, language teaching can be narrowly European, allow prejudices and ignorance to masquerade as cultural awareness or even neglect the cultural dimension entirely.

Textbooks often deal in stereotypes: the Frenchman with his striped pullover and string of onions; the Englishman with his umbrella and briefcase; the woman in the kitchen preparing the meal for her husband when he comes home from work; a Spain of sun, beach, fiesta, siesta, flamenco and bullfighting. Such stereotypes may seem harmless or even amusing to some people but they are in reality damaging. First, they are the negation of education in that they encourage ignorance and prejudice; instead of promoting understanding of other cultures in all their complexity and diversity, they give one single, often pejorative image which masquerades as knowledge. Secondly, they are demotivating. Why should students wish to communicate with the narrow, two-dimensional figures with which they are so often presented?

It is therefore essential to adopt a philosophy of language teaching in which countering prejudice of all types has a central role; O'Shaughnessy (1988; 1989) describes how an anti-racist policy can be developed and put into action. France, for example, needs to be presented as a complex, highly developed country; a multicultural society with a history of white and of black immigration; a society peopled by rounded individuals. But that is not enough; through French we can introduce children to the French-speaking world and allow the inhabitants of that world to speak for themselves. Similarly, the global dimension of other languages and the ethnic and linguistic minorities within other societies need to be recognized and acknowledged. Learning English provides access to the experience of a girl of Asian origin living in London or to that of a Nigerian or South African; to neglect this dimension is to sacrifice something fascinating and enriching.

Language learning and language syllabuses should not become so narrow that the language becomes an end in itself rather than a means to an end; for, as Shotton (1991) reminds us:

> The principal value of learning any language, be it native or foreign, does not lie in the language itself, but in the world which then becomes accessible to the learner.

Language has to be taught with culture or, rather, the two have to be *integrated*:

> It would also mean repeating past mistakes if culture would simply be attached to existing language courses in ways that background information has been introduced into many language courses in Britain.

(Buttjes, 1991)

# LANGUAGE LEARNING, TRADE AND DEVELOPMENT ISSUES

Some of the new enthusiasm for language learning is associated with trade and commerce. Clearly students need to be well equipped to deal with the world of work, but we should not allow ourselves to become mere language trainers rather than teachers, or simply to offer narrow courses in 'French for business' or 'Spanish in the office' or 'English at work'. We must remain educators, people who prepare students for their role as citizens in the local, national and international community.

This means that languages should be studied in their social and cultural context; students need to be prepared to discuss common issues and problems, to be able to compare their culture to other cultures, and not just be able to do business with people abroad. Ultimately, of course, there should be no real contradiction between the broader and narrower vision because, to do business successfully, you need to be able to interact socially with business partners and understand the culture and society in which they work.

Indeed, the study of languages in a work-related context can make a significant contribution to development education. Commerce and industry have local, national and international dimensions that can be exploited in a wide range of ways. For example, pupils can be taught to present their own communities to foreign tourists or to visiting business partners. They can consider the broader social and environmental effects of industrial location. One activity that works well is for pupils who have learned the necessary vocabulary and studied relevant texts in the foreign language to stage a debate over whether to accept the building of a factory by their village. Pupils engage more in the spirit of the debate if they are allocated roles: one can play an unemployed person looking for a job, another a concerned parent whose child's school is near the factory site, another the representative of the company and so on.

Pupils can study, through the foreign language, the dimensions of international trade and the products of different countries. When looking at how a product might be marketed in a foreign country pupils might be asked to consider stereotyping in a range of advertisements in the foreign language; they might then develop their own advertisements. Pupils obviously need to take account of cultural differences when preparing such work, as material suitable for one culture is not always appropriate in a different society.

Similarly, students on non-vocational courses need a broader approach than preparation for a visit to a pen-friend or as a tourist. This narrow role not only brings with it a limited range of language but also encourages students to see foreign countries merely as tourist destinations rather than as rounded societies. We cannot accurately predict which countries students will have contact with, nor what sort of contacts they will have, so it must be our responsibility to prepare them in the broadest possible way for contact with other cultures and societies. If we widen their horizons when they are young they may indeed have richer and more varied contact with other countries later on.

It is important then to understand the real people around the world who speak the languages that we study and equip children to understand their lives, their work, their societies and issues that concern them. In this way language teaching can make both a general and a unique contribution to development education. We can broaden and deepen pupils' understanding of other countries and make them more aware of their own, but we can also do what no other area of the curriculum can do: we can allow the inhabitants of those countries to speak for themselves in their own language, to present themselves as rounded human beings. Development issues should never be considered in a way that is divorced from their human and cultural context; language teaching can help establish this context and permit a direct dialogue between individuals.

# AN INTERNATIONAL APPROACH TO THE NATIONAL CURRICULUM

So far we have reflected on some general issues that relate to syllabus design and to language learning policy, but good policies without action are worth very little. What will now be considered is how the content of language lessons can be adapted to address development issues. We will do this in two stages; first through an examination of the proposed areas of study for modern languages in the National Curriculum for England and Wales (DES, 1990), and secondly, through a review of some materials and discussion of some classroom activities that might be developed from these materials.

The modern languages National Curriculum document moves away from the defined content syllabus of GCSE courses and replaces it with flexible areas of experience that pupils should 'visit' at least once between the ages of 11 and 14 and again between 14 and 16. The seven areas of experience are as follows:

A    Everyday activities (e.g. home life, shopping)
B    Personal and social life (e.g. family, festivals, religion)
C    The world around us (e.g. houses, towns, climate)
D    The world of work (e.g. local jobs and trades, tourism, industry)
E    The world of communications and technology (e.g. writing letters, benefits and dangers of technology)
F    The international world (e.g. travelling abroad, stereotypes, international organisations, co-operation and conflict)
G    The world of imagination and creativity (e.g. fashion, pop culture, sculpture).

(DES, 1990: 39–40)

The specific content is left to teachers but it clearly permits either a narrow Eurocentric approach or an approach which supports development education.

All the required areas can be covered by looking at the everyday life of a white French family, their religion and festivals, their home, town and work. Pupils might write to such a family or communicate through electronic mail; they might look at the European community, at French pop music, at Degas or Renoir and at Truffaut. Yet the same areas might alternatively be covered in a much more challenging and interesting way: one that opens pupils' eyes to the broader Francophone world and which stresses cultural diversity. Here are just some of the possibilities:

1 Home life and daily routine in the Ivory Coast.

2 The festivals and religion of Senegal where Islam is the majority religion but where one can also find Christianity and animism.

3 Homes and housing in Tunisia. City and town life in West Africa.

4 Tourism in a developing country: what that country might offer the tourist (basic level); tourism's contribution to the economy and effects on the country (higher level).

5 Pupils have pen-friends in a range of French-speaking countries and exchange information on all aspects of life.

6 Pupils examine and challenge not only the stereotype of the Frenchman with his onions but also the common stereotypes that pupils hold of Africans and Arabs, for example, the African as passive victim of disaster; the Arab as fundamentalist fanatic, as terrorist or as oil–rich oligarch.

7 The different forms of dress in different French-speaking countries in the world.

8 Cultural products of other French-speaking countries. Some of the immensely rich African oral tradition has been gathered and translated into French and is available in published form; novels in French from the Arab world, West Africa, Canada and the Caribbean are now beginning to appear on examination syllabuses for older students.

9 Use of development education or related materials either in the language of study or in the pupils' mother tongue.

10 Use of ethnic minority groups within the classroom to provide alternative perspectives and experiences, and, possibly, a knowledge of another language; these can serve as a useful point of comparison.

French, English, Spanish and Portuguese have much in common, as ex-imperial languages that left a lasting mark. They are now spoken in many countries around the globe and thus can be used to gain direct access to a wide range of cultures. Not all languages will be open to the same treatment and not all will have this international dimension, but all western European countries have recent or established migrant communities. Within Europe there exist a wide range of ethnic groups with a rich diversity of cultures and experiences. Study of any national language should permit a study of these groups who will be speakers of that national language. Each country also has a range of voluntary development agencies that can provide useful materials for teaching about development issues around the world.

Many teachers will have within their own classroom pupils from ethnic minorities whose awareness of another culture or language can be used – minority groups add an extra dimension to any classroom but they should be specially welcome within the language classroom where their presence can be drawn upon to illustrate cultural and linguistic variety and thus pave the way for language study and cultural awareness.

Quite clearly pupils' understanding of complex development issues will need to be built upon a more basic awareness of the concrete realities of everyday life. Language teachers are all familiar with the notion of a spiral curriculum whereby one considers the same area several times throughout a pupil's period of study, each time increasing the breadth and depth of treatment, and moving from simple language skills to those needed for analysis, presentation of opinion, discussion and debate. Thus, for example, the proposed National Curriculum topic of 'houses and housing' (DES, 1990: 40) might involve the following stages:

1  Where I or others live;

2  Describing my house or the home of someone in the country of study;

3  Description of my local area now and in the past;

4  Description of towns in the country of study; preferably with the help of a pen-friend;

5  General features of living accommodation in the countries under study;

6  The difference between town and country life in different societies;

7  Homelessness and government policy in different societies.

Development issues at local, national and international levels can be built into this progression so that pupils first develop a simple awareness of where different speakers of our language live; they move on to simple descriptions and then consider broader questions of change, quality and contrast; finally they reach the level of debate and discussion on issues of policy. The same pattern of progression could take place for every area of content, moving each time from the concrete to the abstract and from the specific to the general.

An example of this in practice can be found in the French textbook, *Arc-en-ciel* (Miller et al., 1990), where pupils begin in Book 1 by building a basic awareness of the contours of the French-speaking world before, in Book 2, looking at differences between France and the Ivory Coast through the eyes of a young Ivoirienne who visits France with her father. Broader issues, such as the environment, are considered in Book 3. Textbooks alone will not provide a rounded development education but there have been encouraging signs in recent years of a move away from some of the more pernicious stereotypes towards presenting more complex images; Starkey (1990) provides a detailed analysis of language textbooks.

# TEACHING METHODOLOGY

Although there is no proven, single method for teaching languages, some key features of good practice, endorsed in the National Curriculum (DES, 1990: 58–62), are:

- regular use of pair and group work in a way that encourages co-operation and interdependence;
- the performance of genuinely communicative tasks in the classroom (where one pupil must convey information that another does not know);
- the use, whenever possible, of the language under study as the general means of communication within the classroom;
- the use wherever possible of authentic texts;
- the development of links with other subject areas in a way that will break down the barriers that separate disciplines and encourage pupils to make connections between what they learn in different classrooms.

All these features of good practice are essential features of the practical activities below.

## Activities based on tourist brochures

Even in the context of tourism pupils can learn much about the world. This activity was designed for pupils of between 14 and 16 years old to work on an extensive group project where each group investigated one country where French is spoken, from a list of four (Ivory Coast, Tunisia, Senegal, Morocco), using tourist materials obtained from national tourist boards or travel agents in Paris. The group divided the following tasks between them:

1 Filling in a fact sheet about the country (collective task using all documents as a team);

2 Producing a magazine advertisement for the country;

3 Writing a postcard imagining they are on holiday in the country;

4 Writing a letter imagining they are an inhabitant of the country corresponding with someone in England;

5 Answering oral questions in French on the country, with the rest of the class playing the role of tourists and them acting as travel agents;

6 Writing a short poem about the country (in a simple form that used only nouns and adjectives);

7 Finding out additional information by use of the library.

Each task was made easier by the provision of a self-access help sheet which suggested the main language structures pupils might need in the completion of the task. The pupils worked from a dossier of authentic materials. Those who chose the Ivory Coast, for example, received some pictures showing different aspects of the country (beaches, markets, local costume, Abidjan – the capital, a city with some striking modern buildings), general tourist information, hotel brochures, excursion details and transport information.

These materials enabled the pupils to learn about a country they might not even have heard of and discover details that could serve as useful background to more systematic attempts at development education. Yet at the same time, materials designed to attract Western tourists can be problematic. On the positive side, even tourist information can carry much useful detail: students working on the Ivory Coast learned about its geographical location, climate, the mixture of religions, the many different ethnic groups with their individual languages, local products and main exports, population distribution, wildlife, hotel infrastructure, typical dishes and traditional costumes. They saw that Abidjan is a large, modern port city that still maintains traditional street markets. These details helped break down some of the more pernicious stereotypes of Africa and assisted in filling some of the huge gaps in pupils' knowledge about that continent.

Yet because the material is designed to appeal to the tourist, it has many failings that the educationalist must consider. First, it does not go beyond the surface, beyond what the tourist camera could capture: brightly dressed people but no details about how they live; attractive dishes but no explanation of the conditions under which the food is grown; historical sites but no talk of contemporary problems. Secondly, it represents local people merely as providers and entertainers of Westerners and not as part of their own society.

bloodthirsty or childlike savage of colonial myth is replaced by the simple friendly 'colourful native' of the tourist brochure. A good example of this can be seen in this quotation from a text selling the Ivory Coast:

> Par ces *couleurs* et les appels *pittoresques* des vendeuses de légumes et de fruits le marché africain représente pour le *touriste* un spectacle dont il ne se lasse pas et une merveilleuse prise de contact avec la gaieté et la *gentillesse* des habitants [my italics].

Tourist-orientated materials can be used to teach children about the developing world as long as we do so in a context which compensates for their limitations. Their useful basic information needs to be supplemented by other sources, and perhaps more importantly, care needs to be taken to educate students about stereotyping. Simple discussion about the quality of the text should take place in the foreign language: for example, 'c'est sexiste', 'c'est raciste', 'c'est stéréotypique', 'c'est exceptionnel', 'c'est une image touristique', and so on.

The skills needed to detect bias, partiality and stereotyping, and to decide which sort of audience a text is aimed at, are important life and language skills which should be developed in all pupils as an essential part of their education. Rather than insulate pupils from reality by carefully selecting texts, one should equip them with the critical skills they will need throughout their lives. The Council of Europe's Recommendation on Human Rights Education, R(85)7, lists among the skills that should be taught:

Skills involving judgement, such as:

- the collection and examination of material from various sources, including the mass media, and the ability to analyse it and to arrive at fair and balanced conclusions;
- the identification of bias, prejudice, stereotypes and discrimination.

# TEACHING MATERIALS

## Using photographs

Many photographic materials are available which can be obtained either in education packs from agencies such as Action Aid, Save the Children or Oxfam, or from magazines like *New Internationalist* (Britain) or *Échanges* (France). Groupe de Réalisations Audiovisuelles pour le Développement (GRAD) sells a wide range of slide packs which cover a variety of topics from human rights issues to the stages in the manufacture of a pair of jeans. These can be used in some of the same ways as photographs and have the advantage that a whole class can view them and discuss them at the same time; the disadvantages are that they depend on projectors or viewers, are less flexible and also much more expensive.

Photographs are a very useful resource for development education because they can be used to give a direct view of certain aspects of life in different countries, to establish contrasts and similarities and to expose stereotypes and preconceptions. They are also a useful tool for teaching languages because they provide a direct stimulus for foreign language production and discussion and can be used to introduce new vocabulary without recourse to mother tongue. They have the great advantage that they can be used equally well with complete beginners or with advanced learners, according to the level of difficulty of the task set.

These ideas for exploiting photographs are an adaptation of a photopack *Images of Africa and Britain* from the British agency, Action Aid, which has various sister organizations abroad that could provide similar materials. The pack contains a range of images from each of the two areas. Pupils are expected to work in groups.

One activity is to give the group a selection of the photographs and ask them to decide whether each is of Africa or Britain and to justify their choice. This is a useful way of bringing assumptions into the open and also to teach or reinforce linguistic structures needed for hypothesizing, for example:

I think it is . . . because I can see . . .
In my opinion, it must be . . . because there aren't any . . .

Another activity is to give the pupils an envelope containing, on separate pieces of paper, a range of adjectives (for example, fertile, infertile, grey, strange, tropical, efficient) and a few photographs and ask them to assign the adjectives to the pictures and then discuss their results with other groups. This is again a useful way of exploring perceptions and preconceptions. Linguistically, it helps pupils learn and use adjectives, as well as develop discussion skills:

I think this is tropical because . . .
I don't agree, I think it's . . .

The group is then asked to write captions for several pictures, jumble them up and ask another group to match the captions to the photographs. Pupils again explore and discuss their judgements while at the same time practising writing and reading skills within a setting of genuine communication; they are producing language for an audience that does not know what they are going to say rather than engaging in mechanical grammatical activities.

Once pupils are reasonably confident at describing the pictures, other, more demanding activities can be added: one pupil can look at a photograph and say where it comes from. The others then have to guess what will be in the picture. A pupil may be asked to give either a verbal or written description of a photograph which only they can see. Another pupil then has to draw the picture from the description.

Alternatively, a photograph or set of photographs can be an excellent starting point for role-play, improvised drama or written composition in a way that encourages empathy with the people depicted. An activity best carried out by the teacher is to cover part of a photograph and then ask pupils to predict what is in the hidden part. This is a very good way of challenging assumptions and is also linguistically useful as it encourages children to mobilize their imagination and their vocabulary resources.

At a more prosaic level, photographs are very useful for more traditional teacher-centred activities such as teaching vocabulary or practising question and answer in a pre-communicative way (pre-communicative because the questioner already knows the answer, so the emphasis is on linguistic form, not on content). Pictures can be used to introduce family relationships, different types of work, foods, clothes, local products and many other things in a way that shows a variety of images and gradually challenges stereotypes. Teacher questioning can be used simultaneously to test language and to draw attention to features of life shown in pictures; for example: 'What are these women doing in this picture?' 'Why are they collecting water?' 'Is it heavy?' 'How far do they have to go?' 'What will they use the water for?'

Photographs are not without their dangers: they can produce negative and uninformed reactions and, without a caption or text, these reactions may go unchallenged. The teacher has to be prepared to challenge assumptions and encourage pupils to go beyond superficial responses.

## Development education texts

Written materials designed for development education can also be adapted for use in language learning; however, because they use the foreign language, they are less flexible than photographs. Care needs to be taken to match the text and the task to pupils' capacities. First, the teacher will need to be selective in the choice of materials, using texts aimed at schools but adjusting the target age group. Secondly, she or he can adopt a series of strategies to make materials more accessible:

- Edit and simplify where necessary;
- Ask pupils to understand rather than be active producers of language;
- Control the difficulty of the task by thorough preparation and familiarization with context and language, by the level of the question set, by the amount of assistance provided before and during the activity, and by the rate of progression required;
- Adopt working methods that encourage co-operation and mutual assistance.

The activities below are based on material produced in France by CCFD (Comité catholique contre la faim et pour le développement) from a dossier called *Éducation au développement: le bassin méditerranéen*.

The first text is designed for use with French children aged 12–13 but could profitably be used by non-native speakers who had been learning French for about five years. It presents in cartoon form a day in the life of Saïd, an Algerian boy (see Figure 1). The pupils are asked to write in French a list of

**Figure 1** Cartoon of life in Algeria

*Source:* CCFD, *Éducation au développement: le basin méditerranéen.*

those aspects of the boy's life which seem similar to their own and another of those which seem different. At this stage it would be profitable for pupils to share their answers in pairs, than for the whole class to establish a list of similarities and differences in a way that should encourage discussion in the foreign language. Although one might criticize this text for artificially cramming a range of development issues into the life of this imaginary child, the text does raise awareness and encourage language use.

Another document from the same dossier, *La population en Algérie*, gives two bar charts showing the population profiles of France and Algeria in 1985. Pupils are asked to imagine that they are the presidents of the respective countries and to say what they would build (des écoles, des centres des loisirs pour les jeunes, des maisons de retraite) and why. This could be exploited in the language classroom in two stages. First, pupils could practise the language of comparison to contrast the two populations:

> En Algérie, il y a plus de jeunes/enfants/personnes âgées qu'en France. En France, il y a beaucoup de . . . / peu de . . .

Then pupils could practise using the conditional tense to explain what they *would* build:

> Je construirais des écoles parce que . . . etc.

Once again it would be useful for pupils to work in pairs or in a group to ensure an exchange of opinions in the foreign language.

One final example is of materials, from the same dossier, that deal with the environment. Pupils are given a table to complete where the principal components of the environment are given: le sol, l'eau, la forêt, le littoral, la mer, and they have to fill in three boxes for each:

> A quoi cela sert-il? (How is it useful?);

Qu'est–ce qui a provoqué la dégradation? (What has damaged it?);
Quelles mésures peut-on prendre? (What can one do about it?).

To answer the third question pupils are given a list of possible answers which they have to match to the correct sector of the environment. Some of the 'solutions' are obviously inappropriate (e.g. 'construire d'énormes complexes touristiques au bord de la mer' – build giant tourist complexes by the sea!) and can be used to establish a list of what not to do. The text has much potential for the language class. It can be used to practise and reinforce the vocabulary needed to discuss the environment. It can be used to teach expressions of necessity (We should . . . We must . . . It is essential to . . . It is vital to . . . . . . is urgent) or of prohibition (We shouldn't / We must not). It can be used for reading comprehension, for writing, for discussion (as pupils share their results) and as the basis for an essay or a discussion on the environment.

## Human rights and environmental materials

There are a number of other agencies producing materials in foreign languages which deal with human rights and environmental issues. Dossiers produced by Amnesty International, recounting the cases of political prisoners, can be used with profit with relative beginners. Routine questions of name, age and personal details take on a new significance if the person is in prison!

Environmental questions are dealt with by all the equivalent organizations to Friends of the Earth and by other similar bodies. Amigos de la Tierra in Spain has a leaflet about how to produce less rubbish and to recycle, called *Para producir menos basura, volvamos a utilizarla*. Although a lot of it is too dificult for many learners, it can be adapted, simplified or used as a source of vocabulary or ideas; in short, it can be recycled!

The leaflet begins with the question '¿Qué hay en nuestro cubo de basura?' (What is there in our bin?) Different categories are looked at: metales, trapos (rags), latas (tins), vidrio (glass), aceite (oil), plásticos (plastic), cajas (boxes), textiles, materia orgánica, otros (others). Pupils can be asked to compile a list in Spanish of what they find in their bins, noting the weight of each item; or alternatively, list the containers of all the products in their house and share the results with the class to establish a table of products and containers. Pupils are then asked to put the containers in several categories:

1 Se puede reciclar (it can be recycled).

2 No se puede reciclar (it can't be recycled).

3 No es necesario (it's not necessary).

4 Contiene productos peligrosos (it contains dangerous substances).

A final column could be added labelled: ¿lo reciclamos? (Do we recycle it?) to encourage some self-evaluation. Children share their results or interview each other.

103

In this way pupils work with some of the typical contents of the language lesson (quantities, household products, containers) while at the same time doing something more interesting than usual and developing their environmental awareness. The same Spanish leaflet contains a list of recommendations for producing less waste. These can be used with more advanced pupils for the traditional style of reading comprehension (question and answer, true or false); for translation or summary; or for some more imaginative tasks. It is possible, for example, to cut up the lists of solutions and then ask pupils to match the solution to the material.

## Own-language materials

For most educators it is probably much easier to obtain material in their own language. There is no reason why this should not be used in the language classroom, for although translation into the foreign language is now (rightly) practised much less than before, providing a summary in the foreign language and explaining details or the gist of a text in one's own language to a foreigner are useful skills which, in England at least, appear regularly in modern language examinations.

With more advanced pupils one can use texts such as those found in the magazine *New Internationalist*. This magazine is particularly useful because it puts many of the topical issues (e.g. life in the city, Aids, feminism, weapons – sale and manufacture) that language students are expected to discuss in an international context instead of giving the normal British, European or Western-centred view. A rounded picture is provided of various developing countries, so that instead of associating them simply with disasters, students can see that life in these countries is just as complicated as in ours and that people have to face many of the same questions, albeit in a different context.

One example of a text that has been used in this way is that on housework: women's unpaid labour around the world (*New Internationalist*, 1988). The text (see Figure 2) was used to contribute to study of the exploitation of women and was used in conjunction with a series of texts in French. Pupils were thus familiar with most of the necessary vocabulary before dealing with the text in English. They were first asked a series of factual questions, with the questions helping to provide the vocabulary needed in the answer, for example: 'Est-ce que les femmes doivent beaucoup travailler dans les pays pauvres? La situation est-elle différente dans les pays riches?' Students then wrote an essay where they focused on the language skill of introducing examples to support generalizations. They were expected to incorporate phrases such as: 'prenons le cas de . . .', 'citons un exemple . . .', 'regardons la situation en Australie'.

Once again all the activities are ones that one would normally use in a language class but the end result is educationally superior because the perspective is broader and the task is more motivating because the input is more varied.

# VISITORS IN THE CLASSROOM

Perhaps more important than language texts is the personal contact that modern language study can facilitate, either directly, by inviting a foreign-language speaker into the classroom, or indirectly, by introducing tape recordings, letters or photographs. Large cities will provide opportunities for the first type of contact as they may receive language assistants from countries as diverse as Senegal, Algeria, Mexico, the former USSR, and the French overseas departments Martinique and Guadeloupe, as well as from ethnic minorities within European countries. In addition, all major cities welcome many foreign visitors, some of whom can be persuaded to visit schools. These human resources are precious and should not be squandered; through them pupils can be brought face to face with representatives of a range of cultures and countries and can establish rich and rewarding contacts.

Pupils should use their language skills to find out as much as they can about all aspects of the lives and countries of origin of assistants and visitors. They can enquire about their daily lives, their family, their beliefs, their leisure activities, their diet, their home and where they live, the climate of their country, the political system, industry, agricultural products, exports and imports, education, their opinion on issues of general interest, their personal concerns. The list is endless but the main message is clear: students can gain a portrait of life in another country in a direct and individual way that is clearly superior to the stereotyped views so often held. This direct communication will complement development education materials by adding a personal element.

If pupils' contact with a native speaker is to be profitable, they need to be set specific, structured tasks and to prepare questions in advance. Interviews can be recorded and used as a basis for later discussion or written work. Without thorough preparation and structuring, meetings with native speakers will not produce the hoped-for results. Such results should be taken for what they are, a valuable and personal insight into another culture. No one individual can represent the totality of a culture, and personal contributions work best when balanced by a range of materials from other sources.

# SETTING UP A NORTH–SOUTH RESOURCE BANK

A further step forward is for a local education authority or group of schools to co-operate in building up a resource bank; this can draw on the whole pool of language assistants in an area, particularly those from the South or European citizens whose origins are in the South. Individual assistants might each be interviewed and recorded on a range of selected topics, and some may be persuaded to provide photographs of their families, of where they live or letters and other accounts giving their reaction to life in Europe. The materials open up the possibility of comparative analysis in a way that will help break down

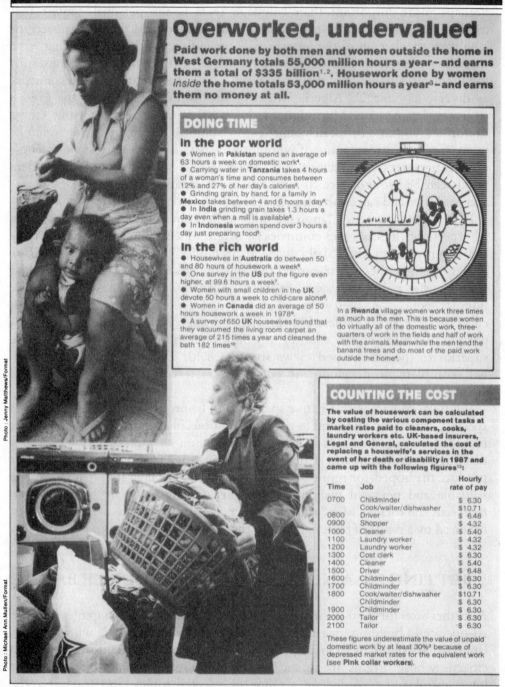

**Figure 2** Housework: women's unpaid labour around the world

*Source:* New Internationalist (1988).

# – THE FACTS

## MAN ABOUT THE HOUSE

### A day in the life

| Hours worked weekly by | MEN | by WOMEN |
|---|---|---|
| Philippines[7] | 41 | 61 |
| Uganda[7] | 23 | 50 |
| Indonesia[5] | 61 | 78 |

### How he helps

● Men in the US do an average of 1.6 hours of housework a day, irrespective of whether their wives/partners have jobs outside the home[13].

● In the UK 93% of the cleaning and 90% of child-care is done by women[10], who also prepare 77% of evening meals[14].

● One survey of UK men found that only 21% had *ever* washed any clothes and only 19% had *ever* done any ironing[15].

### His 'n' Hers

Research into who uses which tools around the house reveals that men tend to use tools for one-off occasional jobs, whereas women use tools for regular frequent repetitive tasks[13].

Used by **MEN:** drill, saw workbench, electric sander, hammer, screwdriver.

Used by **WOMEN:** stove, carpet sweeper, vacuum cleaner, pressure cooker, iron, electric mixer, washing-machine, sewing-machine, tumble dryer.

## PINK COLLAR WORKERS

### Woman's work

Outside the home women tend to be employed in occupations that mirror the kind of work they do inside the home.

● In the UK over 90% of clerks, cashiers, maids, nurses, canteen workers and sewing machinists are women[13].

● In Latin America and the Caribbean women working in the service sector outnumber men by over four to one[4].

● In the USSR 82% of workers in the health service and 74% of teachers are women[4].

● Women in Australia, Norway and the US are five times as likely as men to be working as secretaries or clerks[4].

### Bosses and secretaries

'Today's secretary also acts as wife, mother, mistress and maid. Office work is the business equivalent of housekeeping – concerned with tidying up, putting away, and restoring order. Filing is like washing the dishes. Typing a perfect letter is as transient an achievement as cooking an egg.'[16]

|  | BOSSES | | SECRETARIES | |
|---|---|---|---|---|
|  | Women | Men | Women | Men |
| GERMANY (Fed.Rep.) | 1.3 | 4.2 | 34.0 | 9.6 |
| HUNGARY | 0.1 | 0.2 | 16.4 | 3.5 |
| UNITED STATES | 3.8 | 10.4 | 27.9 | 5.5 |
| JAPAN | 0.4 | 6.4 | 18.2 | 9.4 |
| EGYPT | 0.8 | 0.9 | 25.0 | 6.5 |
| SINGAPORE | 1.2 | 8.2 | 14.9 | 5.7 |
| VENEZUELA | 1.6 | 9.2 | 16.7 | 7.6 |

% of male and female labour force in administrative and managerial (bosses) and clerical (secretaries) jobs.

Source: ILO

### Woman's worth

Because housework is considered menial and unskilled (partly because it is unpaid) the equivalent work in the market-place is also considered unskilled, and paid for at a correspondingly low rate.

● In the US a secretary with 18 years' experience earns less than a parking lot attendant[17].

● Research in 24 industrialized countries in 1982 found that women in manufacturing earned an average of only 73 cents for every dollar earned by men doing equivalent work[4].

● A nurse in the UK earns $14,000, that is $6,000 less than a fireman (*sic*)[16].

## CAREER CHAOS

Career structures and working hours in most countries assume the worker has no domestic responsibilities. This is why women, though half of the world's adult population, are only a third of the official cash-earning labour force[4].

### Part-timers

Housework, especially that concerned with child-care, prevents many women working full-time.

● In the UK 41% of employed women and 2% of men are working part-time[4].

● One in 25 woman teachers in the UK and one in 12 woman nurses has had to abandon her career and now works part-time in a cleaning or catering job[13].

● Women's responsibility for housework prevented them earning $27 billion in overtime payments in the UK in 1987[19].

### Love or money

Housework prevents many women putting in the number of hours necessary for promotion in their careers. Women with careers often have to sacrifice their private lives.

● Women professionals in the UK are over three times as likely as men to be unmarried[20].

● 50% of top women managers in the US are childless[17].

● Women in the US are three times as likely as men to interrupt their careers in order to take care of children, typically dropping out for 9 years. A 2-to-4-year break depresses earnings by 13%; a 5 year break by 19%[17].

● In 1985 bringing up two children was estimated to cost the average UK woman $88,200 in lost earnings[22].

### The price of a wife

Other research has come up with the following values for a woman's unpaid domestic work in the home:

● US: $6,500 per year in 1977. That's 6 times the US military budget and half of total GNP[7]. If being 'on call' for child-care is counted, the cost rises to $700 per week (1979)[7]. A 1980 estimate put the annual value at $14,500[4].

● CANADA: $6,000 per year in 1978, which adds up to $26 billion or 27% of GNP[11]. A survey in 1975 found that 49% of people thought women should be paid for housework[8].

● UK: $360 (£200) per week for child-care alone, which would total $27 billion or 6% of GNP (1984)[8].

1 World Bank, *World Development Report, 1987.* 2 International Labour Office, *World Labour Report,* Vol.3, 1987. 3 L Goldschmidt-Clermont, *Unpaid Work in the Household,* International Labour Office, Geneva, 1982. 4 D Taylor (Ed.), *Women: A World Report,* New Internationalist/Methuen, 1985. 5 B Rogers, *The Domestication of Women,* Tavistock, 1983. 6 B Cass (Ed.), *Women, Social Welfare and the State,* Allen and Unwin, Australia. 7 L Leghorn and K Parker, *Woman's Worth,* Routledge and Kegan Paul, 1981. 8 D Piachaud, *Around About 50 Hours a Week,* Child Poverty Action Group, UK, 1987. 9 Reported in the *Toronto Star,* 31 May 1975. 10 *The 1,001 Dirt Report* survey of 650 housewives. 11 Reported in the *Toronto Star,* 20 June 1978. 12 *How the Insurers put a Price on a Wife,* in *The Times,* London, 28 March 1987. 13 W Faulkner and E Arnold, *Smothered by Invention,* Pluto, 1985. 14 HMSO, *Social Trends,* UK, 1987. 15 Association of Market Survey Organizations, *Men and Domestic Work,* UK. 16 M K Benet, *Secretary: An Enquiry into the Female Ghetto,* Sidgwick and Jackson, London, 1972. 17 S A Hewlett, *A Lesser Life: The Myth of Women's Liberation,* Michael Joseph, London, 1987. 18 Reported in *The Observer,* 10 January 1987. 19 Research by the General, Municipal and Boilermakers' Union, reported in *The Guardian,* London, 19 January 1985. 20 A Oakley, *Housewife,* Penguin, 1976. 21 Survey reported in *Woman's Own,* UK, 20 March 1976. 22 Research by the Centre for Economic Policy Research reported in *The Guardian,* London, 19 January 1985.

perceptions of the Third World or South as a monolithic bloc.

Further activities can be designed: for example, the assistants might provide a sketch or a plan of where they live accompanied by a written description; the results are jumbled up and students asked to match the descriptions to the correct plan or sketch. A grouping exercise can be devised where assistants' comments on life in their host country are recorded; students are then asked to sort the reactions into positive and negative ones. Such an exercise might form the basis of further work where the students express their own feelings about where they live. At a higher level, the assistants can provide a range of opinions on a wide range of issues for comprehension work and as a stimulus and resource for discussion.

We should not underestimate the difficulty of what is suggested above; the production of worthwhile materials demands time, resources and co-operation. Questions to be considered before such a project begins include:

1  From whom can backing be obtained?

2  Will the assistants and teachers be released to do the work?

3  Who will pay for time on release, resources and materials production?

4  Who will provide technical support?

5  How will the materials be developed and by whom?

6  Who will co-ordinate the project?

7  Who will be the users of the materials?

8  Can materials of a sufficiently high standard be produced?

## SCHOOL LINKS

Pen-friend links with countries beyond Europe require fewer resources but still demand sustained effort and organizational skills. Ideally, links should be established and maintained by co-operating teachers in two countries; experience suggests that when pupils are left to their own devices only a small percentage continue writing over a long period. All the topics mentioned in connection with language assistants can be explored and photographs, plans and sketches exchanged. Results are much more fruitful if the teacher co-ordinates activities so that all the pupils receive letters on a particular topic, say families, at the same time and can make comparisons. If the co-ordination is good, teachers can arrange for materials to be received to fit in with the programme of study.

There are some published materials which can be used to gain direct access to someone else's life in the foreign language. One example is the French text

*Nous venons d'Algérie* (Finifter, 1986) which forms part of a series 'Les copains de la classe' (classmates), looking at various aspects of the life of ethnic minorities in France, including their impressions of life in that country and those of the country their parents left behind. Generally the children speak for themselves but the text also provides necessary background material. The result is a complex picture, reflecting the diversity of opinions and biographies that one finds in real life. The accounts are largely in simple langage that would not deter a reasonably competent language learner. The following conversation might be used as a straightforward reading comprehension or discussed in French:

> – Ma mère fait le Ramadan, mon père il le fait pas. Moi, non plus.
> – Mon père, il mange du porc, il fait pas le Ramadan.
> – Nous, on n'a jamais fait entrer de porc chez nous, jamais!
>
> (Finifter, 1986: 101)

> – My mother observes Ramadan. My father doesn't. Nor me.
> – My dad eats pork and he doesn't observe Ramadan.
> – We've never had pork in the house, never!

Extracts from this book can be used to build up a rounded, varied picture of children of Algerian origin in a way that challenges stereotypes of Muslim communities and demonstrates that media images of Islam, which often focus on fundamentalism, do not accurately reflect the lives of ordinary Muslims.

## CROSS-CURRICULAR ACTIVITIES

If teachers are able to portray people within their cultural contexts then the potential for development education is increased; songs, poems, and a wide range of literature and folk tales bring other cultures and peoples to life. For example, traditional African folk tales which have been translated into French can be used to encourage the important skill of reading for pleasure and can also help teach children that having an oral culture does not mean having no culture. Moreover, they can be used to encourage cross-curricular work, for example in art and drama.

Once subject barriers come down, many possibilities open up. Language teachers can work with other subjects in a way that promotes development education. Geography is an obvious choice; pupils might, for example, study a locality in French-speaking West Africa and develop a more complex understanding through co-operation across the two subjects. Work in history might enable pupils to understand why certain languages are spoken around the world. Modern language study can also support history and allow pupils to look at historical documents in the original language: the original version of the 'Déclaration des droits de l'homme et du citoyen' adds authenticity to study of the French Revolution. Students of French who translate the document for other classes have a genuine audience, making the task more realistic.

Immigration, a topic sometimes studied in history or social studies, may be profitably explored using the modern language to gain direct access to the experience of immigrant populations. Human rights issues can be studied through minority communities' experience of racism. Pupils can compare the experiences of minorities studied in the foreign language with the lives of minorities in their own country.

In each case the language class can be used to provide the authentic voice(s) of another culture and to give an all-important human context to development education work. Other subjects provide opportunities for children to explore in their own native language some of the complex development issues at a level that children could not manage in the foreign language. Such support is invaluable to the language teacher, who needs to be particularly careful not to promote negative images or stereotypes by partial or limited visions. Individual teachers or departments can achieve a lot, but ultimately, development education is best done within a broad framework of commitment and co-operation across a school.

## SUMMARY

Co-operation is a good word to finish on. Co-operation is essential at all levels: co-operation between pupils in their approach to learning; co-operation by teachers at departmental level to improve practice by consent and mutual support; co-operation by teachers to break down subject barriers; and co-operation between schools and with local education authorities to build up banks of resources and to share ideas. No one school can afford the time or the money required to research, obtain and/or buy materials. Development agencies cannot give free gifts! Co-operation, finally, is needed between countries to exchange materials and to establish precious individual contact, first, between schools in Europe and schools in the developing world and secondly between schools within Europe, so that teachers in Spain and England, for example, can help each other gain access to agencies and sources.

Through such co-operation modern language teachers can make a unique contribution to development education in the following ways:

- Teaching language in its cultural and social context;
- Using languages to gain access to the experience, lives and culture of the people in the range of countries where the language is spoken;
- Encouraging links with language learners abroad and welcoming native speakers into the classroom;
- Avoiding Eurocentrism and countering prejudice and stereotypes while helping pupils develop the skills to do the same;
- Exploring the lives of ethnic minorities abroad and using them to gain access to other cultures and languages;
- Drawing on the linguistic and cultural awareness of ethnic minorities within our own society;

- Bringing development issues into the language classroom by broadening the content of our lessons, by using progressive textbooks, and by drawing on materials from development and other related agencies;
- Encouraging cross-curricular links to explore different aspects of development issues.

# REFERENCES

Buttjes, D. (1990), 'Teaching foreign language and culture: social impact and political significance', *Language Learning Journal*, **2**, 53–7.

Council of Europe (1985), *Recommendation R(85)7*, Strasbourg: Council of Europe.

DES (1990), *Modern Foreign Languages for Ages 11 to 16*, London: Department of Education and Science Welsh Office.

O'Shaughnessy, M. (1988), 'Modern languages and antiracism', *British Journal of Language Teaching*, **26** (2), 20–5.

O'Shaughnessy, M. (1989), 'Implementing an anti-racist policy in modern language teaching', *World Studies Journal*, **7** (2), 20–5. (NB It is well worth consulting the whole issue of the journal as it is devoted to languages and world studies.)

Shotton, R. (1991), 'Cultural studies in foreign language education', *Language Learning Journal*, **3**, 68–70.

Starkey, H. (1990), 'World studies and language teaching', in Buttjes, D. and Byram, M. (eds), *Mediating Languages and Culture*, Clevedon: Multilingual Matters.

# RESOURCES

Action Aid, *Images of Africa and Britain: Photopack* (catalogue reference, IAB).

Amigos de la Tierra, *Para producir menos basura, volvamos a utilizarla.*

CCFD (Comité catholique contre la faim et pour le développement), *Éducation au développement: le bassin mediterranéen* (catalogue reference, DES 90.91).

*Échanges* (magazine de la coopération française), No. 5, December 1990.

Finifter, G. (1986), *Nous venons d'Algérie*, Syros, France.

Miller, A., Roselman, L. and Bougard, M.-T. (1990), *Arc-en-ciel 3* (pupils' book), Cheltenham: Mary Glasgow Publications, Stanley Thornes.

New Internationalist (1988), Life sentence: the politics of housework, *New Internationalist*, 181.

## Useful Addresses

Action Aid, Hamlyn House, Archway, London N19 5PG.

Aide et Action, 78/80, rue de la Réunion, 75020 Paris.

Amnesty International (British Section), 99–119 Rosebery Avenue, London EC1R 4RE.

Amnesty International (French Section), 4 rue de la Pierre-levée, 75553 Paris.

Ayuda en Acción, calle Españoleto 13/1, 28010 Madrid.

Cimade, Département Développement, 8 boulevard Bonne Nouvelle, Paris 10.

Comité catholique contre la faim et pour le développement, 4 rue Jean Lantier, 75001 Paris.

*Croissance* (development magazine), 163 boulevard Malesherbes, 75017 Paris.

*Échanges* (magazine de la coopération française), Kaolo News, 68 rue Carnot, Suresnes 92150, France.

Enfants et Développement, 13 rue Jules Simon, 75015 Paris.

Federación de Amigos de la Tierra, avenida de Betanzos 55, 11, 1 Madrid.

Frères des hommes, 20 rue de Refuge, 78000 Versailles, France.

GRAD (Groupe européen de réalisations audio-visuelles pour le développement), 12 rue Pertuiset, 74130 Bonneville, France.

International Save the Children Alliance, 147 rue de Lausanne, CH–1202 Geneva.

Orcades (environmentalist approach to development), 12 rue des Carmelites, 86000 Poitiers, France.

Oxfam (Youth and Education Section), 274 Banbury Road, Oxford OX2 7DZ.

Save the Children, 17 Grove Lane, Camberwell, London SE5 8RD.

Terre des hommes France, 4 rue Franklin, 93200 Saint Denis, France.

# CHAPTER 6

# Watching the World:
# Curriculum Strategies for Teaching about the Media

*Catherine Midwinter*

> Dawn – and as the sun breaks through the piercing chill of the night on the plain outside Korem, it lights up a biblical famine, now, in the twentieth century. This place, say workers here, is the closest thing to hell on earth.
> (Michael Buerk, BBC TV News, 23 October 1984)

Most European adults will recognize these words and be able to conjure up the images which introduced this unusually long and graphic news item that began an unprecedented period of intensive media coverage of an African country. The plight of Ethiopia, or more precisely the UK's response to the famine, became temporarily a topic of everyday conversation. The images of 'Africa's starving millions' became media currency and the Live Aid concert ensured that these images became a shared First World second-hand experience of the Third World.

The 1984/5 representation of Sahelian Africa is probably the best known and the most *analysed* example of media coverage of the South in the 20 years or so since the emergence of development education. The 'negative' images of African dependency prompted one British development educator to say that development education had been set back by ten years (Davis interviewed by Hicks, 1991). A development educator from Zimbabwe felt equally strongly:

> What such an approach has done is to strip us Africans of our real dignity. When we move into the streets of Western countries we are seen as Africans who are running away from famine, from a dictatorship or some disaster. That's the impact of the image which is now embedded in the Western public's mind about my people. Now those people who are responsible for the images are not taking the responsibility for the consequences.
> (Nyoni interviewed by Wiles, 1988, in Wiles and Nyoni, 1988–9)

But why should development educators be concerned with the media and the production of images? How can media representations of the South be analysed and understood? What are the benefits for young people of learning about media and development issues?

This chapter aims to answer these questions with particular reference to 'The Media Project 1985–8', an EC co-funded formal education sector project at the Development Education Project (DEP) in Manchester, in the north of England. This curriculum development project aimed to encourage teachers and their pupils to explore and examine the ways in which the media created, reaffirmed or challenged images of countries, cultures and peoples of the South and North.

The first part of this chapter will outline some of the research into media portrayals of the South and the impact on young people, followed by a rationale for incorporating media literacy within development education. The second part will set out the aims and methodology of 'The Media Project' and present some of the ideas, techniques and activities developed. The third part will draw some conclusions from the project, briefly evaluate its impact and discuss ways forward.

## REPRESENTATIONS OF PEOPLE, CULTURES AND COUNTRIES: THE POWER OF IMAGES

Media representations are images of the visible world brought to us through television or newspapers, magazines, films, comics and so on. The media often show us places, people and events that we have not experienced first hand. They are representing reality, but it is a constructed reality that is the product of choices that have been made on our behalf. If we take these products at face value we are denying the complex series of decisions that have been made about the intended messages, and we are disregarding a variety of interactions that construct the meaning of the image for us. We must recognize that we bring our own values and cultural background to an interpretation of these messages. Images are also read within a context: even photographs are viewed within a particular set of circumstances, whether it be a newspaper front page, or a textbook which is studied as part of a particular syllabus.

Images are not simple. The notion of representing implies an action performed by someone, a process that requires a perpetrator and an audience. It is, though, a process that we all experience and can understand. Take the example of a holiday snap. Your friend wants to take a picture of you standing in front of the hotel. She tells you where to stand, waits until there is a gap in the passers-by and takes the picture. Later you look at the picture and exclaim: 'Oh, I look really fed up, but I wasn't.' Your family comment that the hotel looks large and grand, but you explain that most of the building is the office block next door. Your friend is pleased because she had caught one of the hotel staff in the picture. She sticks it in her album with the caption: 'The people at this hotel were very friendly.'

This process, of interpreting images, is enacted every time we engage with media representations. As we consume images and fit them into a framework, we bring to bear personal and other concerns which include politics, history, culture and economics. Sithembiso Nyoni underlines the power of images:

> I think that images are crucial. They inform the relationships that people have with each other, the way they view you, the way people think about you, the way they describe you, the way they relate, the attitudes they have and the attitudes they disseminate. Images also affect the way people *think* they understand you. Images are very complicated to identify.
>
> (Nyoni interviewed by Wiles, 1988)

However, if we learn the skills we *can* identify the process of construction; deconstruction is possible once we know how to look for the apparently invisible seams.

Being bombarded by images and consuming information is a part of all our daily lives. It happens at many different levels and from a variety of sources, although given that the average British adult spends 75 hours every week with television, radio, newspaper and magazines (Tunstall, 1983), the media are inevitably the major source. About one in five young people at all age levels regularly watch an early evening news programme and about one in ten between the ages of 8 and 15 watch 'World in Action', a weekly documentary programme (DES, 1983).

The media were at the top of the list of sources of images of Africa in the research carried out with young people for the *Images of Africa* UK report (van der Gaag and Nash, 1987). A four-nation study, *Young TV Viewers and Their Images of Foreigners* (Halloran and Nightingale, undated), shows that the media provide the most potent source of views about other peoples.

This chapter is particularly concerned with young people's interaction with the media images of the South, and the implications for development education practice. So what do young people learn from all this media input; what do they know of the South?

It is noteworthy that most research that can help us answer this question relates to Africa. It is interesting to speculate why this should be but more than passing consideration is outside the scope of this chapter. Suffice it to say that in the 1980s, at least, young people probably had greater awareness of Africa than of, say, South America. Africa had a relatively high media profile and development educationalists often found themselves accepting a media-led agenda. Researchers followed suit.

## Images of Africa

In a 'mental maps' exercise with young people undertaken in 1986 for the *Images of Africa* UK report the predominant images were of 'Africa starving' or

'Africa primitive' (van der Gaag and Nash, 1987). The idea of 'primitive' peoples, of shields and spears and slavery, competed for space with images of poverty and famine splashed in big letters or drawn large across the whole of Africa. Wild animals were another important feature. (See examples in Figure 1.)

Another piece of research asked 6-, 10- and 14-year-old pupils (or teachers on pupils' behalf) to fill in a questionnaire which included asking for a response to the word 'Africa'. Of 278 replies 'the only positive response to the word Africa came from a 14-year-old boy who had lived in Kenya and spoke of feeling a sense of loss at having left there'. Otherwise, words like 'starvation' and 'charities' were common. 'More traditional associations such as jungle, wild animals and tribes were also often stated, but the whole perception was exceptionally negative and there were many comments such as "it's a bad place", "it's horrible" and "I would hate to live there"' (Jungkunz and Thomas, 1986).

Jungkunz (1988) followed this up with in-depth interviews with 6-, 10- and 14-year-olds. The 6- and 10-year-olds' responses to questioning about Africa and Ethiopia were in keeping with the 1986 results and included 'people starving as the sun is too hot to grow anything', 'heat', 'deserts' and 'not enough rain'. The 14-year-olds' responses showed more sophistication but were nevertheless Eurocentric; for example, South Africa 'is more modernized than the rest of Africa' and has 'our type of housing' as opposed to 'very primitive shacks made out of mud and straw'. No 6-year-olds had heard of the 'Third World' and 14-year-olds painted a gloomy picture of 'famine', 'drought' and 'disease'. All 51 subjects interviewed put television as their main source of knowledge for their answers. It is notable that when asked to list names of countries, Africa was the most frequently mentioned 'Third World country', although in 1990 further work relating to this research (Thomas and Chapman, 1991) shows that 80 14-year-olds mentioned China 56 times, 7 times more than Africa.

## Other images of the South

There is evidence to show that children's perceptions of other countries of the South are also stereotyped and narrow. In Jungkunz's (1988) research the pupils were also asked about countries such as China, India and Jamaica. A 6-year-old said they ate 'different food' in China; a 10-year-old said 'Indian people don't live like us' as they 'can't buy clothes in shops or go to the supermarket'. On the whole the 14-year-olds were better informed but one 14-year-old knew only that Jamaica was 'hot' and that 'black people live there' and it might be 'in the Mediterranean'.

It does appear that 'many 6-year-olds and some 10-year-olds are uncertain as to what constitutes a "country". By 14, though, the concept of "country" is more fully understood' (Jungkunz, 1988). In another exercise, 84 14- and 15-

**Figure 1** Children's ideas of life in Africa

year-olds in the north of England were asked to mark Ethiopia on a world map. Although the majority located it somewhere in Africa, only 27 were able to place it accurately; others put it in such diverse locations as Borneo, Greenland and Romania (Moore, 1987). There was also very little awareness of the size of some of the African countries; for example, Ethiopia was seen as being 'smaller than Britain'. Young people in the UK not only seem to have stereotyped views of countries of the South, but also seem to be somewhat hazy about the geography of the South (and quite possibly of the North as well!).

## Interpreting photographs

Attitudes become even more apparent when young people are shown photographs of the South. In the case of Africa, the historical relationship between Europe and Africa put images in a particular context that has its roots in colonialism. Thus a photograph of a scene in Addis Ababa with cars and high-rise buildings was labelled 'Western influence in the streets' (van der Gaag and Nash, 1987). When asked *why* a photograph of the famine had been taken the answers were 'to get sympathy', 'to show their condition', and once 'to show they carry on despite the suffering'. Another piece of research (Grant, 1986) provided a striking example of narrow ethnocentricity. The majority of responses to a photograph of a smiling woman and her child in Burkina Faso were that if they looked contented 'we must have helped them'. Africans had become 'aided Africans'. In other words, if Africa is not starving it is only because the West has helped.

In a study of 320 primary school children's responses to photographs, (Graham and Lynn, 1988) they were shown a photograph of two black women, one in European dress and one in traditional dress, taken at Nairobi airport. Both women appear prosperous and well-to-do. With few exceptions, children thought the Western-clad woman was an air stewardess or secretary, while the native-clad woman 'gathered twigs to make brooms' or 'cleaned houses'. According to Graham and Lynn, the children thought that most African people 'slept in mud huts whatever they did during the day' and the inclusion of modern city scenes in the pictures did not alter the children's perceptions. A photograph of schoolgirls in Columbo has a telegraph pole and cable in the background but 'at least 90 per cent of the children failed to observe these at first, claiming there was no electricity'. This research notes: 'These children were kind and generous in their attitude to "Third World" people but the unquestioning acceptance of our superiority was overwhelming.'

Sensational pictures of disasters, wars and famines will, for the foreseeable future, dominate media coverage of countries of the South. The impact cannot be ignored as from research findings we can conclude that visual images dominate the perceptions, and, although the context can lend the images variable significance, most people asked to comment on a picture will describe the *content* without relating it to text or information from other sources. As one photojournalist put it, 'people will always quote the stereotype' (van der Gaag and Nash, 1987).

Stereotypes won't disappear tomorrow: they are a useful shorthand that we all use from time to time. Does this really matter? The answer must be yes if they are allowed to go unquestioned and unrecognized; such stereotypes can be misleading, hurtful, destructive and can fuel racism. For example, the words most often used to describe Africans in press coverage of Africa in 1984–5 were 'rebel' and 'victim' (van der Gaag and Nash, 1987). News values lead us to expect that sensational events will be reported, but what appeared to be lacking in these reports was any context for the reader; there was no exposition of African countries and African lives and the political complexities of a situation were simplified. The 'rebels' and 'victims' were not given a voice and the connotations were those of 'uncivilized' people and 'primitive warriors', echoing the old colonial images.

This kind of reporting has considerable implications for the British public's perceptions of Africa, Africans and black people in general. Not only does it reinforce an ethnocentric attitude towards Africa as underdeveloped, primitive and dangerous, but it engenders a racist and neo-colonialist attitude towards black people in Britain and overseas.

## Southern perspectives

It is important to note that the Africans involved in the FAO *Images of Africa* project felt that 'misinformation about Africa in Europe was essentially a European problem'. The synthesis of four African reports from this project points out that:

> The European public perceived the food crisis in Africa as a dramatic and catastrophic event. On the contrary the African reports emphasise that, viewed from their perspective, the crisis was a process over an extended period of time not an immediate happening . . .

> the question of famine is not considered within the wider issues of political and economic structures and international linkages. Global problems of power, control of means of production, inequitable distribution of resources are split artificially into a distorted image of Africa as an isolated, hungry continent on the one hand and an equally distorted mirror image of Europe as a generous benefactor on the other.
> (FAO/Freedom from Hunger Campaign, 1988)

As Sythembiso Nyoni, one of the Zimbabweans who worked on the project, says: 'I'm a Zimbabwean and therefore the image of the majority of my people becomes my image.' However, she adds:

119

I am aware that the image of Africa is very tarnished . . . like every country Africa has problems. But it is not the whole story . . . Where I work, the image I know is of a dynamic village population who are struggling to recreate their world . . . When that is not spoken of, is not revealed, is not articulated, then I grow angry, because I think that the images that are being thrown around to represent me and the people of Africa are distorted.

(Nyoni interviewed by Wiles, 1988)

The implications of this distortion are far-reaching. It matters not only because young people are failing to appreciate the diversity of life in other countries, but also because they are quoting media-derived stereotypes to reinforce negative and narrow views and attitudes, even when presented with contradictory evidence. This is not merely of interest to development educators; it has huge significance for all teachers, not least with respect to the effects of this stereotyping on black children's perceptions of themselves and white children's perceptions of black people.

In a recent video *Developing Images* (IBT/Double Exposure, 1988) a student, Rita Sharman, says:

People associate me with the 'Third World' and it makes their view towards me very patronising because they feel that the 'Third World' is all about charity and helping them. And me being from the 'Third World' – it's almost as if they are being charitable by letting me be in this country. And that can fuel all sorts of resentment – racism. And it just makes it difficult for all black people in this country to see those sorts of images.

Nyoni argues cogently:

I am taking the responsibility as an African . . . But we are living with that negative image. What is it doing with us? And what is it doing to the Western public? It really has done more damage. It has reinforced racism, it has reinforced the colonial mentality of looking down on Africa which is a damaging attitude if you want to engage in a dialogue about human development with the West . . . Something urgent needs to be done in my opinion.

(Interviewed by Wiles, 1988)

The effects of television and other media as powerful transmitters of ideas and images cannot be denied. The research findings quoted above show clearly the implications of the effects. If our aims within development education encompass understanding the links of economic, social and political forces which shape lives throughout the world and developing the skills, attitudes and values which enable us to bring about change and work towards a more just world, then we cannot ignore the impact of media representations.

## Media literacy

We may agree with Nyoni when she says something urgent needs to be done, but that it should be done in the classroom through media education may be considered controversial. However, it can be argued that all teachers are already media educators to a certain extent, in the same way that all teachers are teachers of language. All teachers use mediated material composed of language and image. Many teachers who are aiming at their pupils' critical abilities will already, as a matter of good practice, be encouraging pupils to question the validity of their sources of information. To extend this questioning to take account of media images and 'texts' in the classroom is a necessary yet simple step in exposing the 'seams' in the process of image construction and thus encouraging a more informed consumption of the media. To discuss with pupils 'Who has produced this? Why? What is its purpose?' begins the process of media literacy and a recognition of the complexity of images. This involves developing skills, concepts and attitudes which support and often overlap with those of development education such as a questioning approach, open-mindedness, tolerance and critical awareness.

Media education need not be an intimidating set of complex notions, full of jargon and mystique. Certainly, the study of the media as a discipline requires some knowledge of theory and practice in order to understand concepts such as institution, audience, narrative and genre. However, many aspects, such as developing students' image-analysis skills, their awareness of media products' construction, their understanding of the concept of stereotyping and thus their 'critical autonomy', are accessible to all.

The case has been made for educating young people about the media and representations of other people, countries and cultures. What then are the theoretical and practical implications of this; what might teachers be doing in the classroom?

# PUTTING THEORY INTO ACTION: THE MEDIA PROJECT 1985–8

My experience as an English and Media Studies teacher from 1974 to 1982 and then as a member of staff at the Development Education Project (a development education centre working with schools) led me to research and set up the Media Project. This was partly established in the belief that media education is a vital ingredient of the curriculum for any young person and partly in a response to the many calls for help from those who, in the course of teaching development issues, had come up against a wall of stereotyped and often prejudiced views of the South, relating directly to media images. Challenging stereotypes also forms a major aspect of anti-sexist and anti-racist teaching, and it seemed that there were few resources for teachers who wished to tackle these issues. Although research was increasing, development education had paid little attention to supporting this area of work.

Teachers and development educators were asking questions such as 'how can we make sense of the conventions and codes used by the media so that we can "read" messages more critically?' A number of questions were identified:

- What is a stereotype, why are stereotypes used and how can they be identified and challenged?
- Why are countries of the South mostly shown in the media only in the context of disaster and conflict? How does the reporting of a country such as Nicaragua (today it might be Iraq or Yugoslavia) affect our attitudes towards it?
- Where do interests within the media lie and who has power and control over what we see, read and hear?

The prospect of encouraging innovative curriculum development was exciting and the time seemed right; by 1985 co-financing had been obtained from the EC and the three-year project began.

The Media Project, therefore, was run by me with the support of the co-ordinator, office organizer and resource centre organizer at DEP. Figure 2 reproduces the promotional leaflet, produced in 1985, and outlines the project aims; these were closely adhered to over the three years of the project, whilst

---

TARGET GROUP

The project will be working directly with teachers of media studies, world studies and related subjects. The processes and materials developed will be for the benefit of students between ages 13 and 16 within English, Social Studies, Personal and Social Education, Geography, Religious Education and General Studies.

---

PROJECT PROGRAMME

The DEP project worker will develop the project with the help of a Project Advisory Group and the teachers involved over a three-year period. This period can be broken into three phases.

Phase I: Preparation Research, initial in-service training course, formation of teachers' working groups.

Phase II: Materials Development Supporting the working groups producing the units (see across). Helping teachers develop ideas in school (team teaching). First trialling of units. Teacher exchange with the Netherlands.

Phase III: Production and Dissemination Revision and second trialling of units. Production and printing. In-service courses/conferences for local and national dissemination.

---

**LINK WITH THE NETHERLANDS**

A similar project will be run by the Polemologisch Instituut (PI) in Groningen. DEP and PI will work together to enable: comparative studies between the Dutch and British media's interpretation of international events; the sharing of educational materials; teacher exchanges between the two countries to learn more about the media and media studies.

---

## PROJECT UNITS

The resulting teaching pack will be made up of five independent, but integrated units.

---

### Media Literacy

- will explore the relationship between medium and message and facilitate understanding of the way we perceive communicated language and images.

---

### Images of Other Countries

- will emphasize, particularly, images of the countries of the "South" and how these are created, re-affirmed or challenged by TV and other media.

---

### Bias and Stereotyping

- will consider images of people both in the "South" and in Britain/Netherlands. The unit will refer to race, gender and class images in the media.

---

### Understanding the News

- will help students recognize fact, opinion, supposition, points of view, editing and style. It will refer to newspapers as well as TV.

---

### Media Democracy

- will deal with issues such as ownership, public access, political control, censorship, technological developments (eg cable TV).

---

**Figure 2**

the methodology developed to fit altered circumstances. The link with the Polemologisch Instituut in Groningen produced some work, but sadly the Dutch project was unable to obtain funding and we were unable to work as closely as we had hoped.

# The project process – phase 1: preparation

The curriculum development project began (after a term of preparatory work) with in-service courses for secondary teachers. Two similar courses entitled Images of the World: Media, Message and Meaning in the Classroom comprising six sessions of one and three-quarter hours each were run concurrently at Teachers' Centres in Greater Manchester. These courses aimed first to introduce teachers to the skills and concepts of media education, using media studies and development education techniques to consider the media in relation to issues of represention of people, cultures and places within local, national and international contexts. Secondly, the aim was to motivate teachers to join small working groups to explore the issues in more depth, contribute ideas for teaching materials and test these ideas in the classroom.

The courses were enthusiastically supported and achieved their aims, despite the ambitious nature of the timescale. However, as one participant pointed out, if the vista of what *could* be done was opened up and people were given the confidence to begin exploring it with pupils and colleagues, then as an introductory course it had been a success. During this phase an extensive resource collection on media issues was established at DEP, which became a British Film Institute Education Regional Advice and Resource Centre.

# Phase 2: materials development

During this phase the ideas and activities that would form the teaching units were developed. The original idea of setting up teaching groups to work on individual units was abandoned. This was due to lengthy industrial action by the teachers' unions which prevented after-school meetings. Also it became clear that all the themes were so interconnected that to work on them chronologically or separately was counter-productive. The process that evolved enabled the project worker to develop ideas through a series of termly day-long courses, workshops, team teaching and consultation with groups and individuals.

For example, the project worked with two teachers from a school in Rochdale on developing ideas for a simulation game to be contained in the *Whose News* unit on media ownership and control. This included running a version of *Crisis in Sandagua*, a simulation game previously published by DEP, with a group of year 11 (15–16-year-old) students at the school. The co-operation followed on from a day course for teachers on news reporting of Central America which included participation in *Crisis in Sandagua*.

During one term, the project worker taught year 11 students alongside their teacher at a High School in Old Trafford over a six week period. This enabled concentrated testing of activities on stereotyping for the *Picturing People* unit. The contact was first established at the preparatory courses.

# Phase 3: production and dissemination

During the spring term of 1988 the content of each unit was established and the publishing process was begun. The curriculum development work resulted in five separate but complementary teaching units for teachers. They include copyright-free material that can be photocopied for pupils' use, such as worksheets and photographs. The whole series of five books is entitled *Watching the World* (Nash, 1989) and comprises:

Unit 1: *Investigating Images – Working with Pictures on an International Theme*
Using the theme of buying and selling in different parts of the world, including Manchester, the photographs and accompanying 20 colour slides provide a basis for activities which develop skills of visual analysis and observation, a vital component for studying the impact of the media. This unit, therefore, acts as a core to the others in the series.

Unit 2: *News from Nicaragua – Fact and Fiction: A Case Study*
This unit explores the way news is gathered from around the world and enables comparison of news from different perspectives, by focusing on Nicaragua. It contains a full-size colour poster with accompanying suggestions for use.

Unit 3: *Aspects of Africa – Questioning Our Perceptions*
This unit explores the kind of images of Africa that people build up from media coverage and whose viewpoints are represented. It aims to challenge stereotyped images of Africa and Africans and is accompanied by 20 colour slides.

Unit 4: *Picturing People – Challenging Stereotypes*
Using the theme of youth, this unit enables understanding of the concept of stereotyping. It considers the uses and dangers of stereotypes and the role the media plays in forming them.

Unit 5: *Whose News? – Ownership and Control of the News Media*
This unit is based on a simulation game, *The Sandagua Connection*. Through the simulation and with the help of classroom activities for preparation, debriefing and follow-up to the game, students explore who and what controls the reporting of the news. Issues such as ownership, the law and censorship are raised. The simulation is designed so that it can be run in long or short sessions. A full-colour poster on media ownership is included.

In the summer term of 1989, day courses were run in the Manchester area to disseminate the *Watching the World* series to teachers and advisers working across the humanities curriculum. These courses were successful in attracting geographers, historians and religious education teachers although the majority of participants were English and media teachers. The evaluation suggested that the materials filled a perceived need for a cross-curricular approach and were useful to media specialists and non-specialists alike.

Workshops were also run at conferences and day events around Great Britain, mainly by invitation. Dissemination has continued beyond the life of the project, through DEP's regular in-service programmes and in response to national requests.

An aspect of the project worth underlining is the user-friendly, 'low-tech' approach and the important part that was played by still photographs. It is perhaps assumed too often that media studies entails using expensive and complicated equipment and that it is necessary to screen lengthy films and analyse whole television programmes. Although it *is* useful to use video and pupils *do* benefit from hands-on experience, one of the main messages of the media project is that a low-tech approach is ideal for this work. In fact it is essential to begin any work on analysing media representations by building visual literacy skills, and this is best carried out by using still photographs.

## In-service and teaching strategies

Here is an example of how the process of building visual literacy skills was explored first with teachers on an in-service course and then developed into teaching activities for the published classroom materials. Teachers were asked to draw 'mental maps' of Africa. These were to be the images that were uppermost in their minds and could include words, pictures and symbols. They had ten minutes to produce their 'mental maps' on large sheets of paper using coloured felt-tip pens. The group then had the opportunity to look at all the maps and make comments; the participants were asked to note similarities and differences between the maps, asking questions such as:

- Do the images show any evidence of first-hand experience?
- Where do these images come from?

This is an excellent way of eliciting the extent to which we all carry stereotypes in our heads and the extent to which they are media derived. This simple activity can be used in the classroom and is a good way to begin work on any place as it shows clearly what pupils do or do not already know or believe.

Teachers (in pairs or threes) were then asked to look at a group of nine photographs of people in different African countries, in a variety of active situations such as working in a factory, or watering some plants in a nursery. Each pair had to pick the three photographs that surprised them most. Pairs then reported back to the whole group and observations were made about photos that had been picked frequently or rarely and why this might be. This activity is a way of challenging stereotypes.

Each pair was then asked to choose one picture from the three that they would use on a fund-raising poster in their school. This raised interesting questions about what kind of fund-raising it might be and which type of pictures were deemed 'suitable' and effective for raising funds. Discussion focused on the extent to which our images of Africa (or wherever) relate to the perceived 'problems over there' because of media and charity representation, rather than any sense of real people's lives and shared concerns.

Following this, one photograph was selected by the facilitator and a photocopy given to each pair, who were then given a context such as 'the front page of a newspaper', 'a family photograph album', 'a geography textbook', 'a campaign leaflet'. Each pair was asked to give the photograph a caption that might appear with it in that particular context and to write it beneath their picture. The whole group then tried to guess what the contexts were and then discussed the captions and their effects. Participants were amazed at the extent to which the same photograph could be given a very different meaning by the addition of a few words. The exercise shows the extent to which the message that we get from a picture is affected by its context and is an important aspect of understanding the concept of representation.

This was followed by an activity to develop observation skills and to make visible the way in which we 'read' pictures. Using the same photograph (or another), each pair filled in an analysis sheet (see Figure 3, pp. 129–31) which asks for observation of specific clues that help to clarify its particular meaning for the viewer. Discussion explored the extent to which it is possible to make assumptions from particular features of the picture and how much our cultural framework and the stereotypes that we are familiar with affect our reading of the picture. It becomes clear that although a picture might be assumed to be a straightforward way of communicating and 'tells the truth', in reality pictures can be far more complex and open to interpretation than words. This is an essential part of understanding the impact of images and it is important for pupils themselves to have made this step in order to analyse more complex media products.

As a way into understanding how television can be understood as a series of still pictures (or chunks of film) the next activity was introduced. Teachers were asked to work in groups of four or five and each group was given 30 small pictures of outdoor scenes in Manchester. It was interesting to use pictures of the teachers' local area but a variety of pictures of any place can be used. Each group was then given a different title for a news item, for instance: 'Manchester voted Britain's most exciting city', 'Manchester faces huge debts' or 'Residents say inner-city Manchester needs cleaning up'. They were given an hour to choose ten photos out of the 30 to represent edited sections of a television news item, and write a commentary to go with them.

Small groups then presented their news items to the whole group, who were startled at how often the same pictures had been used but to make dissimilar and sometimes opposing points. The activity points clearly to the extent to which editing and selection plus a commentary can alter representations and produced a biased view. This understanding can then be transferred to television output and representations of other places analysed to establish the viewpoint, taking account of what may have been left out.

**Figure 3**
**Image Analysis Key Questions: Worksheet 1**

PEOPLE

1  What sex are they and how do you know? _____

2  How old are they? _____

3  From what part of the world might they originate? Why? _____

4  Where in the world do you think they are in this picture? _____

5  Do they seem poor, wealthy or neither? _____

6  What can you tell about them from their clothing? _____

7  What can you tell from their expressions? _____

8  Who are they looking at, and why? _____

9  How are they positioned, and why? _____

10  What are they doing? _____

11  Are they posing for the camera? How do you know? _____

PLACE

12  What can you see in the foreground? _____

13  What can you see in the background? _____

14  What kind of place does this suggest? _____

15  What is the relationship of the people to the place? _____

PRESENTATION

16  Describe the technicalities of the picture (cross out those of the following that do not apply)

colour/black and white/sharply focused/blurred/partly focused/clear/grainy/very dark/ strong shadows/plenty of contrast/very light/indoors/outdoors/long shot/medium shot/ close-up/high angle/low angle/telephoto/wide angle

17  What is the main focus of attention in the picture? What do we look at first? _____

_____

18  Has anything been missed out or cut off ('cropped') at the edge of the picture? _____

_____

**Figure 3 (continued)**
**Image Analysis Key Questions: Worksheet 2**

UNDERSTANDING THE MEANING

1 How are the people in the picture relating to each other and the things around them? ⎯⎯⎯⎯⎯⎯⎯

⎯⎯⎯⎯⎯⎯⎯

2 How are the people relating to the camera? ⎯⎯⎯⎯⎯⎯⎯

⎯⎯⎯⎯⎯⎯⎯

3 Do you feel you are part of what is going on in the picture or are you an outsider? Why? ⎯⎯⎯⎯⎯⎯⎯

⎯⎯⎯⎯⎯⎯⎯

4 Can you tell the story in the picture?

⎯⎯⎯⎯⎯⎯⎯

⎯⎯⎯⎯⎯⎯⎯

5 What are the clues that suggest this story? ⎯⎯⎯⎯⎯⎯⎯

⎯⎯⎯⎯⎯⎯⎯

6 What are you supposed to feel about this place and/or these people? ⎯⎯⎯⎯⎯⎯⎯

⎯⎯⎯⎯⎯⎯⎯

7 Is there anything that is difficult to understand in the picture? ⎯⎯⎯⎯⎯⎯⎯

⎯⎯⎯⎯⎯⎯⎯

8 How do you make sense of what is in the picture? ⎯⎯⎯⎯⎯⎯⎯

⎯⎯⎯⎯⎯⎯⎯

9 Can you relate any parts of the picture to your own life? ⎯⎯⎯⎯⎯⎯⎯

⎯⎯⎯⎯⎯⎯⎯

10 What kind of additional information would help you understand the picture more fully?

⎯⎯⎯⎯⎯⎯⎯

11 Would you understand this picture differently if you lived in Africa? Why? ⎯⎯⎯⎯⎯⎯⎯

⎯⎯⎯⎯⎯⎯⎯

12 Why do you think this photograph was taken? _____

_____

13 Who do you think took this picture? How can you tell? _____

_____

14 What do you think this photograph would be used for? _____

_____

The final activity was to analyse the title sequence for a documentary. The title sequence can easily be video recorded and is a short, compact, but vital sequence with plenty of clues about what is to come. It is infinitely preferable to work in depth on a short piece of film than to try to grapple with a whole programme feature. Participants were asked to note down what they might expect to see in the title sequence of a documentary about South Africa. After they had watched the sequence through once, it was then repeated and paused at each 'cut'. For each image participants were asked to write down three words that came to mind. The sequence was then shown again and the participants were asked to note down the topics that the documentary might be expected to cover, who would be presenting it and what points of view might be expressed. Teachers were then asked how their original expectations for the title sequence matched up with what they actually saw, then to examine how the subsequent expectations had been engendered by the title sequence.

It is valuable to note the extent to which subconscious awareness of the codes and conventions of television leads us to know pretty much what to expect of a documentary title sequence. The specific ways in which a very short piece of film can say a great deal is a good focus for discussion and is a manageable introduction to looking at the power of television images. This last activity is also a good preparation for showing a documentary and arouses more interest than just showing it 'cold'.

The above activities are just one route to developing visual literacy skills using the minimum of equipment and making the most of still photographs. Clearly these kinds of exercises have hundreds of variations and can be used to go down a variety of different paths. As they are mainly skills based they are aso transferable and can be used with different content and to cover issues as well as places or people and cultures. These activities lend themselves to experimentation and teachers found them as valid and useful in the classroom as for themselves. The fact that they had tried them out previously gave them added confidence.

# DRAWING CONCLUSIONS AND LOOKING FORWARD

The project was hugely enjoyable and stimulating to work on and indeed proved to be a timely choice as many media–related issues, such as the use of 'positive' images, became more central to the work of development educators in the late 1980s. There are a number of general observations that can be made about the process of the project.

The project enabled closer links to be made with educational fields other than development education, in particular media education and multicultural education. Other people were engaged in work which embraced issues of media representation and the discovery of the various approaches was mutually beneficial.

Some teachers and advisers are very committed to media education; these people were open to the 'globalizing' of media work and proved very rewarding to work with. They had often been aware of the rather Eurocentric view within media teaching resources but had been unsure of how to challenge it or where to find alternative resources. However, the amount of media education work within each local education authority (LEA) varies enormously depending on the commitment and support of the LEA. In many places the excellent work of many teachers happens in an uncoordinated way. It seems that a significant number of teachers are keen to explore the kinds of issues that were covered by the Media Project but are desperate for support and encouragement. The Media Project highlighted the need for structured training and resources, properly funded.

The project attempted to introduce a cross-curricular approach and this was particularly successful. Although media work has always been seen mainly as the province of English, the project set out to challenge this. As has been shown, the perceptions of the world that children bring to the classroom cannot be ignored by any teacher dealing with humanities subjects, at least. The project also contained a clear element of teacher education so that teachers of all subjects might become aware of their contribution to the students' store of images. It became evident from the project work that the *Watching the World* series could be used within a variety of subject areas and educational initiatives such as Technical and Vocational Education Initiative and other curriculum areas such as personal and social education.

A recent survey (Dinn and Midwinter, 1992) shows that in 1991 teachers were using the *Watching the World* series very flexibly, selecting activities for a variety of subjects, age ranges and purposes, including adult education. This accords well with the intentions of the resources, which were not written as a course of study, but more as a bank of material that could be returned to again and again, given that coverage of media issues has always been a rather random affair in schools. It will be interesting to monitor any changes in the use of the materials as the National Curriculum becomes established within the secondary school.

It is also difficult to gauge impressionistically the extent to which young people who have been exposed to this kind of media education have altered their views of the world or become aware of media issues. Without particular research no great claims can be made for The Media Project but it is undoubtedly the case that there are more young people whose perceptions are being challenged than five years ago. There is a need, though, for research which investigates not only young people's images of the South but also their imaging of development issues. The notion of debt or aid may well have very different associated images when related to North and South. This seems a vital next step in learning how to present effective educational material on media and development issues.

Themselves an aspect of development education, media issues have become increasingly important. There has been a growing awareness of the importance of media education and of a variety of methodological approaches. This can be established from the growing number of books, journal articles, conferences and workshops devoted to analysing the relationship between the media and development issues. Associations such as Third World First, the National Association of Development Education Centres, the Education Network for Environment and Development and the International Broadcasting Trust have all run major conferences around media and development issues in the last four years and there have been many requests for contributions to such conferences based on the experience of the Media Project. Research continues, as does the debate about images used for fund-raising and the helpfulness and meaning of the term 'positive images', indicating a greater degree of awareness than in 1985 at the start of the project.

An important part of development education work is to ensure that it is disseminated in such a way that other people can carry the messages further. There seem to be many more people within development education who are confident to tackle media issues and, although it is difficult to know how much might be attributed to the Media Project, the approaches in the teaching materials are widely used by development educators. Although the project has ended the issues are still very much alive and the continued requests for information and dissemination of the project's work are a measure of its success.

## CONCLUSION

This chapter has noted concern within countries of the South over the way they are portrayed. The Southern participants at the Images of Africa Project Conference in 1988 made it clear that it is up to Europeans and northern countries to examine their use of images and implement changes. The Media Project has regarded the raising of consciousness over use of images of people, countries and cultures as a priority, and it is encouraging that it has moved up the development education agenda. It has been given weight by the Code of

Conduct on Images and Messages relating to the Third World produced by the NGO–EC Liaison Committee in Brussels. This code underlines the conclusions of the *Images of Africa* Project and provides recommendations and practical guidelines. It is an important indication that it is increasingly not only grass-roots development education that recognizes and is prepared to struggle against the 'hell on earth' images of the South. However, it is only by questioning perceptions and challenging images at personal, local, national and international levels, in partnership with those in the South, that we will move forward.

# REFERENCES

Department of Education and Science (1983), *Popular TV and Schoolchildren: The Report of a Group of Teachers*, London: DES.

Development Education Project, Manchester, 'The Media Project 1985–8: report to the Commission of the European Communities', unpublished report.

Dinn, R. and Midwinter, C. (1992), *The Development Education Materials Survey*, Manchester: Development Education Project.

Food and Agriculture Organization/Freedom from Hunger Campaign (1988), *The Image of Africa: Synthesis of the African National Reports*. Rome: Commission of the European Communities and the Directorate for Development Cooperation, Italian Ministry for Foreign Affairs.

van der Gaag, N. and Nash, C. (November 1987), *Images of Africa: The UK Report*, Oxford: Oxfam.

Graham, J. and Lynn, S. (1988), Children's Images of Third World Countries, Research project, London: South Bank Polytechnic.

Grant, R. (1986), 'Band Aid: help or hindrance?', BA dissertation, University of East Anglia.

Halloran, J. D. and Nightingale, V. (undated), *Young TV Viewers and Their Images of Foreigners: A Summary and Interpretation of a Four Nation Study*, Centre for Mass Communication Research, University of Leicester.

Hicks, B. (1991), 'World in crisis', *Times Educational Supplement*, 31 May 1991.

Jungkunz, T. (1988), *How Schoolchildren View 'Third World' Countries*, Oxford: Development Education Unit.

Jungkunz, T. (1988), *How Schoolchildren View 'Third World' Countries*, Oxford: Development Education Unit.

Jungkunz, T. and Thomas, O. G. (1986), *Young People's Perceptions of Other Countries*, Oxford: Development Education Unit.

Moore, J. (1987), 'The formative evaluation of the Media Project in secondary schools', MEd dissertation, University of Manchester.

Nash, C. (1989), *Watching the World*, Manchester: Development Education Project.

Thomas, O. G. and Chapman, J. (1991), *Fourteen-year-olds' Images of 'Third World' Countries: A Comparison of Two Research Methodologies*, Oxford: Development Education Unit.

Tunstall, J. (1983), *The Media in Britain*, London: Constable.

Wiles, P. and Nyoni, S. (Winter 1988–9), 'Images of poverty: a view from Zimbabwe', *Journal of the Child Poverty Action Group*, **71**, 6–10.

# CHAPTER 7

# Managing Whole-School Change

*Chris Leach*

Schools exist in a changing educational climate and a changing world. Effective schools have to be able to adapt and manage change so it enhances the education they provide. The wider world presents us with many issues such as injustice, exploitation, the misuse of power, and environmental degradation. Education is about developing understanding, skills and values to address these issues. Development education is concerned with global issues and should therefore form an integral part of a school's curriculum and practice. Development education is also about an approach to learning and teaching which is based upon individual rights, active participation, evaluating change and empowering people to be actively involved in their own futures. These are notions which involve the whole school community and which permeate classroom practice, management approaches, school policy and ethos. They are also notions which can inform change in a school's approach to teaching and learning.

The introduction of a development education approach is likely to raise a number of challenges for teachers and children in schools. The adoption of this approach may challenge established views and approaches to teaching and learning and require colleagues to examine their own personal views. As development education can cause people to examine their views about the world, their teaching and the nature of the curriculum, it is closely linked to the notion of change in education. Change can occur in isolation, in one classroom, or with a few individuals, but the scope of change is often limited by the wider school context. For change to be effective the whole school must be involved in the process; it must be a shared experience, with commonly held understanding.

The process of managing whole-school change needs careful planning and consideration if developments are going to affect the whole curriculum and reflect the consensus of opinion within the school. Teachers need to be working together with a sense of common purpose and a feeling of a common aim and ethos for the school.

This is the challenge in many schools, and what is offered here is an analysis of an approach developed in one Birmingham school, attempting to turn policy into practice. This may enable people to share in this process and may perhaps inform their own approach to management. It must be emphasized that this is a dynamic process which is constantly evolving to reflect the changing needs of the school, the pupils and the community it serves. This is only a 'snapshot' of the process at work within one school at one particular time.

Development education offers the opportunity to develop a curriculum which involves children in their global context, in their relationships with other peoples and, ultimately, in working towards their future as custodians of the planet. Coupled to this is the notion of equipping children with the understanding, skills, and values to take action for positive change. Development education may involve children in developing the awareness that they can and will have power, as consumers and as citizens of their local area, country, and their planet.

This is closely related to developing a curriculum which focuses on active, child–centred learning where children take more responsibility for their learning both as individuals and as part of a group. This type of approach is directly linked to the ethos of the school. Development education materials and approaches were seen as something which would support the development of the school community. The approach would inform the whole curriculum right across the school. It therefore formed an integral part of change within the school.

## THE CONTEXT

Benson is a primary school with a nursery unit; it takes children from 3 to 11 years old. The school is a classic Victorian building, built in 1889. It sports a grade 2 listed tower, steeply pitched roofs and neo–Gothic architecture. The school has twelve classes with about 30 children to each class, children being grouped in age bands. The nursery unit has 60 places: 30 full–time places, and 60 part–time, giving a total of ninety children. This gives a school population of about 430. During the 1970s the school received additional funding from the Van Leer project, set up by a rich industrialist who wished to further develop links between the school and community. In material terms this added a new wing to the school which was built in order to house community rooms and a playgroup; the school was also given new toilet blocks. More importantly, a major initiative was undertaken to develop stronger links with the community, and a range of events and groups were set up. These still exist and have developed to provide a strong community link for the school.

The school population reflects the rich cultural diversity which exists in the locality. Children come from a range of religious backgrounds: Hindu, Sikh, Muslim, Buddhist, Christian and secular. Children also have their roots in a wide variety of areas: India, Pakistan, the Caribbean and Ireland. Cultural diversity is an important part of social life and is celebrated through assemblies, festivals, language, literature, the arts, food and shared experience.

The school has a staff of over 20 teachers, who include a home–school liaison teacher, two teachers of English as a second language and a pre-school worker. There are also nursery nurses, classroom assistants and domestic staff, all of whom are involved in the development of the school ethos. Staff range from the very experienced to newly qualified teachers just beginning their teaching careers and come from a range of cultural backgrounds. At the point of this snapshot the school had appointed five new teachers, including a new deputy headteacher and a co-ordinator of the infant department.

The management approach in the school is one of consultation, negotiation and shared responsibility. The headteacher and deputy work closely together, in consultation with the nursery, infant and junior co-ordinators, and the curriculum co-ordinators.

The ethos of the school can be summed up in the following statement, which is given to everyone who joins the school community:

> This school pledges itself to be a place where children of all races and religions will find safety and respect for themselves, their families, and their traditions.

This is supported by policy statements on equality of opportunity and anti-racism, which are reflected in practice throughout the school. The emphasis is on shared, active, group-based learning and teaching which values co-operation, shared responsibility, trust and respect for others.

The school also operates within the wider context of the English education system, which is currently undergoing radical review and change. This is manifest in the introduction of a new National Curriculum which sets targets for each age band within each of the prescribed curriculum areas of mathematics, English, science and technology, history, geography, music, physical education and art. This is coupled to the development of a programme of assessment of children designed to ascertain which level they have achieved within each area.

The rapid pace of change created a climate of anxiety and uncertainty for teachers, putting pressure on staff to opt for a fragmented curriculum, compartmentalized in subject areas rather than reflecting the integrated, holistic, global system which exists in the 'real' world outside school.

## THE WRITER'S BACKGROUND

I had recently moved from another Birmingham school where I had been a junior co-ordinator and had participated in the development of a whole-school approach to curriculum development, led by a newly appointed headteacher. Development education materials and approaches had played a major role in that process. At the time of my appointment as deputy headteacher at Benson School I was also involved in a project run by the Birmingham Development

Education Centre which looked at examining learning and teaching about other places (see Chapter 13). These experiences came together to inform my contribution to the management of change at Benson.

# THE CHALLENGES

The needs of the school were, and still are, identified through the formation of a School Development Plan. This is a document required by the local education authority which identifies the needs of the school in terms of curriculum, training, resources, classroom practice and the building. The plan is developed through consultation with all the staff, who help identify specific needs, set priorities for the school, and plan how needs will be met.

This raised a number of challenges for the school. The introduction of the National Curriculum was a major external challenge as it represented a whole new approach in English schools: a shift away from the school's traditional autonomy to choose its own curriculum to meet the needs of the local area, to the adoption of a curriculum which is designed to reflect national needs as perceived by the government. This asked teachers to work in areas where they often felt they had little expertise or experience.

In addition the school wished to build on existing good practice: developing strong links with the community; providing a curriculum that was relevant to the needs and experiences of the children; and placing value on equality of opportunity and anti-racist work, through an integrated curriculum.

To further support the above practice a curriculum was needed which looked at issues such as injustice, stereotyping, interdependence and global links, and which could result in positive action by the children and the community. This implies a need to raise the awareness of the staff to such issues and to develop strategies whereby they could be introduced in the classroom. It was seen as important to identify and develop an approach which would enable senior staff to introduce change into the school in a non-threatening way. Change needed to be effective in the curriculum, in classroom practice and in raising staff awareness of global issues. The staff had previously worked on whole-school projects and this experience was seen as a potential vehicle for change within the school. The senior management group, through consultation, agreed that this would be a valuable way to effect change and support colleagues.

# A GLOBAL APPROACH TO THEMEWORK

A global approach to themework is one in which the whole school works together towards a common theme. This crosses all age groups and is done through an integrated curriculum. For example, the theme of 'Health' could be used as a focus for work in science, on our bodies and keeping healthy; in geography, on global issues about health in developing countries and on global pollution; in history, on the development of health care and traditional or alternative medicine; and in religious education, looking at spiritual health.

There are a number of advantages to this approach:

- The whole school is working together on a common theme. This gives the school a sense of common purpose.
- Learning in one area supports learning in another.
- Children across the school have a common experience and can therefore share their learning outside the classroom.
- In-service training can relate directly to the classroom situation, and experience gained can be transferred to the classroom directly; it is relevant to the work in hand.
- Resources can be held centrally and colleagues can share ways of using them.
- Good practice can be directly shared between colleagues.
- Displays around school can have a common theme with means they can become a learning resource for *all* members of the school community.
- Assemblies are a time at which the ethos and philosophy of the school can be set. These can be planned to relate to a common theme. They are therefore relevant and can be readily followed up in the classroom.
- The National Curriculum can be introduced a stage at a time, so that all can share in the experience and challenges as each new area is developed. This can be supported by meaningful in-service training.
- Issues can be explored and awareness raised together. This can offer support. It also contributes to the development of the sense of the staff as a team working together.
- Parents can share in the sense of common purpose and contribute to learning across the whole school through involvement in the project.
- Classroom practice and organization can be examined within the context of a common theme. This can be looked at by colleagues working together, thus heightening consistency of approach.
- The approach emphasizes the holistic view of knowledge. It emphasizes the link between one area of the curriculum and another.
- An integrated approach enables curriculum areas to be combined: English work can be linked with science and mathematics. In a practical sense this helps ease the pressure on an already full timetable.

## CHOOSING A THEME

A number of criteria for choosing the themes for the year's work were selected. These arose from the needs identified in the school deveopment plan, statements about the ethos of the school, policy statements on equality of opportunity and anti-racism, and the needs of the National Curriculum. Our criteria were:

- Does the theme create opportunities to meet the needs of the National Curriculum?
- Does the theme reflect the ethos of the school?
- Are issues about stereotyping, racism, interdependence, development, diversity, and justice raised by the theme?
- Does the theme reflect and celebrate cultural diversity?
- Does the theme help to create positive images of the children, their community and non-European groups?
- Is the theme relevant to the children's experience?
- Does the theme create opportunity for teachers to meet the learning needs of the children?
- Does the theme create opportunities for in-service training, especially in areas highlighted by the development plan?
- Does the theme help to develop classroom practice?
- Does it create opportunities for parents and the wider community to become involved in the learning process?

By the application of these criteria, themes can become a vehicle which carries forward change in line with the needs of the school and curriculum, and is rooted in practical experiences in the classroom.

Each theme has a different emphasis, in which certain criteria play a more dominant role. It may be a focus on an in-service issue, on classroom practice, or a curriculum area; the emphasis is decided by the needs of the school as identified in the school development plan.

For the first year of development we chose the themes of 'Our Community', 'Communication' and 'Food and Health'. The second year's cycle was 'Journeys', 'Change' and 'Spaceship Earth'.

Figure 1 shows how a theme works. Each strand of the theme supports change in the school.

**Figure 1**

# PROJECT GUIDELINES

The project guidelines are written by the deputy headteacher in consultation with senior staff and give guidance to staff about the overall aims of the project; in other words, they indicate where we as a staff and a school are trying to go. Their contents reflects the needs identified by the senior staff within the school – postholders with an overview of the curriculum – and needs identified by the whole school staff in the school development plan. The guidance is given to indicate the range of the curriculum to be included in the project, the duration of the project, and what is required of individual teachers in drawing up forecasts or plans for their groups. The guidelines also indicate where and when training will support the project and how this can be used.

This gives people a clear framework in which to plan their work, supporting colleagues with their planning and helping to ensure consistency of approach across the school. Teachers use a range of pro forma for planning; the first gives an overview of the whole project showing where cross-curricular links can be made. There are two pro forma for curriculum areas, one identifying work in core subjects, the other in foundation subjects. The pro forma breaks planning down into a week-by-week plan for the term and identifies which attainment targets are to be addressed – the aim of each activity, its content, the nature of the activity and what resources are needed. A final pro forma is used to indicate planning for visits, assemblies, assessment and displays.

# FACTSHEETS

People need practical support with the development of themes; factsheets aim to help with this. These are prepared by postholders for each curriculum area: mathematics, English, science and technology, history, geography, religious education, and art and design. Information on how community links can be developed are also included. This draws on the individual expertise of specialists within the school staff team; people are also given an opportunity to research the theme following lines of their own personal interests, which can give themes added vitality. Postholders use this opportunity to indicate what and how aspects of the National Curriculum can be developed or introduced. This has often been linked to in-service training from LEA support staff or our own in-house training.

To ensure continuity and progression across the schools, postholders keep an overview of their area of the curriculum, clearly identifying what the objectives are for each age group, indicating how and when these can be developed through the whole school themes. Factsheets play an important role in terms of 'ownership' of the project. Teachers are making a concrete contribution to the development of the projects through their factsheet, enhancing commitment to the project's development.

The potential issues raised by the project are also kept in sharp focus by the factsheets. This takes the project beyond the basic requirements of the National Curriculum. For example, when we looked at 'Spaceship Earth' a lot of work focused on global links and interdependence; our responsibilities towards the planet; and reflecting on other people's perceptions of the planet such as the Native American view of land ownership. In the project on 'Journeys', children explored their own life experiences and considered alternative futures for themselves, for others and for the planet.

Development education plays an important role throughout the process as development education materials are referred to within the factsheets, and staff are introduced to these new resources in a practical and meaningful way. Factsheets also provided a valuable resource for future projects which draw on similar themes.

## ASSEMBLIES

Assemblies are designed to complement each theme and raise issues on a whole-school basis. This helps to reinforce the whole-school ethos. Each assembly gives staff material which they can follow up in the classroom. Assemblies give issues status within the school, and their consideration a high profile. Each assembly also tries to present positive images of other cultures, and to break down stereotypical views. It also creates a platform for celebrating cultural diversity within the school. Stories, information and drama draw from the traditions of many cultures, widening the children's perceptions of other people and their religious views.

This multi-faith approach gives the projects an important spiritual dimension. Relationships with other people and the planet are explored in this way, contributing to the children's spiritual development, building this into the theme as an integral component.

For example, when considering the theme of 'Journeys', the notion of pilgrimage was explored. Also considered were the journeys people make, either by choice or under duress, as travellers, followers of nomadic life styles, as migrants or as refugees. At a deeper level, the journey of life was considered, looking at the different perspectives of the purpose and way of living life offered by different religious schools of thought.

## RESOURCES

New resources are essential to the management of change within the school. Each theme is resourced with new materials. New resources are exciting; teachers want to use them if they are seen as relevant to the work they are doing in the classroom. It was found that teachers shared resources across the school and shared ways of using them. They are often referred to in training sessions or factsheets so teachers can see how to use them in the classroom.

As well as resources which relate to one specific theme, we also introduced a range materials which would help to develop people's awareness of development education and the global curriculum: *Earthrights* (Greig et al., 1987); the series *Teaching Development Issues* (Development Education Project, 1986); *Global Teacher, Global Learner* (Pike and Selby, 1989); and *World Studies 8–13* (Fisher and Hicks, 1985). These were used for in-service training and form the core of a readily accessible resource area within the staffroom.

Materials specific to each theme are chosen to fulfil some of the following criteria:

- They present positive images of a range of cultures and groups.
- They raise or explore issues central to the theme.
- They give accurate, up-to-date information.
- Material in them is accessible to children or staff.
- They present information in the children's home language if possible.
- They are exciting to use.

Resources include books, posters, music tapes and maps. The community, parents, visitors and the locality are also seen as a valuable resource to support projects.

Good resources can enable people to look in detail at new issues; there is time for reflection and consideration. They can offer new practical ideas which can be used in the classroom; this can open people up to new ways of working. The most valued resources are those which begin with practical classroom activities. These can be adopted for lesson ideas and soon teachers begin elaborating on an initial idea, making it their own, meeting the needs of their children.

New resources also give themes status with staff and children. In the classroom children enjoy bright new materials and it stimulates them to enquiry. The investment also makes a statement about the school's commitment to the theme and the children, enhancing their self-image. Children's positive self-image is further developed if resources reflect their cultural background; a book is a powerful medium for making language, traditions and stories legitimate currency in the classroom.

## IN-SERVICE TRAINING

School-based in-service training (INSET) was planned to support the development of the project. Themes are chosen to create a forum for training and staff development. Needs for INSET were identified through the school development plan.

A key element of INSET was teachers' personal development. An informed and interested staff with a sense of commitment to the ideals of the school, which in turn reflects issues raised through development education, enhances teachers' involvement in, and commitment to, the process of change. Many of the issues within development education are challenging, and this, coupled with the urgency of the National Curriculum, could have created a great deal of anxiety among the staff. INSET aims to relieve this anxiety by providing information, examples of good practice, practical ideas that could be developed in the classroom, ways of using new resources, and support in the classroom. We often start by reflecting on current good practice in the school, reinforcing the point that we are not starting something entirely new; people already have skills in this area which can be developed. This helps to build confidence and reinforce good practice. As one colleague commented: 'The science training day was excellent, I could use the ideas straight away in the classroom. It's much easier when you've had a go yourself.'

The introduction of the National Curriculum puts a major emphasis on curriculum development in the school; when tackled through themes this can be achieved within the context of the school ethos and designed to reflect development education issues. INSET is practical as it relates to the theme in hand and is set in the context of the school. Often INSET is provided by staff within the school; this gives them additional status and contributes to the climate of success within the school. External provision was also brought in to reflect wider issues within education and to see practice in other schools.

Development education had a major influence on in-service training, informing the approach to training and providing practical approaches to the issues in the classroom. Training sessions tried to create situations which placed the emphasis on participation, all the staff contributing to the development of an idea or approach. Resources like *A Sense of School* (McFarlane and Sinclair, 1986), the photopack *Behind the Scenes* (McFarlane, 1988), and *Themework* (McFarlane, 1990) were invaluable here. Getting staff working, for example, with photographs, examining issues, brainstorming ideas, doing ranking exercises, working collaboratively, helped to build confidence with new ideas. This also reflected the type of practice in the classroom which would support the ethos of the school.

When looking at the theme 'Communication' INSET was provided on using photographs in the classroom. *Get the Picture* (Davies, 1989), a resource book which examines ways of looking at images with young children, was extensively used, first in a training session then in the classroom, with teachers feeding back their experiences to the whole staff. This created the confidence to use photographs in a variety of ways in the classroom.

The on-going programme of INSET has a common thread throughout: try out, use, reflect, share, evaluate, and build new practice. This operates in the context of whole-staff meetings, cross-phase groups (teacher working in a range of age bands), faculty groups (teachers with different but related areas of curriculum responsibility working together), phase groups (for example, teachers of infants) or in age bands, creating scope for teachers to work together, share experiences, and develop confidence in a range of group situations.

Themes have provided scope for a range of INSET activities which have begun the process of policy development and innovation in classroom practice. These have included:

- using images
- technology
- science
- information technology
- collaborative teaching approaches
- religious education
- music
- English, reading and writing
- maths, classroom practice
- gender and equality of opportunity
- outdoor education
- geography and the global curriculum
- assessment and pupil profiling.

# DISPLAYS

Very often parents, visitors and children make their first judgements about a school through its displays. They can say a great deal about school philosophy and priorities, and the status of children's work. In addition to this, displays fulfil a number of other functions. They are an excellent medium for presenting positive images, and can raise children's sense of self-worth if their work is given status alongside other positive images. Displays convey information and can present challenging issues.

A display which one class put together while following the theme of 'Journeys' was about travellers, and showed a range of images and information about travelling people. This provoked a lot of questions and statements from parents, for example: 'I didn't know Gypsies had to have different bowls to wash clothes, food and themselves; I thought we were clean!'

Another display, during a project on 'Our Community', showed a Rastafarian. A parent, herself a Rastafarian, commented: 'It's so good to see my way of life shown in school. Many people don't take us seriously, they think we're a bit odd.'

When the school is following the same theme, displays can also be used as a resource by other children; they can go and visit displays made by other classes and use them as a learning resource. This further enhances the status of children's work.

Good displays can also interact with people; issues which the curriculum is dealing with can become common currency around the school through the use of display. Skilfully used they can help to break down stereotypical views and raise awareness.

As part of the forecasts which staff produce, we asked therefore for people to plan for displays as an integral part of their project. These would include children's work, information, positive images, home-language labels, questions about the issues in the display, and books. The common theme throughout displays creates a sense of common purpose throughout the whole school, enhancing the sense of a whole-school philosophy.

## COMMUNITY INVOLVEMENT

Project themes were chosen to be relevant to the needs of the children and the community. This automatically provided a role for parents and other members of the community, as educators with expertise within the school. Visitors to the school, and visits the children make as part of their project, add status to the community. They show that the school values the community it serves. This makes statements about the value which is placed on cultural diversity.

The themes also created a forum to celebrate cultural diversity in school: music, dance, food, traditions, customs, religion all formed an integral part of the theme and were often expressed through special events in the school. All of this is carefully planned by teachers working closely with the home–school liaison teacher and formed a natural part of the themework.

## ASSESSMENT, EVALUATION AND PROFILING

The National Curriculum and the priorities of the school both emphasized the development of a school policy and procedure for assessment and profiling. The use of whole-school projects meant that the development could take place within a context of common experiences. Ideas about moderation of children's work could be shared across the whole school as children were all working in similar areas of study. Staff plan for a schedule of assessment as part of their project planning; no one is working in isolation, all are supported by other colleagues. A major part of phase-group meetings is given over to this process. The same was also true for the development of a system of pupil profiles: teachers shared experiences and tried different models to develop the system that the school now operates.

In a wider context, each project was evaluated when completed, staff being given opportunity for formal feedback on the project. This helped to inform future planning and project development. Yearly, the process of developing a school development plan creates an opportunity for staff to reflect on the themes they had worked through. Currently a working party of teachers is engaged in reviewing the planning and delivery of the curriculum. This results in a constant 'fine tuning' of the approach to meet the changing needs of the school.

# SCHOOL ETHOS, AIMS AND POLICY

The school ethos, aims and policy put issues on the agenda in the classroom, the project themes acting as a vehicle for this to happen. There is a two-way relationship here. School ethos and policy informs the development of teaching and learning. In return the examination of issues in the classroom informs the development of school policy. For example, a class may examine gender issues in their class. They may then ask: 'What is the school policy on equality of opportunity and is it effective?'

Policy development should always be a two-way process, reflecting practice and showing where practice should be leading. Development education has informed the development of school policies, some written, some unwritten, which contribute to defining the nature of the curriculum in the school. Specifically the following have been addressed:

- gender
- anti-racism
- equality of opportunity
- issues about development
- environmental issues
- creating positive images
- combating stereotypes
- co-operative and collaborative approaches
- child-centred, active learning approaches.

The school policies have also been influenced by the requirements of the National Curriculum, local education authority policy, and the school governing body.

Importantly, school policy is not something which is abstract, removed from the school curriculum and practice in the classroom. Whole-school themes have enabled policy to be an integral part of the life of the school, development education philosophy making a direct and practical contribution.

# REFLECTIONS

The whole-school themework approach has had to respond to the changing requirements of the National Curriculum. The approach was established partly as a vehicle for this development. The history National Curriculum, however, specifies two requirements which seem to run contrary to a whole-school theme approach. At Key Stage 2 (7–11-year-olds), children are required to learn very specific historical knowledge; for example, about the Victorians, and the Tudor and Stuart period. This requires children to follow different historical themes in each class. This would seem to challenge a whole-school theme approach as it moves towards compartmentalizing the curriculum.

The history curriculum the children are required to follow is largely based on

147

British history and is, on first appearances, very Eurocentric. Initially this would seem to be at odds with the criteria the school has for the selection of themes and the nature of the curriculum in the school.

However, there seems to be quite a lot of scope within each of the history study units to build in an examination of the issues we are concerned about. The targets for knowledge and understanding of history and the interpretation of history are very much concerned with looking at bias, stereotyping, evidence, divergent views of one event, consequence of actions, power relationships and other issues which are at the heart of development education.

A schedule has been drawn up for classes to look at each of the history themes outlined by the National Curriculum within the context of the whole-school themes, and teachers are evaluating this process. We are also looking at ways of exploring the history study units in a way that reflects the needs of our school and the community it serves. Study units like Food and Farming, Exploration and Encounter, Homes and Places of Worship, Britain since 1930 have a lot of potential for examining issues and perceptions. There is further scope here for development education to make an impact on the school curriculum.

Since the development of the approach, a number of changes can be seen in the school. There is certainly a feeling of all working towards a common end, although this may be perceived in different ways. There is a sense of continuity in the school. The children are used to the approach and do seem to enjoy sharing their learning experiences, and working together. 'It was great working in a group, we had lots more ideas and could share out the jobs. It really gets you thinking, doesn't it?' commented one 7-year-old. There are a wide range of new resources being used in school, and people enjoy using them. A lot of collaborative planning and working goes on and this has resulted in more effective planning. Our colleague commented: 'It's a lot of hard work at the beginning of the term, but it is worth it. You know where you're going and what you're going to do, how you're going to do it and who is going to help you with it.'

Teachers try to include issues in their project planning and look for ways of developing these with the children. As another colleague put it during the project on 'Spaceship Earth': 'Children are concerned about these things, they are worried about the future of their planet; we can look at this through this project.'

Visitors to the school quickly pick up on the ethos of the school and the approach to the curriculum. When a theatre group, which specializes in presenting stories from other cultures with challenging messages, visited the school, its members commented: 'We could tell as soon as we walked in that the children would be receptive to our work. This school is obviously concerned with presenting positive images of other cultures.'

A group of children recently looked at a range of photographs of homes from all over the world, using the *Doorways* pack (Shelter, 1987); one observed: 'Most people seem to build their own home out of things they can find near where they live, I wish we were that clever.' Another asked, on looking at a photograph of homeless people: 'It doesn't seem to be fair – some people are so rich, while others seem to not even have a job, what can we do to change things?' It seems that children are aware of issues, are concerned about them, and want to learn more about them.

Development education raises a range of issues which are challenging for any school to address. It asks staff to examine their own views and attitudes as well as raising questions about the nature of the curriculum a school provides. It often calls for review and changes in practice. This requires a management approach which can give people the security and confidence needed to take on new ideas, and give them practical ways to apply them in the classroom. People need to be involved in the process and be given opportunities to make their own contribution. At Benson School the whole-school themework approach has proved to be an excellent context for teachers to address these issues themselves, building them into the curriculum and the children's learning experience.

# REFERENCES

Davies, M. (1989), *Get the Picture: Developing Visual Literacy in the Infant Classroom*, Birmingham: Development Education Centre.

Development Education Project (1986), *Teaching Development Issues*, 7 vols: Perceptions, Colonialism, Food, Health, Population Changes, Work, Aid and Development, Manchester: DEP.

Fisher, S. and Hicks, D. (1985), *World Studies 8–13: A Teacher's Handbook*, Edinburgh: Oliver & Boyd.

Greig, S., Pike, G. and Selby, D. (1987), *Earthrights: Education as if the Planet Really Mattered*, London: WWF/Kogan Page.

McFarlane, C. (1988), *Behind the Scenes*, Birmingham: Development Education Centre.

McFarlane, C. (1990), *Themework*, Birmingham: Development Education Centre.

McFarlane, C. and Sinclair, S. (1986), *A Sense of School*, Birmingham: Development Education Centre.

Pike, G. and Selby, D. (1989), *Global Teacher, Global Learner*, Sevenoaks: Hodder & Stoughton.

Shelter (1987), *Doorways*, International Year of Shelter for the Homeless and Save the Children, London.

# PART 3

# CASE STUDIES IN DEVELOPMENT EDUCATION

PART 3

# CASE STUDIES IN DEVELOPMENT EDUCATION

# CHAPTER 8

# Environment and Development: A Cross-curricular Project in a Swedish School

*Margaretha Thyr*

Humans are active, creative and curious, and these are important factors that must be considered in the educational situation. We learn when we are really motivated, when we think something is important, and we learn by experience and affection more easily than by reading or listening to lectures.

Ask some people if they have learned anything new in the last week or month, ask them *why* they learned this particular thing and *how* they learned it. Then compare the answers you have received and I am sure you will find some common denominators.

If you ask a child or teenager what he or she thinks is important to learn about, you can be fairly sure about the answer. What is important to young people is to learn to be prepared for the future, to survive. Another word for this could be development education.

Apart from the interest of the students, there is another, more formal reason to work with development education in Swedish schools; the principles of development education are enshrined in the principles and aims of the Swedish National Curriculum for schools.

The Swedish curriculum makes it very clear that development education is of great importance, that the school is responsible for giving the students knowledge about the global situation, about natural resources, environmental issues, developing countries, international understanding and solidarity; in particular to show local and global links and interdependence. The curriculum guidelines indicate that between solidarity and marketing, the two different aspects of international teaching, solidarity should be given priority; although both aspects demand the same knowledge and skills, the difference is more a question of attitudes and motives.

The Swedish curriculum is a positive support to teachers who want to work with development education; any obstacles are likely to come from unfamiliarity with the methodology on the part of the teacher or, in secondary school, the organization of the school day into short lessons with many different teachers making cross-curricular work harder to plan and organize.

Anyway, I felt encouraged to start my project in my class of 30 students, aged 12–13, an ordinary Swedish class in a middle school. I asked the students what issues they thought were important. I took these issues and connected them with local and global links; we searched for answers and found new questions through an interdisciplinary and investigative way of working.

# PLANNING THE PROJECT

My class of 30 students and I decided to follow our local stream from the spring to its outlet in a bigger lake in Sweden. We planned to work for a year. We felt free to use as much time as we needed, because with this way of working I knew we would cover much of the traditional content, but in another way. Looking back, I think we used approximately one day a week for the project. As I taught almost all the subjects in the class, I only had to co-ordinate our work with that of teachers for sport, handicraft and music; all were supportive of the project. The work was largely planned with people outside the school.

The idea of working on this project arose because there had recently been a terrible environmental catastrophe in the River Rhine at Basel. All life in the river north of Basel was wiped out. One of the children said: 'Imagine if this happened to our own local stream; who would care about that? We are the ones who have to care for our own environment.' I realized that I had the motivation for a big project for my class.

According to the Swedish curriculum, teachers and students are able to and should choose those areas that are engaging and of interest, and connected to the reality experienced by the students. The teacher's task is to lead his or her students from their own interests to a wider perspective by letting them ask questions, investigate, experience, read, reflect, organize, reach conclusions and use their new knowledge (see Figure 1).

The idea is not just to adjust completely to the students' wishes but to build a bridge between interest and aims (see Figure 2).

## Aims

To allow students to work from their own interests does not mean that students do whatever they want; rather that the teacher is a facilitator who must be very clear about the aims and give the students distinct frameworks, guiding them from their interests towards the aim of the work.

My aims were as follows. I wanted my students to:

- work from their own ideas and interests;
- work in an interdisciplinary way and through research;

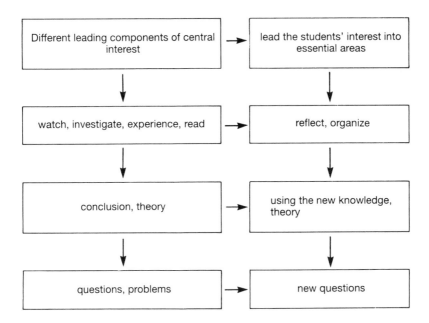

**Figure 1**

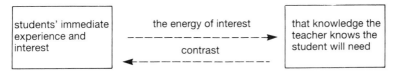

**Figure 2**

- meet the community outside the walls of the school and connect with professionals from different areas within school;
- develop an interest and knowledge about their native place and environment;
- gain self-confidence in asking their own questions;
- become conscious of the fact that they could affect the situation in their own village;
- extend their interest to the global situation through knowledge about the local situation; to see if and how our little village is dependent on the rest of the world, but also to see that our village has an impact on the world;
- take responsibility for their own work by picking out problems and solving them within given frameworks of aims, equipment, skills and time;
- follow through a project from beginning to end, giving them the joy of creativity, pride and self-esteem.

I decided on three headlines for the project:

- Cultural history that links you with your roots
- Environmental issues
- Local and global links.

We also had the idea of producing a book and putting on an exhibition to disseminate information about the results of our work.

We really felt inspired to work with our own stream. It was important. We were ready to do real research. We could find out things, and document facts that nobody had done before. What a challenge! It certainly sounded more exciting than: 'Now children, let's read page 54 and then answer the questions in your exercise book.'

## Community partners

Helmer, a grandfather of one of the students and very informed about local history, was willing to help us. He was the first 'guest worker'. As time went by, more than 20 people became involved in our stream project: people representing institutions, different professions and knowledge, retired villagers, military personnel, politicians, shop assistants, farmers and parents. They were all needed to meet the different challenges we met. A professor from Java, a specialist in the water cycle, was the partner who came from the most distant place. We could not have anticipated how many co-operating partners we would need. As the method is through research you only realize your needs as the work progresses.

## How we collected information

We used our visitors' information and we took notes or recorded:

- own research
- interviews
- excursions
- telephone calls
- correspondence with our partners
- library work.

## ORGANIZING THE WORK

To start with, we had a discussion and made a mental map of ideas before identifying headlines for our work; that gave us the 'chapters' for our book (see Figure 3). Depending on the task the pupils worked individually, in small groups or bigger groups.

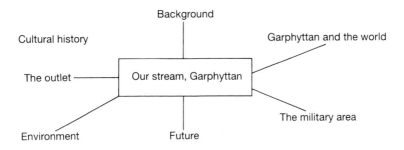

**Figure 3**

# Who?

We made a mental map of each chapter. Everybody was involved in every chapter:

- Students chose tasks in the chapter according to interest.
- Groups sometimes had to be adjusted to spread the work a bit.
- What expert help did we need?
- Who does what?

# How?

Each group chose the methods and a place for their work. Sometimes they worked in the classroom, at other times outdoors, in the library or at home.

The group chose how their work would be presented, used and documented.

# When?

The group made a schedule for their work. Time was needed: classroom time, homework, when to meet partners, etc.

# Feedback

A group representative or the whole group presented their plan to the teacher. We discussed contents, equipment, who was to do what, methods, particular skills in the group, expert help, time available, costs.

As the facilitator, I received a copy of each group's plan, and we decided on particular times for feedback and checking up.

We structured our work by mental mapping (see Figure 4).

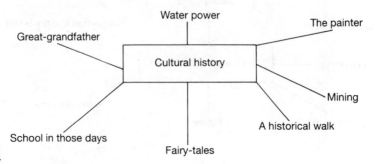

**Figure 4**

# SOME EXAMPLES

## Investigating the stream

We could find the spring in reality; we had maps and our strategy was to follow the stream back until we found the spring. One problem we had to solve was, which of the small branches was the real start of the stream? What is a water-diviner? After many discussions we chose one of the branches. The spring was in a military area, where Bofors, well known for its affairs in India, has a test area. All students made themselves acquainted with the stream on the map. Before we went out we also started our documentation by writing about the stream and its flow through the landscape.

This is what one girl wrote:

> We met at the school. Weather was just fine. We went by cars up to Krokmossen, a bog. We passed different military areas. We parked our cars, we got our maps and our fieldbooks, and then each group started their expedition following their own strategy with the aim of finding the spring.
>
> My group decided to follow the little stream back to its source. After half an hour we found what we decided was the source of the stream, wet land with a little water pool in the middle. After the rains it was very wet. We stopped there for a while, writing, taking pictures. Then we had our packed lunch and went back to the cars. It is 9.50 a.m., on 12 September 1987. We wonder if anybody before has ever done this expedition. Probably we are the first ones in the world.

I knew very little about local history, although I had lived in the area for 15 years. But Helmer knew a lot. We had nice walks with him, and he told us about his childhood in the village, how things had changed, about the mining history of the area, about the factory in the village. Helmer told us many things. We made choices about what to investigate in depth.

Another student wrote:

We took a walk through our village with Helmer. He told us about the nine dams; one is Sagardammen. There is a waterfall. We made a map of all the dams that had been in Garphyttan. Another thing Helmer told us was that 10,000 years ago, at the end of the ice age, Garphyttan was on the shores of the sea formed by the melting ice. There are some rare leftovers from that time such as Gotlandsag, a grass that grows only on Gotland now, and the hazel-mouse.

I had certain aims with my work, but I also had good spin-offs. Parents and relatives of the children became very interested in our work, and the project became a focus of discussion in the local community. Parents came with old pictures and photos and newspaper cuttings. One student had a great-grandfather: 'I would like to tell you about my great-grandfather who worked at the factory at the power-station. Nils was born in 1928. He had seven children. One of them was my grandfather Eric . . . My grandmother gave me this information.'

Some new ideas came up during the work. When we were studying a mining place we saw the foundations of a house; it had been a hunting cottage of a famous painter. That gave us a reason to visit the city museum to study his oil paintings.

As we live in a forest and mountain area there are a lot of stories about trolls and witchcraft. We delved into these things, searching in the library, asking old people and documenting the old fairytales.

## Investigating the military area

We had great trouble in entering the military area. We had to go there on a Saturday when they are usually free, because the military hold their exercises on weekdays.

We prepared our questions:

• Had it always been a shooting area?

No, it had not. There had been a big political discussion at national level more than 40 years ago and one of the politicians, now retired, came to our school and told us about how his party lost this discussion.

• What happened to the people living there?

They had to move.

• Were any of them alive today?

After many phone calls we found Aunt Fanny, born in 1899. She was happy to tell us how she had to move. One student interviewed her:

I lived up there with my husband and five children. In 1945 we had to move because they wanted to make a military area up there. We got Kr 12,000 in compensation, a rather good amount of money at that time. I was very worried, because I did not know where to move. But in the end we were offered a choice of two houses.

The stream flows through a military camp. This led our thoughts into issues such as defence, arms and peace.
We interviewed a lieutenant:

- What kind of exercises are you doing?
- What is it all about?
- What do you want to be skilled in?
- Is it hard to shoot?
- Have you had any accidents?

This made us interested in studying armaments at a global level. We found that 2 per cent of today's armaments are enough to destroy all life on earth. A new question arose: What are the other 98 per cent for?
We also considered the fact that the education of a child costs the same as 3 minutes' fire with a modern automatic rifle; a modern tank costs as much as 1,000 classrooms for 30,000 children in a developing country. Is it a good choice to invest in a tank or education?

# THE ENVIRONMENT: A PARTICULAR INTEREST

We made a mental map that consisted of different questions that we wanted to have answered (see Figure 5).
We divided the work first by interest, and then we had to adjust a little to get more even groups. We had many jobs running at the same time. Everybody was out examining small animals in the water, and we also engaged other classes in the school as we wanted to check five different lakes along the stream and water system.
One student wrote:

Now we will work in another way. We want to check the quality of the water, if it is acidified and why it is acid. We will study by looking at what species we can find, especially mayflies. It is Joackim, a specialist from the environmental department, who has taught us this method.

We went out to different places. It was rather far to walk. We found different animals. When we had worked for a while we had some refreshments. When we came back to school we checked and identified the animals.

We can't claim that this is a scientific investigation. We were out just one day and it is possible that we couldn't identify all animals correctly. And we just checked at one place in the water. We don't know if there are

160

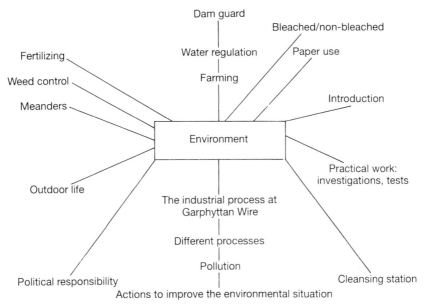

**Figure 5**

other animals in other places in the lake. But what we have done has proved to be a good method of checking the quality of the water. There are other good methods. We had a nice day and we brought refreshments to eat.

## Garphyttan Wire: the biggest workplace along the stream

Garphyttan Wire, the factory in the village, has traditions from hundreds of years back. Today its main product is valve springs for cars. Every third car in the world has a spring from Garphyttan. Many of the children's parents work there. It was very hard to us to be allowed to visit the factory. The students wanted to talk with the director. We met a kind of indifference: they didn't take the children seriously.

Our questions were:

- What are you producing?
- How is it done?
- Are there environmental problems?
- Have you taken any action to decrease pollution?
- Have you planned environmental improvements?

Martin from the County Department, who was responsible for environmental control of the factory, let us follow him in his routine check of the outlet from the factory. First he came to our classroom and explained about the processes in the factory, such as acid-bath cleaning, pulling of thread, hardening, grinding and cleansing stations. We got reports, we sent questions we could not understand and he answered. We saw how they passed out a metal-rich effluent to bury 50 metres away. We estimated that the volume of what they buried every year was the same size as our classroom. We found it strange that they buried something that they had worked so hard to get from the water. The question about this from one of the students was not answered.

We were worried and angry. Who had responsibility? What about the local politicians? We asked them if they knew that two temporary dams for effluent were there without any fence and that they were leaking. The politicians had no responsibility, they said, but next summer we noticed that there was at least a fence, so that small children could not fall into it.

One day when we came to test the water we could not reach it. The beach was muddy, because they had regulated the water. This gave us new questions:

- Why is water regulated?
- How is it done?
- How is the water used?
- Does it give much electricity?
- Why does the new owner regulate more stringently than the local one, who was responsible before?
- Does it mean anything for the animals in the lake?
- What is a power-station, a water wheel, a modern turbine?

We turned back to the local politicians and asked them more questions about their responsibilities and points of view. We also interviewed a farmer who had land along the stream. We knew that fertilizing is a big problem for the environment, but this time we were happy to find farmers who really tried to care for both animals and environment.

## The nature reserve

The river meanders to an end in a beautiful area. We decided to go there. It was a late October day, frost was almost there and the trees had dropped their leaves. Some of our working partners came along to have a nice day. We made a fire, did some cooking and we wrote poems:

Weather is beautiful
The frost has just started to come in the night time
All the trees have lost their leaves.
They lie on the ground, brown.
Just now I stand where our river meets the black river
The stream flows slowly and calm.
Here is so beautiful.

Here we conceived the idea of arranging a hike and to go canoeing, staying overnight in the springtime the following year.

## The world in Garphyttan

In our class we had thought of what Garphyttan would look like if we had no contact with the rest of the world. We had learned from Helmer that about five hundred years ago Germans came here to help us with iron mining. So without that contact the factory would not have been there, maybe.

Another thing we did was to go home and check in different rooms where the things around us had come from. We also went to small shops and looked at the shelves for things from abroad. We realized that without the rest of the world our shops would be almost empty.

In an interview we found out that Garphyttan Wire sells its products to almost all the countries in the world, but mostly to Germany, England, France and the USA. Its main product is valve springs for cars. The raw material comes mainly from France and Japan.

That Garphyttan Wire is selling to India is extra-interesting to us, as our class is sponsoring a child in India. To this could be added that people in our rural district are supporting a day care centre in Jamshedpur, Bihar, a city with the biggest steel plants in India.

Every year 800–900 foreign trailers come to our village to load. These trailers go to Gothenburg from where the load is shipped further to France, Romania and Belgium, for example.

The person responsible for the loading does not know what the drivers do when they are waiting for their time to load. Those from East Europe do their cooking in the truck. We had the idea of interviewing some truck drivers, but we became short of time and we had no interpreters to help us.

Some other questions that arose were:

- Who owns the company?
- What is a subsidiary company?
- What is a multinational company?

## THE FUTURE

We discussed what life might be like in Garphyttan in 50 years when we are retired. We acted out a little play about the future and different ways of reaching the future, the consuming and lazy way or the more thrifty way, in which solidarity is also an important part. What will happen in the future if the rest of the world had the idea of consuming as much as we do? Is it right to live like we do?

We asked all the people who helped us the following questions concerning the future:

- What is important for yourself?
- What is important for your local area?
- What is important for the world?

Helmer could exemplify the answers we got:

I want to be healthy and spend much of my time together with my family and grandchildren. Garphyttan must be kept as the beautiful place it is. We must be rescued from war and catastrophes and we must help the poor people in the world.

# DOCUMENTATION

We always started up with mental mapping; that is, focusing; organizing; associating. In the following, s = students, t = teacher, p = partner, of = office.

| | |
|---|---|
| s | writing in the fieldbook or recording |
| s | write out, comparing with co-worker |
| t | read through the rough draft, asking questions, giving comments about content, additions, cancellations, language, spelling |
| s | further research, by telephone, books, letters, our partners, often to clear up details |
| s | tidying up the work |
| t | feedback. Note that the students themselves are always responsible for the text. |
| of | putting the text on a computer |
| s | making drawings and sketches |
| s1, s2, s3 | correction reading: checking spelling, sentences, layout, headlines, pictures |
| p | reading the text to check that facts are correct and that they are correctly quoted |
| of | final draft of the text |
| all | calculating costs for printing, number of pages, drawings, size of edition, choice of paper. |

The book was printed.

As it was written on non-bleached paper we checked how many people really are using non-bleached paper. We asked in the shops about their selling statistics, we read books and we interviewed 50 people doing their shopping.

Every Swedish person uses 222 kg of paper per year. That is the same as three trees per person per year, so our class is using 90 trees per year. Sweden is one of the countries in the world that consumes most paper. And that is not all. Of the 222 kg, 130 kg is thrown in the waste bin. That means 14 million trees for Sweden as a whole. Maybe we could save some.

We also put on a big exhibition where every student made a screen, pictures, drawings, texts, layout. The students also translated the exhibits into English to make it understandable to the Javanese professor who visited us a couple of times. The exhibition was shown in our school, in the local museum and in the district library.

We wanted to sell the book to spread information about our work. We also needed to earn some money for an excursion, so we decided to get some income from the selling of the book. Half the income was for the class and the other half for the saving of the rain forest in Costa Rica.

## CONCLUSION

We had an interesting year working with this project. We had time for all the other necessary courses in the curriculum. In fact, in this work we covered many traditional 'subjects'.

The stream is still flowing slowly through our little village of 500 households. Recently the newspapers wrote about the waste from the factory. A group connected with the old homestead museum have made a trail through the cultural relics in the village.

I would not hesitate to start a new project with another class. And I would not call it a project, because this is what ought to be the normal way of teaching. If I were advising colleagues, I would encourage them to go ahead and see. If you follow the students' interest and questions, they are carrying you in the work. If you are following your own questions, and do not listen to the students, you have to carry them.

> Each person is active, creative, able to and eager to take responsibility and to search for knowledge, and, in co-operation with others, understand and improve their own and fellow-beings' conditions for life.

> The content and way of working in school must be shaped in such a way that it promotes this view of society and of human beings. School has the duty to give the students increasing responsibility with growing age and maturity.

These are the introductory words of the Swedish National Curriculum and a good support for the teacher who wants to work with and out from development education.

There may be objections from parents and colleagues, but these should be seen as a challenge you have to take, being sure of your goals and the aim of teaching – to prepare for the future, a better future.

# CHAPTER 9

# Development Education in a UK Secondary School: A Cross-Curricular Approach

*Ingrid Abrahams-Lyncook*

This chapter illustrates, through a case study, how a development education approach was introduced within a large secondary school and incorporated into a number of curriculum areas. It examines the relationship between these areas and development education.

With the recent introduction of the National Curriculum many schools are finding it increasingly difficult to find timetable space to teach the core and foundation subjects and to incorporate the equally important cross-curricular themes. Moreover, since the National Curriculum was developed as a set of separate subject areas, it is often difficult to find ways of making links between them.

The challenge was to design a cross-curricular project which would increase pupils' awareness of global issues and draw on their interests, while at the same time meeting the demands of the National Curriculum. The project co-ordinators wanted to develop a project which would not only cut across traditional subject areas but also develop the affective side of learning.

This chapter outlines the aims of the project and explores how it was introduced, highlighting some initial barriers to success. It explores how some were overcome and how the project was adapted or reshaped to cope with others. It seeks to demonstrate how development education can be introduced through a flexible structure to meet the particular needs of a school.

The project was evaluated by pupils, staff and project co-ordinators. Their various perspectives are considered and some recommendations made for future curriculum initiatives.

## THE SCHOOL CONTEXT

Greendale is a mixed 11–18 comprehensive school with over 2,000 pupils on roll, of whom 170 are in the sixth form, and over 100 teaching staff. The school serves a suburban residential area; it is oversubscribed and has good support from both governing body and parents. In the curriculum, particular emphasis is placed on good examination results, traditional subject teaching and setting in a number of subject areas.

The school regularly takes students for teaching practice from the education departments of local universities. The local authority advisers served the school fairly well until the school left local education authority control but there has been little joint curriculum development with other authority schools. Consequently, curriculum innovation and development have been almost entirely dependent on the expertise of the teaching staff, earlier projects being co-ordinated on an *ad hoc* basis by a small nucleus of teaching staff.

Four members of staff from Greendale Compehensive School in Birmingham planned a cross-curricular project on development issues and images in Britain and Ireland as a result of involvement with a Birmingham Development Education Centre (DEC) humanities initiative, linking local teachers and teachers from Dublin and Belfast.

The DEC initiative highlighted the benefits of teachers working creatively together, confirmed the potential of work carried out thematically and acted as a catalyst for the school-based project. Contacts made with teachers in Irish schools were particularly beneficial. Staff from Greendale were asked to examine the constraints and possible effectiveness of introducing development education within the school context. It was therefore intended that the project would illuminate key areas of concern for development education.

# PROJECT AIMS

1  The first, and perhaps most important, aim was to increase awareness about global and development issues for the pupils at Greendale Comprehensive, focusing initially on issues in Birmingham and Dublin.

It was intended that the project would incorporate issues in a local, national and international context. It was hoped that the pupils would be able to recognize that issues concerning land development, injustice and minority group treatment are found at the local as well as at the international level, and that the project would instil a sense of personal and individual commitment and responsibility towards these issues and so engender a respect for others.

2  A second aim was to unite a number of subjects for a more experiential approach to the learning process within a recently devised curriculum structure.

Five faculty groupings had been established eighteen months previously as a more effective means of delivering and communicating National Curriculum requirements. The five curriculum co-ordinators have responsibility for curriculum management and implementation according to targets agreed with the deputy headteacher responsible for curriculum.

It was envisaged that the five curriculum co-ordinators would assist in the planning and teaching of the project, but in the event the project leaders had to rely on the goodwill of staff, volunteering their time to implement this curriculum initiative.

The framework of the project was intended as a means through which teachers with shared interests could work together at curriculum design. Teachers were therefore given considerable flexibility as regards their topic and approach, and did not necessarily work within their own subject specialism.

3 Thirdly, the project sought to transmit cross-curricular issues in response to National Curriculum guidelines.

In July 1989, the National Curriculum Council (NCC) announced its intention to provide non-statutory guidance for the teaching of cross-curricular issues and in Circular 6 (October 1989) expanded the concept of cross-curricular provision by identifying three categories: 'dimensions', 'skills' and 'themes'. Project planners felt that precise statements defining each element were necessary, in order to clarify terms when the project information was disseminated.

The cross-curricular *dimensions* are concerned with the promotion of social and personal development. The project used equalizing opportunities and education for life in a multi-cultural society as media through which to promote development.

Cross-curricular *skills* were seen as transferable skills which could be developed through all subjects dependent on content. Here oracy, literacy, numeracy, graphicacy, problem solving and personal skills were highlighted.

Cross-curricular *themes* were accepted as the elements which enriched the experience of the pupils. The project focused on three of these: citizenship, (individual, family, community, national), careers education and environmental education.

It was felt that the broad cross-curricular scope of the work would have a number of positive benefits, for example, many of the Technical and Vocational Education (TVE) entitlements would be addressed including equal opportunities issues and pupil-centred learning.

## PROJECT CO-ORDINATION AND PLANNING

The project was the first of its kind in the school to involve all pupils within a year group and was also innovative in the way it enabled staff and pupils to work together.

The project was initiated and co-ordinated by three English teachers and the head of religious education. All four members of the co-ordinating team are actively involved in development education, which they see as essentially about identifying, debating/discussion and analysing political perspectives and choices in relation to world development . . . ultimately, development education is about good education in a global framework.

(Regan and Sinclair, 1986: 5)

As the project was to be targeted at year 10 pupils (14–15-year-olds), it was decided that a degree of management support would be necessary to deal with such issues as timetable changes, resources, funding and curriculum overview. A member of the senior management team therefore acted as liaison person and linked with the co-ordinators. The headteacher was kept fully informed throughout; his enthusiasm for the project led to a number of guests being invited to view pupils' work.

## Cross-curricular planning issues

By their very nature the cross-curricular elements do not belong to any one subject or area of experience. Some commentators (for example Chitty, 1987, 1989) have noted that HMIs' eight areas of experience, outlined in Red Book 1, could be used as an alternative basis for curriculum construction and translated into a worthwhile timetable for pupils of all ages.

The cross-curricular skills, themes and dimensions expand the notion of a narrow subject-dominated curriculum. The National Curriculum places equality of opportunities on the agenda of change as an entitlement for all pupils across all subjects. This should ensure curriculum review in all establishments and also encourage staff to review their own practice. As Duffy (1990: 89) points out:

this impetus to cross-curricularity lies in the not unexpected discovery of the subject working parties that 'subjects' are not the most appropriate descriptors of the learning process.

However, although it is clear that a single-subject curriculum approach does not provide an effective medium for the teaching of cross-curricular themes, at the same time content overload in these same subjects threatents to marginalize them; in many secondary schools organization for pupils at Key Stage 4 (age 14–16) was proving problematic.

The project addressed these issues by making the cross-curricular elements the main focus as separately timetabled themes over a period of seven weeks, rather than teaching through subject areas. This followed the model timetabling arrangement 'C' suggested in *The Whole Curriculum* (NCC, 1990: 14f). During the early stages of planning no one cross-curricular element predominated but the place of each became more evident as the project progressed.

A curriculum audit was carried out to ascertain which cross-curricular elements were already being taught in each subject area, when and to which year groups. It emerged that at Greendale, although some aspects of the themes were already being taught through the core and foundation subjects, many teachers felt that there was a lack of central focus for each issue. In many subject areas, teaching the cross-curricular elements was regarded as a peripheral activity, with Personal and Social Education (PSE) being the most natural focus.

The problem of finding space for cross-curricular work in an already crowded timetable was another area of concern. Anxieties were further increased by the option system for year 10 pupils, who also had to adhere to rather rigid GCSE syllabuses. The perceived overcrowding for year 10 pupils was overcome in the planning stages of the project by matching the proposed work schemes to National Curriculum attainment targets in certain subject areas and by identifying suitable GCSE criteria for assessment purposes.

## PROJECT STRUCTURE AND CONTENT: ISSUES AND IMAGES IN IRELAND AND GREAT BRITAIN

After brainstorming possible issues for the project, five themes were chosen as dynamic teaching structures around which to build subject matter and therefore content. Each theme was relevant in the local, national and international context, and material was gathered and collated from Birmingham, Dublin and international aid agencies such as Oxfam and Christian Aid.

In many respects the project co-ordinators felt that they were breaking new ground with this project structure. This project had set out to develop a global approach and integrate subject disciplines. The development process was as follows:

1 The four co-ordinators devised a structure around which to deliver the project. This consisted of two main presentations. The first, at the beginning of the project, centred around the idea of stereotyping and featured a role-play set in a community where a decision to locate a Travellers' site has been made. It proved to be thought-provoking and contentious (see Figure 1). The second, scheduled for the end of the project, concentrated on the theme of 'Land in Conflict' and pupils presented creative writing on the theme of human rights and justice developed out of their work on the Charter of Travellers' Rights.

On both occasions year 10 pupils were timetabled for a whole morning session in one of the main halls. Disruption to the timetable was to be kept to a minimum by incorporating the year 10 social studies lesson into this timeslot. Outside speakers were invited to speak to the pupils and a high degree of staff and pupil participation and involvement in both presentations was apparent.

2 Next a strategy was devised to assist teaching the central theme of the project across specific subject areas; the main theme was divided into five broad

# The Travellers' Committee

You are living in two extended family groups in caravans on an illegal site on waste ground at the edge of town. You are without toilets, water supply, rubbish collection and electricity. The site is a sea of mud in wet weather and is infested with mice and rats and consequently you are concerned for the health of your children. Your children are attending the local primary school but overall they have little contact with the settled community who regard you with mistrust and outright hostility at times.

You make a little money from dealing in scrap and from some seasonal labour but the majority of you rely on social welfare.

You have already been moved forcefully from a previous site and you are now demanding a permanent serviced site with regular rubbish collection and a storage area for scrap. You do not want conflict with the local community but you are determined to resist being forcibly moved on again and you want the site developed in the chosen area.

# Observer Group

Your job is to hear and evaluate the evidence made by the five other groups. You should record the arguments in favour of the site chosen and those against it or other proposals presented. You should discuss the arguments amongst yourselves and make a recommendation to the entire group. You should explain the reasons for your decision.

# Social Workers

You are employed by the local Council. Your job is to liaise between the Council and the Travellers; to help decide what their needs are; to provide information and statistics to relevant bodies and to ensure the full involvement of the Travellers in decision making affecting the site.

You are concerned to minimise conflict with the settled community whose goodwill is crucial. Yet you are determined that the Travellers' rights will be observed. You believe that much of the opposition to the Travellers is based on hearsay and myth and that a proper debate and discussion will resolve the issue.

**Figure 1**

*Source:* McDonagh, M. et al. (1988), *Pride and Prejudice: The Case of the Travellers*, Paper No. 131, Economic and Social Research Institute, pp. 32–3.
The second presentation is overleaf.

## The Local Residents' Association

You have been elected to represent local residents living in either council or private houses. You are concerned that the development of a serviced Travellers' site in proximity to your homes would lower property values; present a permanent health hazard and generally affect the local environment. You have heard that in other areas where sites have been developed petty crime and vandalism have increased. You are also concerned that a serviced site will attract larger numbers of Travellers' families into the area. You are annoyed because other areas do not appear to be taking their fair share of Travellers.

You regard the present site as both an eye sore and a health hazard and you have petitioned the local council to do something about it.

You do not feel Travellers should be victimised but you are determined to resist the development of the proposed site.

## Local Councillors

You are caught in the middle. Your parties have agreed that sites for Travellers should be provided but you have to decide where they should be located. You are worried that if you support a site in one location you will lose the votes of settled people there. You have, therefore, come up with a plan to locate the site away from a settled neighbourhood in a nearby industrial estate. You realise that the Travellers do not favour this site but you feel this is the only realistic possibility.

## County Manager's Office

You have responsibility for supervising the planning and construction of the proposed site. You are determined that the county should provide a proper site but you cannot afford to lose the support of the settled community or of the local councillors because of its implications for other areas of your work. You believe that the site chosen is the best one given the circumstances and the opposition and power of wealthier neighbourhoods. You are determined that the site should be provided.

cross-curricular themes, outlined below. In order to explore these themes in greater depth, much work was undertaken by the co-ordinators to provide interested staff with stimulus material, factual information and resources.

## (A) Images

- Cartoons and written evidence
- Pupil work on stereotyping
- Pupils' written perceptions of each other – correspondence

- Images of early-nineteenth-century Ireland
- Pupil exchange – first generation immigrant experience (Black/Irish)
- A sharing of cultural and religious viewpoints – discussion
- Exploration of music and dance in Ireland and Britain (traditional to contemporary)

## (B) Developing cities

- Heartland – an inner-city area of Birmingham (glossy brochure)
- Docklands – a development project in Dublin (glossy brochures)
- Urban renewal – the planning and siting of housing estates
- Model design and/or project writing
- Ordnance survey maps – Birmingham and Dublin

## (C) Land

- Time-line – considering the partition of Ireland
- Colonization – historical issues of movement from town to country, controversial issues of boundaries/ghettos/physical barriers
- Formation of 'ghettos' – 'Liberties' in Dublin, cluster groupings of minority sections
- Political theories on distribution of land: poll tax, rating systems, management of councils

## (D) Justice

- UN Declaration of Human Rights – discussion of issues and aims of the Declaration
- An examination of various charters – Travellers' Charter (see Figure 2), Children's Charter, Greendale Pupils' Charter
- Biblical texts relating to justice/injustice
- An examination of literature concerned with the theme of justice – fables
- Exploration of the origins of the welfare state and the philosophy behind it
- Role-plays
- Speakers from various organizations – the penal system, Amnesty International

## (E) Minority groups

- Speakers representing various minority groups – the Travellers
- Role-play – a case for the Travellers

# Charter of Travellers' Rights

This charter was prepared by the Irish Centre for the Study of Human Rights in University College, Galway and was adopted by the National Council for Travelling People in 1984. The charter sets out the rights Travellers share with all others – rights which are, the charter claims, 'largely denied to Travellers mainly because of the failure to recognise the central right of Travellers, the right to be themselves . . .". The charter is intended to constitute a set of principles for policy and for action.

## Article 1: Travellers as a minority

Travellers, as individuals and as a group, have a right to

- the realisation of their own identity and to follow their traditional way of life.
- their separate identity and to the protection of the state.
- be consulted on and involved in decisions affecting themselves.

## Article 2: The right to move and the right to stop

Travellers have the right to

- free movement and the state is obliged to act against threats to their health, their dignity, etc.
- until proper sites are provided, local authorities or others shall not dump materials or erect barriers on sites currently used.

## Article 3: Accommodation

- Travellers have the right to decide whether or not they wish to continue their nomadic way of life.
- The state has the ultimate responsibility to provide accommodation for Travellers whether travelling or settled.
- Travellers who should not be forced to accept sub-standard or inappropriate accommodation.
- Sites for Travellers should not present risks or hazards and should take into account family groupings, trades and occupations.
- For Travellers wishing to continue travelling serviced sites should be provided close to all facilities.

- The state should protect customary sites from interference and compensation should be paid for past interference.

## Article 4: Economic needs

Travellers have the right to

- a standard of living adequate for health and wellbeing (food, clothing, accommodation, medical care, etc.).
- work and to fair conditions.
- protection against discrimination in work.
- support to pursue traditional ways of life.
- social security services and entitlements.

## Article 5: Health

Travellers have a right to

- life.
- physical, social and environmental conditions which support improvement in the quality of their lives.
- action by the state to remove causes of ill health.
- water supplies, sanitation, refuse collection.
- medical and hospital services.
- advisory and educational facilities for the promotion of health.

## Article 6: The family

The Traveller's family has the right to

- appropriate social, legal and economic protection.
- protection against discrimination.
- legal protection against measures which force them to move on.
- social protection for mothers, especially during pregnancy.
- special treatment for handicapped members.
- opportunities for the physical, mental, moral, spiritual and social development, especially of children.

## Article 7: Education

Travellers have a right to

- equality of education at all levels which recognises their history, culture and identity. All education should challenge prejudice and discrimination against Travellers.

**Article 8: The law**
- Travellers have the right to equal protection before the law.

**Article 9: Political rights**
Travellers have the right and the opportunity to
- participate in public life.
- have access to the public service.
- special provision for the exercise of these rights necessitated by mobility or illiteracy.

**Article 10: Free expression**
Travellers shall have, with others, the right to
- freedom of opinion and expression.
- legal protection from attacks upon their honour, reputation and private and family life.

- reply in equal measure to inaccurate or offensive statements made about them.
- action by the state against those who incite hatred or discrimination.

**Article 11: Privacy**
Travellers, in common with all others, have the right to
- respect for their person.
- legal protection against interference with their private or family life.
- respect for their property.

**Article 12: Discrimination**
Travellers are entitled to the full exercise of
- their rights and should not suffer any distinction, exclusion or restriction based on the fact that they are Travellers.

---

**Figure 2**

*Source:* McDonagh, M. et al. (1988), *Pride and Prejudice: The Case of the Travellers*, Paper No. 131, Economic and Social Research Institute, p. 7.

- An examination of the role of women world-wide – literature search
- Women and religion; Catholic, Muslim, Sikh, Jewish

Interested staff, after hearing about the project, met with the co-ordinators mainly to decide their preferred area of the project. Specific staff were then approached for their subject specialism or individual expertise. Through staff and departmental meetings, colleagues were kept well informed and teaching took place in subject areas. A range of teaching methods were used and these included team-teaching, collaborative teaching and pupil-centred activities.

A number of departments were represented (English, religious education, history, geography, art/craft, design, drama, home economics, music and mathematics. Information technology was seen as important in supporting the teaching of many topics. Display work was produced in individual subject areas and also by the art department. The project itself lasted seven weeks, fitting adequately into half a term, but the planning and preparation period began a whole term in advance.

## REFLECTIONS ON THE CURRICULUM THEMES

1 'Images' brought in the fun element, where pupils were encouraged to use humour as a weapon to combat isolation and prejudice. This is an important aspect of schooling, and, according to Davies (1990: 174), one that is often overlooked in educational theory and management.

Pupils also become aware of how humour can be used make serious points when in one class an English teacher asked pupils to explore, discuss and summarize powerful political cartoons from *Thin Black Lines* (Regan et al., 1988). The pupils saw how stereotypical roles were often reinforced by the use of cartoons. Such material needs to be handled with great sensitivity and chosen with great care, for:

> The problem is deciding what can be dealt with lightly and what requires heavy treatment, which can be joked about and what offends. Sexist and racist jokes are offensive to someone.

(Davies, 1990: 175)

These points were reinforced when a local headteacher was invited to speak to the pupils; he spoke at length about the inequalities experienced by a foreigner living in Great Britain. The pupils were visibly shocked when they were informed that the foreigner was his own father, who left Ireland in the 1940s.

2 The 'Developing Cities' theme was approached through team-teaching. Staff who had visited Dublin presented an Irish urban renewal project, while some members of the geography department looked at local equivalents. Pupils were given the opportunity to visit development sites and interview local residents. Glossy brochures sent out by city developers were scrutinized and there were also instances of project writing and model designing.

3 The Human, Social and Spiritual (HSS) curriculum area expanded the theme of 'Land' by considering the issues involved in colonization and in migration from country to town. As the community charge for the Birmingham area had just been agreed, pupils were able to investigate political theories on the rating systems. The local Member of Parliament for Perry Barr was also invited to speak to pupils in the style of a debate on the BBC's 'Question Time' programme.

4 The theme of 'justice' brought in a number of outside speakers, from the school chaplain to members of Birmingham City Mission and Amnesty International. Audio-visual aids were obtained from the Central Library, the Development Education Centre and the regional Religious Education Centre at Westhill College. The pupils who were taught this theme were happy to draw up their own Greendale Pupils' Charter after reading the United Nations Convention on the Rights of the Child.

5 Finally, work on 'Minority groups' proved to be the most personal and the most sensitive area included. A series of lessons was planned on the Travellers, an Irish minority group. Their plight, and the sensitivity of the issues, were further highlighted when pupils in an imaginary scene were told that they were going to have five families of Travellers living on a site

opposite Greendale School! Both Osler (1989) in her book *Speaking Out* and Mac an Ghaill (1988) in his book *Young, Gifted and Black* illustrate clearly how second-generation pupils from ethnic backgrounds feel about the British education system and the inequalities which they have experienced. The pupils participating in the project were moved to write their own accounts of the positive and negative treatment they had endured.

In many schools, including Greendale, there is a piecemeal approach to the teaching of such studies. The difference here was that it was taken up as a topic for further development, and the project leaders all saw the distinctive value of development education and realized just how marginalized it had become in the mainstream curriculum owing to conflicting national and local priorities.

## Perspectives on curriculum change

The project planners were reluctant to take a whole-school approach as the school did not have experience of other projects of this nature. There was, however, the feeling that the project should be introduced to as many staff as possible. This was one of the tensions felt at the planning stage. At the outset, the group had held differing views about the methodologies which they wished to include but no discussion was held on the theoretical basis of the planned project. However, the group had almost certainly adopted a theoretical perspective and had firm ideas about the processes that would bring about the desired results; as Sutherland (1988: 4) suggests:

> a theory of education is a statement of what should happen and which actions are most likely to bring about this effect (actions being modified when they demonstrably do not bring about the intended effect) . . .

> teachers should clearly know what they are trying to achieve, why they teach certain things to pupils and use certain methods of teaching

It was generally agreed that an improvement of the quality of teaching was at the heart of the planning but the term 'quality' has proved difficult to define. It might imply a searching for elements of 'goodness' to exploit for greater success. The project team shared a commitment to student-centred learning, which is an important aspect of development education, involving methods such as learning through experience and by discovery. We had designed a project where this teaching methodology could be developed.

> Successful student-centred learning usually involves a structure and framework within which the learning takes place. It is the teacher's responsibility, preferably through negotiation and dialogue with the students, to facilitate the planning and development of a framework for learning and to manage the learning process within that framework.
> (Munby, 1989)

177

The framework required the establishment of an arena in which teachers and students could together highlight the curriculum issues which they identified. For example, in a lesson about the treatment of minority groups, a pupil disclosed how her Irish parents were verbally abused after the Birmingham pub bombings. This opened up the whole issue of prejudice and stereotyping, especially towards individuals who are themselves white. It was evident that the curriculum up until then had not encouraged individual pupils to disclose personal details about themselves and their family in a way that might be regarded sympathetically by others.

## Evaluation: management issues involved in the project

### Management of cross-curricular themes

A small-scale investigation was undertaken to ascertain how other schools within the local TVE Partnership were meeting the requirements of the National Curriculum and the delivery of cross-curricular elements. Preliminary enquiries indicated that, lacking official guidance, schools in the area were developing trial-and-error strategies. Through a number of informal interviews it was possible to gain a general impression of a school's perception of cross-curricular themes. Two main questions were asked:

(a) Who managed the cross-curricular themes?

(b) How were the themes managed?

In most cases there was a named individual with responsibility for the management of the themes but with a variety of management structures:

1 Single-leader model, usually TVE co-ordinator, who acted as a promotional agent, often introducing one theme at a time.

2 Single-leader model, usually a deputy head, where a host of themes are timetabled at the beginning of the year and are then promoted, developed and evaluated by the deputy.

3 Named co-ordinators who take responsibility for a particular theme based on teacher specialism.

4 Working parties set up for each theme by individuals who state a particular interest in that particular theme.

It was felt that the first model meant that a school could cover few or as many as four themes in a given year. The last model might de-contextualize the themes by removing them from the subjects and making them cross-curricular. Greendale operates the third model but this method alone did not seem sufficient for such a large school with over 2,000 pupils.

One important difference, however, was that the project leaders were simply staff who held a common interest in development education and cross-curricular issues; they had no whole-school brief or post of responsibility in this respect.

# EVALUATION

In both presentations and taught lessons, a high degree of pupil participation and enthusiasm was evident in the whole year group, some 360 pupils.

To give the task of pupil evaluation a structure, two pupils were chosen at random from each class. In a large forum pupils and two project co-ordinators discussed the strengths and weaknesses of the project. The following questions were posed and pupil comments were then taped:

- Which part of the project did you most enjoy?
- Which part of the project did you least enjoy?
- Did you feel that you were allowed to participate fully in the project?
- What were the strengths of the project?
- What were the weaknesses of the project?

There was unanimous agreement that the presentations provided the greatest source of enjoyment, entertainment and knowledge:

> The Travellers role-play really made you think about the different viewpoints and how [the viewpoints] can all seem to be right.

> I don't think I'll be telling Irish jokes again . . . they really do lead to stereotyping.

> I liked to see the teachers acting things out, it makes you see another side to them.

It was also apparent that the pupils least enjoyed the presentation on human rights, when the pupils who presented the various charters were inaudible in the large hall. This was purely a mechanical problem but one which was nevertheless picked up by the pupils.

One main area of concern for students was the fact that while certain pupils had been taught approximately 80 per cent of the project content in a number of different subject areas, there were some pupils who had only seen the presentations and had no formal input in subject areas. This was largely due to the fact that staff who had volunteered their time and specialism also had freedom of choice concerning the format and methodology of their sessions. Some of the pupils present were quite vociferous in their condemnation of the way the project gave certain classes special attention.

One year 10 pupil pointed out a possible advantage to the variety in organization and content between classes:

> at least we talked about our lessons at breaktime and were then able to find out what other groups had done. That's it, the project got us talking about school work . . . when was the last time we talked about what we did in a geography lesson?

A brainstorm of ideas from pupils concerning the strengths and weaknesses of the project was written out on a flipchart.

## Strengths

1 The pupils enjoyed seeing staff engaged in drama with their peers.

2 The opportunity to look at local, regional issues as opposed to case-studies in far-off locations was commended.

3 Through the study of themes, some pupils were able to recognize/identify links between subject areas.

## Weaknesses

1 Unequal coverage of the project themes across year 10 forms.

2 Some pupils commented that they had not had enough time to complete their work on the themes while other pupils thought that seven weeks was far too long!

## Staff evaluation

At the end of the project, staff who had involved themselves in the proceedings were asked to complete a questionnaire (see Figure 3). It was intended that this form of evaluation might be more suitable for staff as they had already attended numerous meetings concerning subject content. The comments were generally fairly positive and it was anticipated that the statements would provide a starting point for future projects of this kind.

## Project co-ordinators

The project was seen as very successful by the senior management team and many staff, but self-criticism by the project leaders was much more severe. Before the staff evaluation returns were analysed the four project co-ordinators began their own personal assessment, in terms of strengths and weaknesses of the project:

## Strengths

1 The resource banks were quite adequate and provided staff with alternative ideas.

2 The project content allowed staff flexibility in choosing areas of specialism.

## MEMO

TO: All Staff involved in anyway with the 4th Year work on Images and Issues in Britain and Ireland.

FROM: Project leaders

We would be grateful if you could complete the evaluation sheet below to give us feedback on this project. We would also like to conduct a pupil evaluation, so we also include a few sheets for any classes you may have taught.

1. Roughly, how many children were you able to target with this work?

2. Would you describe the coverage you were able to give it as comprehensive, limited or slight?

3. What do you estimate to be the main benefits to the pupils?

4. Were there any major limitations in the programme?

5. Were there any main school systems or structures that were not utilised?

6. Were you able to use any of the work in formal assessments? If so, in what ways?

7. Do you consider that the formal presentations were a useful introduction/conclusion to the work?

8. What were the best features of the presentation?

9. How could they be improved?

10. Do you consider this work was conducted with the most appropriate year group?

11. Do you see a natural progression forward from what has been achieved?

12. Is there a source of finance you can think of for generating some funds to present curriculum initiatives of quality?

13. Any other points?

**Figure 3**

3  Assessment objectives were met by the use of specified content.

4  References to the project were incorporated into Record of Achievement (ROA) work.

**Weaknesses**

1  It was felt that had the curriculum co-ordinators played a more active role, the project would have been more far-reaching.

2  Owing to organizational difficulties involved with the timetable, there were limited opportunities to combine classes for greater pupil participation.

3  A tremendous amount of laborious extra-curricular planning time had been used at the outset.

# REFERENCES

Chitty, C. (ed.) (1987), *Defining the Comprehensive Experience*, London: University of London.

Chitty, C. (1989), *Towards a New Education System: The Victory of the New Right?*, Lewes: Falmer.

Davies, L. (1990), *Equity and Efficiency? School Management in an International Context*, Lewes: Falmer.

Duffy, M. (1990), 'A view from a secondary school', in Brighouse, T. and Moon, B. (eds), *Managing the National Curriculum: Some Critical Perspectives*, Harlow: Longman.

Mac an Ghaill, M. (1988), *Young, Gifted and Black*, Milton Keynes: Open University Press.

Munby, S. (1989), *Assessing and Recording Achievement*, Oxford: Blackwell.

National Curriculum Council (1990), *The Whole Curriculum*, York: NCC.

Osler, A. (1989), *Speaking Out: Black Girls in Britain*, London: Virago.

Regan, C. and Sinclair, S. (1986), *Half the Lies Are True*, Dublin and Birmingham: Trocaire and Development Education Centre.

Regan, C., Sinclair, S. and Turner, M. (1988), *Thin Black Lines*, Birmingham: Development Education Centre.

Sutherland, M. (1988), *Theory of Education*, Harlow: Longman.

CHAPTER 10

# Peace Education in the Danish Gymnasium-School

*Anne Helms*

I finished my university education in 1980. Since then I have been employed in a Danish gymnasium-school, where I teach English and religion.

To be an English teacher in Denmark at gymnasium level means that you are a language teacher and have to train the students in knowing, understanding, and using the language as freely and correctly as possible. When I get them, they have already had five or six years of English and have mastered the language pretty well. Furthermore, according to the curriculum regulations issued by the Ministry of Education, they have to become acquainted with the general cultural (economical, political, literary, social, technological) conditions of a number of English-speaking countries by reading approximately 600 pages of different literacy genres.

As a teacher of religion I have to give the students knowledge and understanding of Christianity and a number of non-Christian religions, religious phenomena and their ethnographical characteristics, ethical problems, and psychological, ideological and philosophical ideas. It is a deep-rooted principle in the gymnasium that it is left to my own judgement what means and methods I employ to pass this knowledge on to the students. I can use any book, magazine, newspaper, tape or video that I want to – the budget being my only limitation. Obviously, I was able to draw on my experience in both subjects when I became interested in peace education.

## THE STUDENTS

The Danish gymnasium is a three-year school. It gives an education which is a qualification in itself, as well as a preparation for higher education. Students who have completed the ninth or tenth form of the *folkeskole* (primary and lower secondary school) can be admitted to the gymnasium if their earlier schools find them qualified. After three years of study they graduate with a *studentereksamen*, if they pass their final examinations; the *studentereksamen* gives access to universities and other forms of higher education.

The gymnasium is divided into two streams, the languages stream and the mathematics stream. In both, most subjects (14) are obligatory, which means that throughout the three years the student spends most of the time with the same group of other students. All in all they have 33 lessons a week. Each student can study three subjects of his or her own choice, either one of the obligatory subjects to a higher level or a non-obligatory subject, for example film. The obligatory subjects cover a wide spectrum: languages, Danish, history, biology, geography, mathematics, social science, natural science, religion, computer technology and physical education.

When the students start in the gymnasium, they are 15–16 years old: an age at which most of them only recently have become actively engaged in the world around them. They are usually very open and ready to experiment with new ideas. They may have a number of fundamental principles, which have sometimes been adopted from their parents without ever having been questioned or reflected upon. I see them as persons who are easily manipulated – by, for example, the media, parents, friends – and teachers, although I am aware that their manipulability varies with their gender and social background. I consider it a major responsibility to give them the tools to form personal attitudes and make personal decisions. I try to do this by training them in systematic thinking, provoking them to discussions, helping them to see the complexity of most issues, questioning 'accepted truths', and, most of all, by feeding them information about the world in which they live.

## SOME BARRIERS TO PEACE EDUCATION

When I wanted to introduce peace education in both my subjects, I had to face three categories of problems:

1   The students were not interested. They found it either old-fashioned (having heard about the nuclear marches in the 1960s) or connected it with 'hysterical women' at Greenham Common. This was not particularly discouraging, since it only confirmed what I already knew – that the interest in the subject of peace rises and falls with the intensity of world crises, but it left me with the problem of motivating the students. At the beginning of each semester students and teachers decide together what themes are to be studied in each subject, so I had to convince the majority of the class that it could be an interesting and useful theme.

2   There was no material available, since at the time (1982) no one had yet thought of producing any books meant for peace education.

3 Many parents – and other adults – opposed the idea. Their attitudes can probably be explained by a debate which was running in Denmark at the time. It was a debate about teachers' responsibility *not* to indoctrinate their students, a debate which quite ignored the teachers' role as educationalists. This debate went on somewhat parallel to the German introduction of *Berufsverbot*, and it had scared many Danish teachers away from touching on political issues or revealing their personal opinions in the classroom. The fear of being accused of indoctrination made many teachers subject themselves to a high degree of self-censorship concerning what to say and do, and what themes to suggest/decide upon. Some parents and students were actually very quick to hint that indoctrination took place as soon as the teaching touched upon non–traditional matters.

## PEACE: A CONTROVERSIAL ISSUE IN THE CLASSROOM?

I myself felt that when it came to peace education the case was very clear: that peace is better than war, creation better than destruction, are basic facts beyond discussion. Since I also feel my role as a teacher covers more than just the teaching of grammar and literature, I see it as my responsibility to be one of the people who helps my students form qualified opinions as to the best ways to create peace and prevent destruction. But to many people the mere mention of the word 'peace' in the classroom – at a time when the cold war was still very much continuing – was identified with communist propaganda. Consequently it was difficult back in the mid-1980s to convince other teachers that peace education ought to be part of the curriculum.

In 1982 I helped found the organization Danish Gymnasium Teachers for Peace (GTfP), and I was a member of the board from 1982 to 1990. It was a country-wide organization which was meant to lend moral and practical support to other teachers, do practical peace work (international contacts, conferences, exchange programmes, general consciousness-raising) while – and by – aiming at making peace education an obligatory part of the Danish educational system.

It was through this organization that the problem of lack of relevant material was solved. We established a 'bank of peace teaching material'. All teachers who sympathized with the issue sent in whatever they had or knew of, and it was amazing to see how rapidly the collection of books, articles, booklists and videos grew with mutual help. It was also interesting to see how the various subjects, which usually live quite separate lives in our educational system, suddenly crossed borders and used each other's material and experience in the process. This was felt as a great relief; the isolation of the individual subject is a common complaint in Denmark, but of course it was only felt as a relief as long as you were among 'friends'. If you had a colleague who was opposed to peace education, that person could with some justice claim that you had taken part of his or her subject in which you are not educated and therefore not qualified to teach.

# RECOMMENDATION TO THE MINISTRY OF EDUCATION

If you study the suggestion made by GTfP to the Ministry of Education (backed by their union) concerning what an obligatory peace education should cover, it is obvious that if one teacher tries to cover it all, that teacher will be moving in and out of several subjects; for example, literature, physics, social science, history, geography, psychology, sociology. Until peace education actually does become an obligatory part of the curriculum, this problem will remain unsolved. The suggestion was as follows.

## Peace education

- Peace education is a part of all subjects in the gymnasium.
- Peace education should aim at making peace consciousness part of the students' attitudes.
- Peace education aims at increasing the students' awareness of peace as a long process which includes among other things:
  (a) an end to war and war threats;
  (b) a decrease of the structural violence through a reduction in suffering, injustice and fear in the world.

Therefore peace education involves

1  passing on knowledge;

2  working with attitudes.

### *Knowledge*

Peace education should include the following:

(a) **peaceful coexistence rather than deterrence**
- the origin and course of international conflicts;
- weapon alliances, political treaties, freedom from alliances, neutrality;
- the interests of the superpowers and the objectives of their foreign policies;
- modern weapons and warfare, including offensive and defensive strategies;
- the role of international trade in peaceful coexistence and conflicts;
- the work and structure of the UN;
- the peace movements;
- disarmament initatives and negotiations.

(b) **development**
- the development of economic relations between industrial and developing countries;
- the relations among developing countries;
- the military expenses of developing countries;
- the role of the East–West conflict in developing countries;
- military expenses and the resource problems of the world.

(c) **freedom movements**
- the political background of the movements;
- discussion of the use of violence as a means of obtaining freedom;
- the role of the superpowers in the movements;
- the state-building process.

(d) **structural violence**
- the power structures in different social structures as a source of latent conflict.

(e) information about countries with which Denmark has a strained relationship.

## *Attitudes*

Peace education should motivate the students to test their own as well as others' attitudes in a critical, self-reflective process. Peace education should try positively to influence and alter those attitudes which in such a test prove unconstructive concerning the peace objective: social prejudices, images concerning friends and enemies, acceptance of the doctrine of survival of the fittest, belief in the absolute truth of one's own norms.

Peace education should also provide students with an opportunity to experience the value of an open mind towards attitudes and norms which are in conflict with their own; a willingness to engage in dialogue as a tool to solve conflicts; and the ability to co-operate in spite of differences of opinion.

## Methods of instruction

- Peace education offers good opportunities for interdisciplinary instruction; instruction centred around themes and projects will be appropriate.
- The school ought to take part in some kind of international and humanitarian activity, such as support for a development project or a UN organization, friendship schools in developing or eastern countries (with exchange of students and teachers).

# STARTING POINTS

All this still left me with my first problem: how to motivate the students. The first three times I convinced a class that this was a good theme, I used a very traditional appetizer: I showed them a movie (for example, *The Day After*) or a broadcast and let the following discussion awaken their interest. However, after I had started that way three times, I felt it was very unsatisfactory to turn a serious topic into a classroom show; by doing that I felt I was doing exactly what I have also accused the electronic media of: making war exciting entertainment! (Just think of how the Gulf war missile firings were filmed.)

I decided I would have to work on several levels at the same time. I wanted my students to realize that the peace issue was not a question of one particular teacher in one particular classroom – but rather something many people were, and had to be, engaged in. The best way to get this effect was to make the peace theme part of school assemblies; each of Denmark's 140 gymnasiums has to arrange eight of these assembles per school year.

Together with colleagues from GTfP I created different programmes and made suggestions for programmes to be used at such assemblies. Obvious suggestions were certain theatre groups, films and slide-shows, but we also arranged country-wide school tours, for example for a delegation consisting of four Christian people, two from the USA and two from the USSR; for the representative of the ANC in Denmark; and for a Russian diplomat.

Back in the classroom my new approach to catch my students' interest was to make them aware of how little they actually knew about a subject they needed to know – and thought they knew – a lot about. I constructed a questionnaire with 13 questions on the UN and its work between approximately 1975 and the present. In Denmark, small country as it is, the UN is generally accepted as a peace-preserving organization without narrow communist sympathies, so there was no immediate political conflict in using it as a starting point. Each of my 13 questions gave three possible answers, and all the students had to do was fill in what they thought was right. My students in the second and third year felt that they already knew a lot about the UN since most history teachers deal with that. The questions mainly dealt with issues treated in the Security Council. An example:

In 1982 Sweden and Mexico suggested a total freeze of nuclear armaments. Denmark voted:
1 in favour   2 against   3 abstained from voting.

The students were shocked to realize how few correct answers they had – to this day the maximum score has been six correct answers. The explanation is that they have been taught about the history and structure of the UN, *not* the actual work and behaviour in detail. The test provides me with an excellent starting point, since the correct answers often clash with the students' immediate sense of logic, and that raises a great number of questions. I still use a questionnaire in a continuously revised version when I start a new class on the peace theme.

# DEVELOPING THE THEME

From this point we can move in many different directions, and I usually leave it to a combination of my knowledge of the class and the first discussions in the class to decide what way to go. In some classes it is important to emphasize facts: figures, statistics, dates, and names. In other classes there is a great need for more philosophical/ethical discussions in connection with the literary texts. When I teach peace in my religion classes, it is, of course, the more philosophical/ethical/psychological aspects which are stressed. This can be done in English classes too, as long as it is done in English, but more often we let the various literary texts inspire us. Also, I always make a point of making the students help collect material: search newspapers, magazines, book-shelves, album covers and so on, for relevant material.

Actually, many factors help me to decide what to include in a peace theme: how the class functions as a group; their ages; the numbers of girls and boys; the themes studied in their other subjects; and contemporary political events. So, depending on all these factors, we will put more or less stress on the following aspects: conflict theories, war psychology, ethical implications of war and violence, psychological effect of war on all its different kinds of victims, environmental considerations, and images of the enemy. Usually I let the discussion move freely back and forth between the 'micro' and the 'macro' level. That makes the problems easier to grasp for the weaker students and the problems more relevant for the groups of girls who make a virtue out of saying, 'I'm not interested in politics.' Since the world keeps changing, and since I have always tried to give the students an understanding of war and conflict as something that goes much deeper than the matter of East–West relations, we spend some time studying the map for potential conflict areas, now and in the future.

In some classes, if they feel they can bear it and/or need it, we will also try to search ourselves (as well as amateurs can) for what conflicts our personalities produce, what associations (pictures, sounds, colours) we have in connection with war. We read a variety of genres: drama, lyrics, essays, speeches, a novel or extracts from novels. If reality becomes too unbearable we can always spend some time discussing the form and characteristics of a certain genre, or the effect obtained by different narative techniques.

I also employ many different ways of working, partly to give relief from a serious theme, partly to give the students a chance to carry out in practice some of the things we have discussed in theory. For example, we might dramatize conflict situations, or have panel discussions (here attitudes are being tested and new roles tried when a student has to defend an attitude which is not necessarily her or his own). I arrange a lot of group work, which prevents my role from becoming too dominant, and we usually start each lesson with a two-minute speech prepared by a volunteer on something of their own choice – as long as it is related to what was discussed in the last lesson.

# EMOTIONAL PROCESSES

As I have already hinted, one major problem with peace education is the gravity of the theme. I still find it difficult to keep a reasonable balance between making it too morbid and too entertaining. In 1987, when I felt I had some experience, I decided to increase the intensity of the work, so that every paper the students had to hand in during this period had to deal with the subject: analyses of texts/pictures, accounts of personal considerations/hopes/fears, reviews of texts, or little home-made stories over a given theme. But after six weeks I decided to change my methods again. Not that the students objected openly – I am not even sure more than a couple of them were conscious of their protest – but when I read their papers I felt their protest strongly. They needed a break sometimes, and to be left alone with this theme in the isolation of each person's own desk at home was definitely to go too far. This held for the 16-year-old in the mathematics stream as well as for the 19-year-old in the languages stream. Since then I have tried to give at least 80 per cent of their obligatory papers a positive title while we discuss serious, existential problems.

It is unavoidable, however, that it sometimes becomes very quiet in the classroom. On good days it only takes simple tricks to lift the atmosphere; for example I throw in questions like: 'Could *When the Wind Blows* take place in any social class?', or 'How would *What Niall Saw* be different if Niall's mother had told the story?', 'Would the situation have been different if women had been in charge?' or – one that really can cause animated discussions – 'If *you* had been on Nevil Shute's beach, would you have spent the last moments of your life on whisky, sex, or worries about the national honour?'

Fortunately there are sometimes also comic situations: once in a first-year mathematics stream class I had given them a British pamphlet on how to survive a nuclear attack. The pamphlet offers detailed instructions on how to choose a fall-out room and build an inner refuge. Everybody in the class agreed it was a foolish pamphlet with incorrect and/or insufficient advice/information. And besides, they all agreed, if a nuclear attack should ever occur, the best thing to do would be to go out in the open and get it over with. They also complained that the text was boring and the words were too difficult. They did not want to work with this text any more. I accepted. The next day I started the lesson by asking how many of them had an adequate fall-out room at home. It appeared that only 3 out of the 24 had not given it any thought after they got home the day before!

When I work with peace in a class, I feel that while everybody becomes a little wiser, they also go through emotional processes in which they share hopes and fears, reveal antipathies and sympathies, tear down old beliefs and build up new ones. This is the process I intend, but I have had to face the fact that I alone do not control its course and effect. It is nice to have created a situation and atmosphere in which people expose their feelings. In some classes this closeness has led to everybody becoming everybody's best friend. But in other classes there has been a tendency to stereotype each other, and the fact that they have fought with themselves to find their viewpoints makes them feel very strongly for them, which does not increase their capacity for tolerance. Sometimes it has made me feel that I have created new conflicts, and I have never really learned to control this development when it starts.

## TAKING ACTION FOR PEACE

One of the things I have worried about and discussed with my colleagues is how to avoid the students ending up feeling that nothing really matters, since we will all blow up some day, anyway. Therefore we have spent a couple of lessons at the end of each peace theme helping each other point out all the good reasons to preserve life; we have tried to define and describe peace to make it an active concept – and usually I'll go from there to a beautiful poem or a good, juicy and happy-ending love story.

In general, the students have liked to work in this way. It inspires them to have an active part in the project: since they have to help collect and produce relevant material, they feel responsible for the lessons; they also feel they become closer to each other, and – as is natural for their age – they enjoy toying with philosophical and psychological theories. They all feel they have learned something. I know they feel this way from what they tell me, what they tell their parents and other teachers, and from their behaviour afterwards. They might for example actually try to use some of our discussions about conflicts when they run into new conflicts, and many of my 'peace-students' have become very engaged in some of the grassroots groups at school. I was also rather proud back in 1985 when a couple of my students convinced the school administration that the school ought to buy the UN flag, and since then, because of pressure from later students, the celebration of United Nations Day on 24 October has become an annual tradition in our school. I should also mention that our school has now 11 friendship schools with annual exchanges of students and/or teachers, and that our school is part of a Scandinavian project in which the students once a year give a day's work for the benefit of a developing country.

## IN CONCLUSION

I, the teacher, continue to teach peace. The media may try to convince us that peace work is old-fashioned and war is exciting. Our material may change, as may the subordinate themes, but to me it still remains a fact that peace is better than war, and I can still share that with my students. I may not have succeeded totally in producing more tolerant students, but I do think I can raise their consciousness and make them aware of the complexity of truth. Later in my life I might become more ambitious, but here and now I will settle for that.

# CHAPTER 11

# A Development Education Project in Irish Primary Schools

*Fionnuala Brennan*

## THE CONTEXT IN THE REPUBLIC OF IRELAND

The Republic of Ireland is among the 30 richest countries in the world with an average per capita income of IR£7,410 for a population of 3.503 million people. At the current level of 16 per cent, it also has one of the highest unemployment rates in the European Community. The Republic of Ireland has the youngest population in the European Community. The country's foreign debt stands at IR£10.2 billion. In 1985 voluntary donations in Ireland provided the largest per capita donations to Live Aid (£30 million from a population of 3.5 million). However, official development assistance levels are comparatively low as budgetary difficulties have resulted in a decrease in the level of expenditure in Official Development Assistance since 1986. This now stands at 0.19 per cent of GNP.

Largely because of the fact that for decades thousands of Irish Christian missionaries have worked in developing countries and have related their experiences to relatives and friends, as well as in magazines and journals with a nationwide readership, there has traditionally been a reasonably high level of knowledge among Irish people about some of the conditions in these countries. It would be fair to say that while this generated a widespread feeling of compassion for the poor and oppressed, there was little public analysis of the underlying causes of global poverty and hunger.

In the 1970s, owing to increased contact with developing countries through trade and personal service overseas, concern about development problems increased in Ireland and there was a growth in the production of educational materials regarding specific topics such as hunger, or the role of women in development.

In the last decade, and in particular in the past five or six years, there has been a significant increase in interest in development education in many sectors of Irish society, including the formal education sector at all levels. A great deal of work has been done by non-governmental organization (NGO) development aid agencies and other organizations to develop programmes and materials for the different interest groups. In-service and pre-service teacher education courses in development education have been organized, teachers' and students' resources have been published, development education programmes and materials for youth leaders and groups, for trade unions and women's groups, for adult education courses and for farming organizations have all been developed.

# FUNDING AND SUPPORT FOR DEVELOPMENT EDUCATION

The first grants for development education activities were made by the Department of Foreign Affairs in 1979 when IR£35,000 was allocated from the Official Development Assistance (ODA) budget. In 1985 the amount expended was IR£287,247 and the following year IR£600,000 was allocated to development education; this adds up to an average yearly increase between 1978 and 1986 of over 50 per cent. In the following years there was a marked decrease in overall ODA funding. In 1991 the amount allocated to development education was IR£380,000. The current trend, however, is upward: in 1992 IR£455,048 was expended on development education.

Apart from official financial support for development education, there is significant funding from development aid agencies. One of the largest development aid agencies in Ireland, Trocaire, allocates 20 per cent of its total annual income to development education. In 1990 this amounted to over one million Irish pounds. Funding from other Irish agencies resulted in a total expenditure of approximately £2 million in that year. There is also, of course, funding for development education made available from EC co-financing budgets.

Up to 1985, there appears to have been consensus between the NGOs and the Department of Foreign Affairs that the Department would limit its involvement in development education to the publication of information materials on government aid projects and would support development education indirectly by providing funding to outside agencies, mainly NGOs. The Department produced information materials on ODA and the Bilaterial Aid programmes, in the form of education materials such as factsheets, videos and posters for schools, study groups and the general public. It also provided travel grants to encourage opinion-makers to visit developing countries and to produce first-hand reports for the general public on conditions in developing countries. This target group was not confined to journalists and other media workers, but included other key sectors in Irish society, the trade unions, employers, farming and youth organizations.

In 1986, in order to strengthen its efforts in supporting development education the Department of Foreign Affairs established the Development Education Support Centre (DESC), which is funded from the Bilaterial Aid

Programme. DESC was given the specific brief to involve a wider range of agencies and institutions in development education, particularly those agencies which have an educational function but which may lack skills or experience in development education. The role of DESC is to provide professional expertise and resources, a consultancy service for teachers, youth leaders, community groups and others in order to assist them in designing and organizing development education projects and activities. DESC also acts as a support agency for those already involved in development education. This service is operated through DESC's two national and regional centres.

In 1990 the National Development Education Grants Committee was established by the Department of Foreign Affairs to allocate funding for development education activities in both the formal and non-formal education areas. Many small, regional development education groups as well as national initiatives are funded from this source.

# DEVELOPMENT EDUCATION IN THE CURRICULUM

In 1971 a new curriculum for primary schools was introduced in the Republic of Ireland. Among the reasons for changing the old curriculum given in a circular entitled *Education for Change* issued by the Department of Education (1971a) to all parents was: 'our children must be prepared for a world of change'. In the introduction to the new curriculum, *Curaclam na Bunscoile* (1971b), the learner-centred approach was recommended: 'the child is now seen to be the most active agent in his [*sic*] own education'. Twenty years ago, it could be argued, there was curriculum support for the content and methodology of development education.

Almost two decades later the curriculum has again come under review. Included in the specific aims recommended by the current Review Body are:

> To help children to understand the society and environment in which they live, the interdependence of peoples and nations, and to foster a spirit of co-operation and the capacity and willingness to contribute in a critical but positive manner towards the development of society.

> To help children to respect, appreciate and understand their own and other cultural identities.
>
> (Department of Education, 1990)

In a submission to the *Fifth Report of the Joint Committee on Co-operation with Developing Countries: Development Education* (Dáil Éireann, 1986: 54–60), the Department of Education indicated that it did not envisage that development education would become a separate curriculum subject, rather that examinations in related subjects would continue to reflect a development education perspective. This view was also that of the Curriculum and Examinations Board (now the National Council for Curriculum and Assessment) in its submission to the above report, in which it was stated that its view of development education was that it does not encompass a particular area but should permeate the curriculum (Dáil Éireann, 1986: 50–3). The Board especially recommended the need for a systematic input at primary level.

There is, then, support in government educational policy statements and among curriculum development experts for the inclusion of development education especially in the primary school curriculum in Ireland.

While work in development education has been going on for over a decade in Irish primary schools, in-service and pre-service teacher education courses have been organized by NGOs and DESC, classroom materials have been produced and many teachers have become involved in development education, the reality is that development education is not part of the curriculum in the majority of Irish schools. Although there are development education electives (optional courses) in teacher education colleges, and development education is a compulsory part of the core curriculum in one university department of education, development education is not yet part of the pre-service curriculum for the majority of Irish student teachers.

Where development education has been practised in schools, the approach adopted has generally been an individual teacher-based one rather than a whole-school approach where there is a commitment by the principal and the entire staff to incorporate development education into classroom practice. This has obviously limited the impact of development education in schools.

## JOINT DEPARTMENT OF EDUCATION/DESC PRIMARY SCHOOL PILOT PROJECT IN DEVELOPMENT EDUCATION

Arising out of the recommendation of the Joint Committee's Report on Development Education (Dáil Éireann, 1986: 21) to target the primary level education sector, and in order to promote a shift in development education into the mainstream of Irish primary school education, an officially sanctioned pilot project was initiated in 1988.

In 1988–9 the Primary Curriculum Unit of the Department of Education in the Republic of Ireland and DESC (the Development Education Support Centre) conducted a nationwide joint project on Development Education in a variety of primary schools. The aims of the Development Education Primary School Project were:

- to pilot the inclusion of a development education perspective in the primary school curriculum;
- to do so in a variety of primary schools using a whole-school approach;
- to examine the outcomes of the project with a view to making a proposal to the Department of Education on the integration of a development education perspective into the primary school curriculum.

# PROJECT METHODOLOGY

Eight schools throughout the country, representing a cross-section of primary schools, were invited to participate in the year-long school project. These schools ranged from a large urban school to a three-teacher rural school; they included all-boys as well as co-educational schools and an all-Irish-speaking school. In the Republic, children start school at four years and leave primary school at twelve so this was the age range of the project. A working group was set up to conduct and monitor the project, to assist in the recording of outcomes and to evaluate the whole exercise. The group was composed of seven primary school inspectors from the Department of Education and three DESC staff.

The working group did not prepare detailed guidelines or blueprints for development education modules in the classroom; rather it was decided to ask teachers, with the help of some of the resources provided, and as a result of the discussions which took place at the initial seminar, to incorporate a development education perspective into their normal school plan which they prepare at the beginning of each academic year. This was to try to ensure that development education would not be seen as a separate addition to the curriculum, and would thus survive when the high level of support supplied by the project team finished at the end of the pilot phase. By not prescribing activities or providing a blueprint, the working group hoped that teachers would introduce development education more naturally and more organically into everyday classroom practice.

Advance questionnaires were distributed to the 80 participating teachers in order to establish a teacher profile with particular reference to their previous experience, if any, of development education. These questionnaires showed that out of the 80 participating teachers 27 had had a limited experience of development education methods or materials or had dealt with development topics during the previous year and that four teachers had worked in developing countries. Thus the great majority of the teachers had no previous experience of development education. The challenge of the project was to support teachers with little or no previous experience in development education to incorporate a global perspective into their classroom practice successfully and in a cross-curricular way.

Seminars were held in each school to launch the project, to which the whole school staff and the Chair of the Board of Management were invited. Parents were not directly involved. In some schools they were informed about the project by the teachers, in others they found out about it from their children. Many parents provided information and support for the project as it evolved in different schools. Further seminars were held during the course of the project to enable teachers to share their experiences, to discuss their problems, to access support services and to enable the working group to monitor on-going developments. During the year DESC staff and Department of Education inspectors visited each teacher once a term in order to provide support and advice, and to monitor the working of the pilot project.

A final seminar was held in each school to agree the content of the whole-school case study report, which was designed to report on the total impact of the project in each school.

## The project at work: themes, methodologies, resources

A selection of the main themes, methodologies and resources used at four different age levels during the pilot project are shown in Figures 1–4.

| Theme | Methodology | Resources |
|---|---|---|
| Clothes | Drama | Oxfam slide sets – |
| Homes | Dance | *The Way We Live* (slides) |
| Festivals | Stories | UNICEF posters of children from different countries |
| Food | Crafts | Photographs of the children's families |
| One World | Small-group work | *Tinder Box* (66 songs for children) |
| Music around the World | Role plays | |

**Figure 1** Ages 4–6 years

| Theme | Methodology | Resources |
|---|---|---|
| Food | Drama | *The Way We Live* (slides) UNICEF slide sets, including |
| Trees | Simulation games | *The Desert Child, The Mountain Child,* |
| Houses | Small-group work | *Child of Latin America, Oscar of Peru* |
| Global communications | Role play | Videos of India, artefacts from different |
| India | Research | countries |
| Peru | Discussion | Library books |
| Fair Shares | Music | Visitors to classroom |
| Kenya | Co-operative activities | Photographs from magazines |
| | | UNICEF: *Games of the World* (1975) Games, including *The Paper Bag Game* (Christian Aid) |
| | | Posters from embassies and aid agencies *Some Crafty Things to Do* (Oxfam, 1985) |

**Figure 2** Ages 6–8 years

| Theme | Methodology | Resources |
|---|---|---|
| Water | Drama | Videos, including *The Big If, Orkendi, Exiles in Their Own Land* (Christian Aid) |
| Peace and conflict | Role play | UNICEF slides<br>Culture Kits India and Africa (boxes of artefacts from DESC) |
| Trees | Stories | Visitors from overseas |
| Sudan | Music | Media stories<br>Macdonald series of books, *Stories from the Muslim World*, etc. |
| Transport | Role play | A. & C. Black's Beans series of books (1984) |
| Food | Research | Posters |
| Recycling | Analysis | Media |
| Our environment<br>South America<br>Us and the Wider World | | *The Trading Game*<br>(Christian Aid) |

**Figure 3** Ages 8–10 years

| Theme | Methodology | Resources |
|---|---|---|
| Apartheid | Drama | Videos |
| Food and Famine | Dance | Games |
| One World | Music | Slides |
| Rights of Children | Discussion | Culture kits |
| Commodities | Research | Visitors |
| Water | Discussion | UNICEF slides including *Health: A Human Right* and *A Drop of Water* |
| Forests | Analysis | Books, including *It's Not Fair* (Christian Aid, 1984) |
| | Art/craft<br>Games | |

**Figure 4** Ages 10–12 years

During the project period teachers undertook as their primary aim to incorporate a global perspective within their lesson plans and to write evaluation reports as they completed each module or theme. Integration of the global perspective in a cross–curricular manner was very important.

Themework, or projects, already a key part of the teaching–learning activities in many primary classrooms, including the project schools, was seen as a valuable way of exploring the global dimension through active learning methods. By organizing themes imaginatively, teachers found that an environment could be created in which children could begin to grapple with some of the issues surrounding them in today's world. Two approaches were used in the selection and development of development education themes: a whole-school theme whereby one central theme was explored by the whole school, and an individual teacher approach whereby a teacher selected a theme for the class and worked on it for a specified length of time, usually one term or six weeks.

Where specific countries were the thematic focus there was a particular reason for choosing that country; in the case of Peru, for instance, a local clergyman had spent years as a missionary there and one of the children's parents had also worked there. The working group discovered that in the past when a theme such as 'water' or 'forests' was chosen, the tendency had been to treat it mainly as part of a geography lesson with some science or history included. However, during the development education project, a much more global approach was adopted and the lives of forest people in the Amazon, for example, as well as the issues of deforestation and global warming became part of the themework. With regard to the theme of water, the issues of drought, flooding or the uses of water in different parts of the world in religious rituals were all included.

In practice the majority of the teachers used the theme as a focus for work in language, science, religious education, music, art, drama and social and environmental studies. A minority integrated the theme into all subject areas in the curriculum rather than as a specific focus for the different subjects. This was particularly true of infant teachers.

Each teacher evaluated the work done according to the following structures: outline of objectives; identification of methodologies; outline of resources; and listing educational outcomes for both teacher and pupils. The selection of theme was based on the children's interests, the teacher's interest and knowledge and previous classroom work done in the area.

Very popular, especially with the younger children, were themes dealing with the lives of children in other cultures. There are relatively few foreigners or people of different ethnic origin living in Ireland so that many children have never. met anyone who is not white and Irish. Thus there is a good deal of curiosity about other cultures and races. There are, of course, many stereotyped images as well.

Some of the themes selected for older pupils were more concept-based. 'Peace and Conflict' is an example of a wide-ranging theme undertaken by one teacher and his class of 9- and 10-year-olds which included some exploration of the conflict in Northern Ireland. The teacher's objectives in dealing with the local dimension of the theme was to show that major conflict exists in our own country as well as in the 'Third World'. A second objective was to enable children to recognize that there are at least two sides to the Northern Ireland conflict. The emphasis was on creating an openness to others, on seeing situations from different perspectives and hence becoming more open to a mutually acceptable solution. The teacher did not intend or think it desirable to treat the Northern Ireland conflict in any depth at this age level. The children explored firstly their own, quite negative, images of Northern Ireland and achieved a more balanced view by finding out some good news from that part of the island. Then, through reading short stories and poems written by children from both sides of the cultural and political divide in Northern Ireland, they came to realize how fear, suspicion and resentment can lead to a vicious cycle of conflict and concluded that an important step towards breaking the cycle would be to listen to what the 'other side' has to say. The exploration of such a potentially controversial theme was, however, unusual. Very few controversial issues were dealt with during the project in other classrooms.

## PROJECT OUTCOMES

At the outset teachers outlined their educational objectives in terms of the knowledge, skills and attitudes they hoped their pupils would acquire through the development education project. In summary, the knowledge outcomes noted by the teachers were as follows:

- The children's knowledge of global issues such as malnutrition and food supply, and of environmental issues such as global warming, was extended.
- The pupils gained an understanding of the concept of community, starting from a local base and extending outwards, and of their own role in the local and wider world community; they became aware of the interdependence of peoples.
- The children recognized the dangers of stereotyping and of discrimination.

One infant teacher wrote: 'They developed a broader concept of themselves and of other cultures than they would have under usual teaching circumstances.' Another teacher, this time of 11- and 12-year-olds, commented: 'They see differences between peoples, countries and cultures as a positive thing, as something which adds richness and variety to life.'

With regard to *skills*, the teachers found that the methodology and content of development education facilitated the development of the skills of:

- group interaction and co–operation;
- media analysis;
- independent research;
- listening creatively;
- sharing information and skills;
- communication;
- debate;
- synthesis;
- self-awareness.

Some of the activities mentioned by teachers in their reports which led to the development of the skills listed above included drama, role-play, simulation games, ranking exercises, stories and music from other cultures, discussion and debate, listening exercises, which developed an appreciation of others' points of view, and research work, whereby a small group of children were responsible for researching and presenting some aspect of the theme.

It should be stressed here that, as in the case of the knowledge objectives and outcomes, the skills objectives were appropriate to the age and ability of the children in different classes.

Teachers found that, on the whole, children participated more actively in their own learning, encouraged by processes such as small-group work, and that this suited children of all ranges of ability and personality types. Through such activities as role-plays, photo-language (the use of photographs to raise issues and to provide students with material for debate and discussion) and through ranking exercises, quieter children became more participative. (Ranking exercises involve participants in selecting from a list of options and prioritizing the most important as they see them; usually the individual then joins a small group whose members discuss their own choices and sometimes attempt to reach consensus.) Less academically able children had opportunities to discover and use other talents and skills. In one class, for instance, during the theme-work on Peru, a group of children researched Andean music. Two of the less academically bright children made excellent and playable musical instruments and spoke enthusiastically about how they had gone about the task. They also worked on tapes of Andean music and were able to play music some of which they based on what they had heard. This was the first time that these particular children, aged eight and nine, had 'shone' in class.

There were two main strands to the teachers' comments on the development of children's *attitudes*. The first of these concerned the children's attitudes to each other: the teachers observed a greater acceptance and recognition of each other's talents, more openness to other viewpoints and a more positive attitude towards sharing and co-operation as a result of the development education process.

Secondly, the teachers noted a more positive attitude towards the poorer parts of the world, the Third World or developing countries, depending on which term was employed. Largely negative media images were balanced with positive views of these countries by use of the Culture Kits, 'Third World' visitors to the classroom and slides or videos showing people and communities in poorer countries working towards their own development. The children showed a dislike of stereotyping and a greater sense of responsibility for development both locally and globally. An example of children's action in one school, following themework on forests which had dealt with the issue of deforestation, was to contact the local representative of Crann, a national tree conservation group, and to organize tree planting near the school during National Tree Week. Another class of children organized a Fair Trade Day on which they invited the local representative of Traideireann, an alternative trading organization, to visit the school to inform them about fair trading practices and how, as consumers, they and their families could act to help to bring about fairer North–South trade.

> The children developed openness to other peoples and cultures, concern for those living in difficult circumstances and enthusiasm and curiosity about the greater world.
>
> (Teacher of first class (6–7-year-old children))

## EDUCATIONAL OUTCOMES FOR TEACHERS

The majority of teachers found that the development education project had broadened their approach to the curriculum. (The Republic of Ireland has always had a National Curriculum.) A significant number of teachers reported that they had developed a more child-centred teaching style, they had improved their group work skills and recognized the value of simulation games and role-play. In the majority of cases teachers had not previously used simulation games in the classroom. Games such as *The Trading Game* and *The Paper Bag Game* (Christian Aid, undated) were found to be a very stimulating way to bring up the issue of some of the causes of global inequalities, and teachers who used them were unanimous in their praise for the level of understanding, discussion and debate which such games engendered.

An important outcome for teachers was the job satisfaction and added support they received from the fact that the project involved the whole school; this facilitated co-operation in planning, sharing resources and ideas. A common remark made by the participating teachers was that both they and the children enjoyed the development education project. One teacher reported: 'It is terribly difficult to give a true picture of our work by form-filling. The atmosphere, excitement and impact of the project are totally lost on paper!'

There was almost unanimous agreement among the teachers that, despite initial fears, development education was not an extra burden to overload the curriculum, rather it was an exciting medium through which integration was possible and through which the basics could be learned.

## EDUCATIONAL OUTCOMES FOR THE SCHOOL

At the end of the project the working group met with the whole school staff for an evaluation of the year's work and to discuss their conclusions and recommendations. To summarize these findings: the teachers said that they had gained a heightened awareness of the importance of co-operation in planning, in sharing resources and ideas, in implementation and in evaluation in relation to the introduction of a development education perspective into the primary school curriculum. The relationship between the school and outside agencies was developed as many visitors were invited into the classroom as resource people. There was a new consciousness of the use and variety of resources and a renewal of methodology, especially in the area of active learning approaches and child-centred learning. Overall there was considerable professional development of school staffs arising from the project. An indication of how staffs might build on their experience of the development education project was given in the end-of-project report in which all the schools reported that they would continue to include development education in their normal work and indicated a willingness to act as nodes of dissemination for other schools in their area. Many teachers said they would be willing to participate as development education 'witnesses' in future in-service courses. One of the principals wrote: 'We believe that each pupil will be a better, more compassionate local, national and world citizen . . . as a result of . . . development education' (Feeley, 1991).

## CONCLUSIONS OF THE PROJECT

The conclusions were derived from an analysis of the data provided by teachers and from the experience gained by the DESC staff and school inspectors during their regular visits to each of the 80 participating teachers. The main conclusions were the following:

- The project showed that development education can be implemented at all levels in the primary school.
- The whole-school approach to integrating development education into the curriculum is most effective.
- Development education succeeds best when it permeates the curriculum and is not treated as a separate subject.
- A global learning approach ensures an enriching teaching–learning experience.
- The content and process of development education provide scope for the less academically able and more reserved children to come to the fore while stimulating the brighter children to greater effort.
- The children and teachers enjoyed the development education experience.

With regard to this last conclusion, it was interesting that there was almost complete unanimity among teachers about the enjoyment factor experienced by both themselves and by the children. The enjoyment was partly attributed to the active learning methodology of role-plays, games, and the increased use of art, drama and music as well as the use of resources such as videos and slides of other peoples and cultures. Another factor was the interest and excitement aroused by the visitors to the classroom, such as past pupils, parents and others in the community who had lived and worked abroad, especially in developing countries. Where children decided to take action as a result of their classroom work a lot of enjoyment resulted. Examples include such activities as the preparations for the One World Day in one school, and in another, winning first prize in a music competition, for which the class had written and performed a musical based on work they had done on India. Teachers reported great interest among the children in bringing in news items from newspapers, watching television programmes for information about a particular theme and involving parents in their research. While this sense of enjoyment might well have resulted from any project, it would seem that the subject matter, the methodology, the topicality, and serious concern for fairness and justice leading to a sense of personal responsibility and appropiate action which informs development education may have brought about the remarkable level of enjoyment experienced by both teachers and pupils.

Many teachers mentioned in their reports that they had enjoyed the project as they had learned a lot themselves about global issues; some of them were surprised by the amount of interest and knowledge that even young children had about the wider world and many felt that their teaching strategies had been enriched. Here are some typical comments: 'I feel that the project has opened me up to listen to the children's views. I learned to expect more from pupils' own opinions and information.' Another teacher, of a class of 10- and 11-year-old pupils, concluded: 'It has given me a greater appreciation of what the children are capable of; for example, their grasp of the concepts involved in *The Trading Game* really surprised me.'

As only a third of the teachers had ever used development education materials or dealt with development topics before becoming involved in the project, and as the working group were deliberately non-prescriptive, there were initial difficulties for some teachers in understanding the concept of development education. While a minority of the teachers felt that they would have preferred a more directive approach from the project working group, most teachers agreed that as the pilot project proceeded they came to their own understanding of development education and were able to integrate it successfully into their classroom practice.

A few teachers found the use of simulation games and role-play and other experiential learning techniques difficult, and were more comfortable with the use of textbooks and the 'talk and chalk' method. These tended to be older teachers who had not had previous experience of games as teaching and learning tools and who may have resisted the affective aspect of learning.

An important constraint in some schools for the teachers of sixth class (the last class in primary schools) was the concentration on English, Irish and maths for the first two terms in order to prepare the children for the entrance examinations for post-primary schools. There is no state examination at the end of primary school, but many post-primary schools hold entrance examinations from which they make their pupil selection. In some areas the competition for acceptance into certain post-primary schools is very strong and thus sixth-class teachers have to prepare their pupils for this. While there is not an inevitable conflict between these demands and the incorporation of a development education perspective in the curriculum, the reality is that these teachers felt that they had to concentrate a lot on the three Rs and Irish and on examination techniques, and that this did not leave sufficient time for themework.

There were other constraints including large class size (one class had over 40 pupils) which led to difficulties in rearranging furniture for role-play or games. Parents' expectations regarding finishing textbooks which they had bought for their children was a constraint in one school. The latter constraint might have been avoided if parents had been more involved at the beginning, had been informed about the aims and objectives of the project and had been reassured that their children were acquiring knowledge and skills even if they were not progressing at a pace through certain textbooks.

Some teachers of junior classes reported a dearth of materials for development education at that level and pointed to a need for more and better visual aids. This claim is justified and is one which is consistently borne out in evaluations at the end of in-service courses in development education. The work in the UK on the World Studies Project 8–13 (Fisher and Hicks, 1985) and the amount of published material produced for that age level and upwards indicates the earlier concentration on older age levels. While there are now some manuals of co-operative games (Mashader, 1986) and such books as *Learning Together – Global Education 4–7* (Fountain, 1990), there are fewer resources available for junior classes. Perhaps another difficulty at this level is that some teachers may feel that development education always has to be about the wider world and that learning co-operatively and developing a positive image of oneself and others does not justify the label of development education. These teachers may be concentrating overly on the content rather than the process of development education.

A small minority of teachers had some difficulty with the idea of introducing young children to complex global issues. Others, on the contrary, were surprised to discover just how much even the younger children had picked up from the media and how interested they were in wider world places, peoples and issues.

As has already been observed, this pilot project in development education showed that, with only one or two exceptions, teachers did not raise or deal with controversial issues in the classroom. The teachers who commented on this felt that children of primary school age are too young for a conscientization process, that they are not yet capable of understanding their position in a wider world context, that it is too difficult for teachers to deal with complex issues without running the risk of being too simplistic and of therefore distorting the picture. One teacher commented that she was wary of being too 'political' and thus avoided controversial issues in her classroom.

The content of development education is complex and some teachers do not have a sufficiently sound knowledge base in development theories and issues to provide a basis for their classroom teaching. There is, therefore, a need for more linkages between those involved in development studies research and teachers involved in development education in order to ensure that simplistic or outdated explanations for global development problems are not given.

If development education is to be taken seriously and integrated into the school curriculum, there is a need for its inclusion in core pre-service teacher education and in in-service courses. As with any curriculum development, teachers need an appropriate level of support and resources.

While there are some funding implications, it must be said that the majority of development education materials produced in the UK and in Ireland are very moderately priced and thus cost should not be a constraint. Sections of existing textbooks can be quite easily used for development education and imaginative teachers and learners can supply their own resources from the media and the community.

While teachers are rightly concerned about the dangers of oversimplifying complex situations and are wary of introducing possibly sensitive or controversial issues with young children at primary school, I would argue that stereotyped attitudes and prejudices are formed in the early years of childhood. Furthermore, as Susan Fountain contends:

> even very young children try to make sense of global trends and problems that their parents and teachers struggle with at deeper levels . . . they are forming rudimentary conceptions and misconceptions about issues of peace and conflict, human rights, racism, sexism, global development and the environment.
>
> (1990: 1)

Thus, while dealing sensitively with controversial issues and avoiding over-simplification, primary school teachers need to address issues of prejudice, human rights, peace and global development.

Finally, as the pilot project described in this chapter proves, development education adds a valuable and enjoyable perspective to the primary school curriculum. As the pace of social, political and environmental change accelerates, thus creating a more interdependent world which the school-children of today must comprehend, it is all the more vital that the primary school should be the site for the preparation of the ground for later development education work at secondary school level. This is the ideal time when prejudice and bias can be addressed, when the learning ethos is created to develop personal confidence, attitudes of tolerance, caring and co-operativeness, a sense of personal responsibility towards one's own society and some awareness of local and global interdependence.

To enable teachers to practise development education, to carry out a fundamental task for all contemporary teachers which is to prepare students to be effective participants in an increasingly interdependent global society, adequate preparatory and support services must be provided. Most importantly, a development or global education perspective must be officially incorporated into the school curriculum.

# REFERENCES

Christian Aid (undated), *The Paper Bag Game*.

Christian Aid (undated), *The Trading Game*.

Dáil Éireann (1986), *Fifth Report of the Joint Committee on Co-operation with Developing Countries: Development Education*, Dublin.

Department of Education (1971a), *Education for Change: A Circular on the New Curriculum,* Dublin: Stationery Office.

Department of Education (1971b), *Curaclam na Bunscoile: The Primary School Curriculum Teachers' Handbook*, 1, Dublin: Stationery Office.

Department of Education (1990), *Report of the Review Body on the Primary Curriculum,* Dublin, Stationery Office.

Feeley, T. (1991), 'Development education in a rural school', *An Muinteoir: The Irish Teachers' Journal*, **5** (2).

Fisher, S. and Hicks, (1985), *World Studies 8–13: A Teacher's Handbook*, Edinburgh: Oliver & Boyd.

Fountain, S. (1990), *Learning Together Global Education 4–7*, Cheltenham: Stanley Thornes.

Mashader, M. (1986), *Let's Co-operate*, Peace Education Project.

# RESOURCES

The following is a list of the most popular resouces used during the pilot project.

**Artefacts:** *Culture Kit India* and *Mulongo and Naryaka's School Kits Kenya*, Dublin: DESC. Large wooden boxes containing everyday objects from other cultures with slides, photos and teachers' notes.

**Books:** Barratt, S. and Hodge, S. (1982), *Tinder Box*, London: A. & C. Black, 66 songs for children.

Bennett, O. (1984), *Brazilian Family*
Kendall, S. (1987), *Amazon Family*
Stewart, J. (1987), *Family in Sudan*
All these are in the Beans Series, London: A. & C. Black.

Drum, J. and Sutton, H., *Watch Festivals*, BBC in association with Heritage Books.

Granfield, F. V. (1975), *Games of the World*, Zurich: UNICEF.

Hale, K. (1985), *Some Crafty Things to Do*, Oxford: Oxfam.

Malvern Group, *Stories from Overseas*, 1982–4 series, Oxford: Oxfam.

MacFarlane, C. (1986), *Theme Work*, Birmingham: Development Education Centre.

Sheehy, I. (1988), *So Everyone Fights? A Teaching Programme on Development Education for 9–13 Year Olds*, Dublin: Irish Commission for Justice and Peace.

**Games:**   *The Paper Bag Game* – simulates the pressures of trying to survive in Calcutta, Christian Aid. 10–35 players.

*The Trading Game* – helps players to understand how trade affects the economic prosperity of developing countries, Christian Aid. 15–30 players.

*The World in a Supermarket Bag* – links our food to the rest of the world, Oxfam. 10–35 players.

Other games and role-plays were taken from *It's Not Fair* (1984), Christian Aid and Trocaire.

**Packs:**   Lyle, S. and Roberts, M. (1988), *An Arctic Child*, Carmarthen: Greenlight Publications. About the concerns of the Arctic people regarding their fragile eco-system.

Lyle, S. and Roberts, M. (1988), *A Rainforest Child*, Carmarthen, Greenlight Publications. Based in Borneo, it helps children to understand the importance of the rainforests.

**Slides:**   *Around the World-Farming* and *Clothing*, with teachers' notes (1981), Acorn Media.

*A Drop of Water, Child of Asia, Child of Latin America, Health a Human Right, The Desert Child, The Mountain Child, The Rainforest Child* – all produced by UNICEF, sets of 24 slides with teachers' notes and activity suggestions.

*The Way We Live* series, including *Children at Work, Crafts, Clothes, Homes* and *Transport* (1981), Oxfam. Sets of 12 slides with accompanying teachers' notes suitable for primary schools.

*Village Industries* (1978), CWDE. 5 sets of slides set in India showing craftspeople at work. Accompanying teachers' notes.

**Videos:** *Exiles in their own land*, 29 mins (1980), Christian Aid. Set in Brazil, it examines the extremes of poverty and wealth in the city of Salvador.

*Orkendi*, 15 mins (1980), Christian Aid. Filmed in Tanzania; about health, education and clean water.

*The Big If*, 9 mins (1982), Christian Aid. Cartoon without words about the economic consequences of the arms race.

*The Living Arts of India*, 30 mins (1989), Christian Aid. Shows the importance of the arts in the lives of Indian people.

*The Living City*, 30 mins (1977), Christian Aid. Life in the bustees of Calcutta.

*Veeravalli*, 13 mins (1981), Christian Aid. Filmed in India; about the outcastes or harijans.

# Addresses

Christian Aid: Christchurch, Rathgar Road, Dublin 6.

Crann: The Woodand Management Trust, Carrigallen, Co. Leitrim.

DESC: The Development Education Support Centre, St Patrick's College of Education, Drumcondra, Dublin 9.

Irish Commission for Justice and Peace: 169 Booterstown Ave., Blackrock, Co. Dublin.

Oxfam in Ireland: 202 Lower Rathmines Road, Dublin 6.

Traideireann: P.O. Box 20, Athlone, Co. Westmeath.

Trocaire: 169 Booterstown Avenue, Blackrock, Co. Dublin.

# CHAPTER 12

# *Pied Crow* Magazine in Kenya:
# A Development Education Spice

*Alfred Ojwang*

CARE International in Kenya (CARE-Kenya) has been producing the *Pied Crow* Environment Special magazine for curriculum support in primary schools as part of a primary education project since 1983. The problem which this project seeks to address, at least partially, is that

> primary school children and teachers nationwide have inadequate appropriate curriculum support materials to enable children to properly improve and increase their life knowledge and skills.

Lack of educational materials has been a key area of inadequacy in Kenyan schools for a long time.

At the invitation of the government, CARE has operated in Kenya since 1968. A Basic Country Agreement signed with the Ministry of Finance authorizes CARE's general activities in Kenya. Agreements are also signed with the District Development Committees for each individual project. Since 1968 the total value of CARE development programmes in Kenya has been approximately US$35,000,000.

CARE-Kenya's multi-faceted programme strategy emphasizes the improvement of the living standards of the rural population through increased water supply, food and fuel wood production, employment and income generation, and skills acquisition through educational assistance. CARE's projects normally rely on simple, appropriate, low-technology interventions which do not require expensive inputs and maintenance. CARE also promotes activities which can be sustained by individual families, groups or communities which find the activity worthwhile to continue on their own. Projects or activities dependent on continued outside support are avoided. In all projects, CARE maintains close collaboration with the government of Kenya at all levels, especially with the District Development Committees.

Currently, CARE is undertaking projects in the sectors of Primary Education, Youth Polytechnic Education, Water Supply, Health Education and Sanitation, Agroforestry, Women's Income Generation and AIDS Education.

# HISTORICAL BRIEF

The *Pied Crow* magazine began its life as an environmental magazine for primary schools, distributing natural resource conservation and environmental education materials throughout Kenya. Following various studies of the needs and the best channels for providing these materials to schools, the African Wildlife Foundation (AWF) proposed an initial three-year pilot project to CARE-Kenya in 1983 for an Environment Special Magazine project. The magazine's format was 16 pages of cartoons, text and pull-out posters. The issues were to be published six times every year and distributed to all primary schools in Kenya, with the aim of reaching pupils between 11 and 14 years of age.

Until January 1985, the magazine was published in collaboration with *The Rainbow*, a monthly children magazine of Kenya's *Weekly Review*. In 1984 the project was evaluated and from 1985, AWF began publishing the *Pied Crow* Environment Special magazine independently of *The Rainbow*. The production of the magazine moved from AWF to direct CARE-Kenya supervision in 1986.

The magazine has been and is still being published in English despite the fact that Kiswahili is the national language and is spoken in the offices and in schools as the medium of instruction.

# PRIMARY EDUCATION IN KENYA

The national ideology for all planned learning seems to be amalgamation of Lawton's two major categories – the classical and the romantic ideologies (Lawton, 1973, 1978). It is classical in the sense that it looks into the richness of the culture, emphasizes examinations and encourages competition, as national documents of educational matters indicate:

> education must foster, develop and communicate the rich and varied cultural heritage of the people of Kenya . . . prepare and equip the youth . . . with the knowledge, skills and expertise necessary to enable them collectively to play an effective role in the life of the nation.
>
> (Ministry of Education, 1981: 6)

The ideology may be described as romantic in that it focuses attention on the child, helping him or her to develop his or her abilities and form his or her own world-views independently: 'education for . . . full development of the individual talents and personality' (Ministry of Education, 1984: 13).

In reality the educational system is more classical than romantic, therefore very rigid and relatively less open to rapid change. However, change is a natural phenomenon and any education system, whether rigid or flexible, constantly undergoes changes. A natural change basically is like the evolution of species: it takes a long, unplanned and irregular path. Curriculum change, on the other hand, is similar to plant breeding. It is planned over time to produce a particular variety – the learned generation.

There is a long history of educational and curricular changes in Kenya. The most notable ones, in brief, have followed from the Beecher Report of 1949, the Ominde Commission of 1964, the Gachathi Report of 1976 and the Presidential Working Party on Second University of 1981.

The Beecher Report dealt with educational and curricular reforms during the colonial era. The Ominde Commission and the Gachathi Report recommended renovation of the colonial educational system to suit the realities of the newly independent nation. After years of implementation of the recommendations of these reports, it became clear that something was still amiss with the educational system. Lack of gainful employment among young people and wastefulness of educational resources, in terms of school dropouts, are two examples.

The general opinion was that the curriculum in existence just after independence was influenced by the needs of a small minority of students who would eventually proceed to universities. It was argued that practical and vocational subjects were not given the emphasis they deserved. The curriculum had to be changed to cater for the majority of students who will conclude their education at primary or secondary level.

With this background in mind, the Presidential Working Party on the Second University was appointed in 1981. Its task was to consider the best possible way of establishing a second university in Kenya and to make suitable prescriptions for the educational malady. One of its major recommendations was that the education system in the country should be restructured from the then 7–4–2–3 system (seven years of primary, four years of secondary, two years of pre-university and three years of university education) to the 8–4–4 system. The latter means eight years of primary, four years of secondary and a minimum of four years of university education. The government accepted the recommendation and the 8–4–4 system of education was initiated in 1985. At the same time the curriculum was broadened to include vocational subjects such as agriculture, woodwork, metalwork, masonry, commercial subjects and others.

The fundamental question being asked by experts and lay people in Kenyan society is whether the changes will develop young Kenyans to fit into society as it is, or develop them to seek and improve it. Modern education should strike a balance. We need an educational system which helps young people to understand their society well enough to get along and work effectively in it, while striving to improve it. If Kenyan youth can be taught effectively to think like environmentalists, to be instilled with scrupulous questing for truth, and to be made more sensitive to environmental matters through scientific experiments, they will be in a better position to improve and change the nation.

Pocztar (1972), Webster (1976), Beecher et al. (1978) and Beeby (1980) all warn of the problems of bringing about any change. New ideas, in education as in life, travel hopefully: many of them become casualties before their intended destinations. This is due to a tendency of education, like religion, to hallow antiquity rather than promote innovation.

Change in any curriculum is a complex and delicate process. The steps that are taken to solve old problems may sometimes result in the precipitation of a similar set of problems. Within the education sector in Kenya, impressive strides have been achieved. By combining government, community *harambee* (self-help), donor and other non-governmental resources, primary education is available for 90 per cent of school-age children. This achievement is particularly impressive given the high population growth rate in Kenya, which has resulted in an ever-increasing number of children needing education. Currently, over 60 per cent of the national population is under 16 years of age.

Already there are indications that the recent curriculum changes are not matched by the training, retraining or in-service education of teachers in the country. The system of cost-sharing in education in Kenya, translated into practice, means that while all teachers' salaries, basic curriculum and school milk programmes in primary schools are provided by the government, almost all other inputs must be obtained by communities, or through other external assistance. This includes the construction of school buildings, the provision of desks, equipment, books, uniforms and other recurrent costs.

Without question, parents and communities are overburdened and unable to provide adequate facilities and materials for their primary schools. In many poorer areas of Kenya, a meagre mud and thatch building, which lacks any equipment, books or materials, graphically represents the physical facilities available for the rural poor.

While the 8–4–4 system covers a wide range of subjects, which students have to study and pass in order to be admitted into institutions of higher education, the majority of the primary school teachers have little more than junior secondary education. Thirty per cent of them are untrained. The immediate results of all these problems are that school leavers have received inadequate education and are ill-prepared for a productive life. Figure 1 shows the 8–4–4 structure of education.

# THE *PIED CROW* ENVIRONMENT SPECIAL MAGAZINE

The design and production of the *Pied Crow* Environment Special Magazine recognizes that the school provides an organized education and operates in a social system. The design of the magazine must therefore draw on, or otherwise be related to, the life experiences of the target group who are still in primary school. These children are at a very critical point in their lives; for many, education is about to conclude and a productive life begin.

Pupils of this age are at a formative stage, entering their teens, curious about life and developing their ideas for the future. In this respect, it is an ideal age

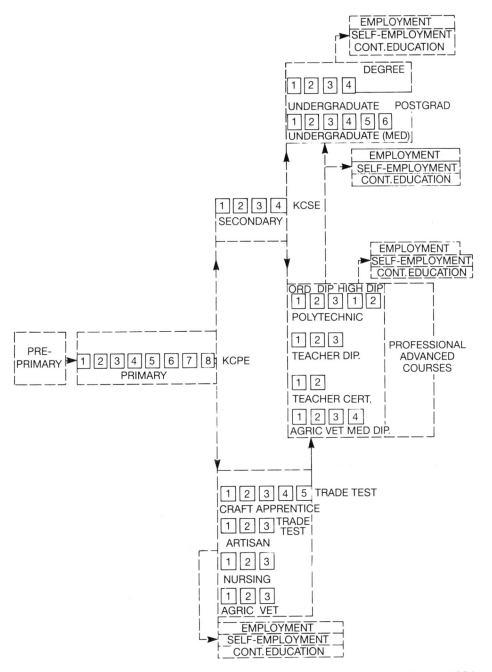

**Figure 1** Structure of education 8–4–4    *Source:* Ministry of Education, Kenya, 1984.

group to target for the provision of life skills, environmental and health education information.

Another target group is primary school teachers. Teachers are not only the educators but often also the model for young people. Armed with appropriate attitudes and knowledge and provided with practical teaching materials,

215

teachers can have a tremendously positive impact on the development of children. Teachers' general awareness becomes a focal point around which major efforts must be concentrated if the magazine is to be successful in changing attitudes and increasing the knowledge of pupils.

Most of our teachers still stand in front of the class, command attention, then talk and chalk. They set a pace which, in their opinion, suits the majority in the class, but leaves the front-runners bored stiff and crawlers agape. This teaching style is mainly due to the kind of general education the teachers themselves have had. Many have had no more than secondary schooling, with little or no period of professional training that might have exposed them to more enlightened teaching methods or resources than those they were subjected to during their own schooling. The *Pied Crow* magazine, therefore, is handy as a development education spice. The objectives for targeting teachers in this project may be summed up as:

1  to provide supplementary resources for the training, retraining or in-service education of teachers, in order to bring a gradual shift from teacher-centred to child-centred approaches in environmental teaching;

2  to bring about change by altering teachers' attitudes through their continuing education in environmental matters.

The *Pied Crow* magazine has been enthusiastically received by local education personnel, teachers and, not least, by children. It has been widely praised by government officials, donors and other development collaborators as a unique environment magazine for children. However, this achievement would not have been possible without the generous financial support from overseas donors.

In particular, the Canadian International Development Agency (CIDA), through CARE-Canada, and the Overseas Development Administration (ODA), through CARE-Britain, have supported the *Pied Crow* magazine since 1987. Other donors include the Norwegian government (NORAD), UNICEF, the Dulverton Trust, the Ford Foundation and the World Health Organization (WHO), which have each provided significant support to the project.

The *Pied Crow* magazine project, over the years, has been managed by a small core staff of six (project co-ordinator, art director, studio manager, secretary, clerk and a driver) under the management structure of CARE-Kenya. The team, led by the project co-ordinator and assisted by the art director, manages the project finances and logistics, and ensures quality artwork, timely production and distribution of the magazine.

The managerial practice adopted by staff is management by objectives (MBOs). The project co-ordinator and the team sit down and discuss an agreed plan of activities over a given period of time. This includes line items to be accomplished (for example, printing of the magazine), their quality, cost and the time involved. After the agreed time, the group reconvenes to assess its achievements and failures. Reasons for not achieving the agreed objectives are then scrutinized in order to improve performance.

The practice admittedly has some shortcomings, such as the lengthy discussions needed to reach consensus; nevertheless, it has enabled the project to achieve its planned objectives to a high degree. It gives the staff a feeling of participation in management and decision-making processes, instead of being recipients of orders from above.

In Kenya, curriculum development and support have been based on a centre–periphery model with a centralized institution deciding all curricular matters and teachers acting as recipients.

The *Pied Crow* magazine project has to operate with this in mind in order to bring about change without necessarily disturbing the power relationships between individuals or institutions. The *Pied Crow* staff have therefore worked closely with the Ministry of Education Inspectorate and the Kenya Institute of Education (the national curriculum development centre), in selecting subjects for the magazine.

Each issue of *Pied Crow* covers a specific topic, introduced by the comic book character that is the magazine's namesake. These topics generally fall under the headings of Natural Resources, Population Growth, Practical Skills, Health Education and Education for Life. *Pied Crow*, for example, has addressed the major environmental concern of deforestation by candidly telling children that chopping down too many trees will leave them without enough wood to build homes for their familes, for furniture, for newsprint for their books or fuel for the *jikos* (ovens). 'Kenya needs more trees, not just axes for chopping down trees', *Pied Crow* tells the kids; and he then shows them how to plant and care for seedlings. However, *Pied Crow*'s approach is not to confront children with global health and environmental issues which they are incapable of solving, but to stress community and action–orientated programmes which allow children to participate in local community projects.

Over the years, magazine themes and content have been developed for six issues of *Pied Crow* per annum. Development has been conducted in close collaborative editorial meetings with the Kenya Institute of Education (KIE), the Ministry of Education, CARE-Kenya staff and other relevant agencies and ministries.

Editorial meetings are run as brainstorming sessions, designed to develop story-lines which can be illustrated by the project's graphic artists. *Pied Crow* staff then produce sketches and text to be examined in subsequent editorial meetings. There is always considerable flexibility in designing broad aspects of the artwork and text, in order to accommodate the varied opinions of the editorial team.

One major drawback of this editorial arrangement was that it excluded readers from the production process. Experience has shown that top-down dissemination of ideas does not always work, owing to the fact that the 'experts' at the top are often ill-informed about needs and conditions at grassroot level. The inclusion of primary school teachers' and pupils' ideas has made the magazine more dynamic and remedied this potential weakness.

Annual magazine distribution to schools has grown steadily from a humble beginning of 212,000 to over 1.25 million copies (see Figure 2).

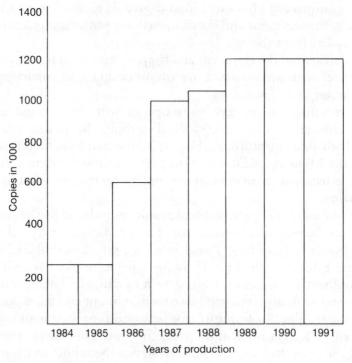

**Figure 2** Annual magazine distribution to schools

Final illustrations, text and colour separations are painstakingly completed by hand by project artists. The final artwork is then taken to a commercial printing firm which prints, packs and delivers the magazine to the Post Office, for distribution to over 14,000 schools throughout Kenya.

Current school readership is estimated to be over two and a half million children, the majority of whom are in the rural areas where the magazine is the only supplementary reading material of its kind.

## MONITORING AND EVALUATION

There have been two major evaluations of *Pied Crow* magazine since its inception. These reviews were taken to assess progress-to-date in relation to planned output, the effectiveness of project activities, and the degree to which the project has met intermediate goals.

The latest, which was carried out in January 1991, revealed that pupils who regularly read the magazine scored significantly higher on a factual environmental test and displayed a more positive attitude towards the environment than those who had not. This is an important development in Kenya, where much of the land is either arid or semi–desert and where productive land is at risk of destruction through inappropriate use.

As the project enters its third phase in late 1991, past experiences have enabled the formulation of realistic intermediate goals. Evaluation of these goals during and after the end of the phase in 1996 will reveal the extent of the project's success. For example, one of the project's intermediate goals is 'the regular delivery and effective use of appropriate curriculum support materials, focusing on life skills, to every primary school in Kenya by 1996'. In order to evaluate such a goal effectively, some measurable indicators have been formulated. These include:

1  the number of *Pied Crow* issues delivered to primary schools throughout the country;

2  the percentages of primary school teachers throughout the country who regularly utilize the magazine as a teaching material;

3  the number of readers' letters which indicate positive reactions to the magazine;

4  the percentage of primary school leavers throughout the country who, at the time of leaving school, remember the topics of at least one of the issues of the *Pied Crow* curriculum support magazine.

The last indicator will have to take into account changes of behaviour due to sources of information other than the magazine, and the time involved. Bringing about changes in behaviour is like tending coconut trees; as any gardener will tell you, there is always a time lapse between planting and fruition. We cannot have the desired changes overnight.

The *Pied Crow* Magazine Unit receives many letters, at a rate of 60 per week, from magazine readers all over the world. Locally, recognition of its need and usefulness have been repeatedly stressed by pupils and administrators of various institutions. Some of the letters show the impact of the magazine on readers. Since the piper calls the tune, it is not surprising that we receive very many letters praising the magazine and asking for more – free of charge! Figure 3 shows an example of such a letter.

## CONCLUSION

Global environmental concern and the health problems faced in developing countries provide considerable motivation for intervention by all people of good will. The role played by *Pied Crow* Environment Special Magazine in introducing changes in environmental awareness at primary level is, in effect,

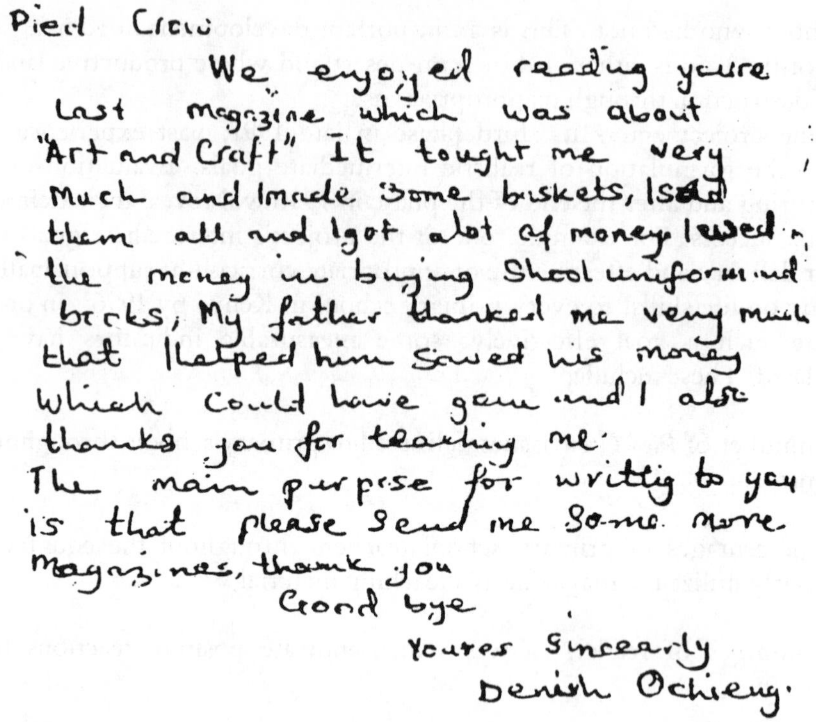

Pied Crow

We enjoyed reading youre last magazine which was about "Art and Craft" It tought me very much and Imade some biskets, Isold them all and Igot alot of money Iused in the money in buying Shool uniform and books, My father thanked me very much that Ihelped him saved his money which could have gaue and I also thanks you for teaching me. The main purpose for writting to you is that please send me some more magazines, thank you
        Good bye
                Youres Sinceartly
                        Denish Ochieng.

**Figure 3** Example of a child's letter

an endeavour to bring about much-needed changes in Kenyan society, through education.

In the short term, piecemeal reforms and innovations seem the most likely immediate developments arising from the *Pied Crow* Environment Special Magazine programme. In the longer term, with proper training of teachers and with proper guidance among Kenya's youth on environmental issues, action taken now may become a key experience in future global conservation.

# REFERENCES

Beecher, T. et al. (1978), *The Politics of Curriculum Change*, London: Hutchinson.

Beeby, C. E. (1980), *The Quality of Education in Developing Countries*, Cambridge, MA: Harvard University Press.

CARE-Kenya (1990), *Multi-year Plan Project Proposal: Pied Crow Skills for Life Magazine Project*, Nairobi, CARE-Kenya.

Lawton, D. (1973), *Social Change, Education Theory and Curriculum Planning*, London: University of London Press.

Lawton, D. et al. (1978), *Theory and Practice of Curriculum Studies*, London: Routledge and Kegan Paul.

Ministry of Education (1981), *The McKay Report*, Nairobi: Government Press.

Ministry of Education (1984), *8–4–4 System of Education*, Nairobi: Government Press.

Ministry of Education (1986), *Development of Education 1984–1986*, Country Report, Nairobi: Government Press.

Pocztar, J. (1972), *The Theory and Practice of Programmed Instruction*, Paris: Unesco.

Webster, J. R. (1976), 'Curriculum changes and crisis', *British Journal of Educational Studies*, **24** (3), 202–18.

CHAPTER 13

# What Is the Value of a Study Visit for In-Service Education?

*Catherine McFarlane*

This chapter explores the value of a study visit for in-service education. It draws on the experience of a group of 10 primary teachers who visited Kenya and Tanzania for a month as part of a longer course looking at teaching about other places in the primary school. The chapter explores some of the key features of this method of in-service, offers some ideas for using this approach and looks at the strengths and weaknesses of using a visit for teacher education.

Recent changes in education in England, such as the introduction of a National Curriculum, have created a demand for greater in-service opportunities for teachers. The majority of short-term courses on offer are directed at immediate classroom needs or skills. Longer-term courses for further qualifications for career advancement are also available. Development education is not seen as a priority in most in-service courses designed to support the statutory curriculum.

In this context a study visit in-service course can offer teachers a different kind of experience of in-service. This chapter explores some of the qualities of such a course for in-service education from the perspective and interests of development education.

## COURSE AIMS

In summer 1989, a group of teachers visited communities in Kenya and Tanzania for a month. This study visit served as a focal point of a two-year inservice course. The course was initiated by the Development Education Centre (DEC) in Birmingham. DEC is an educational charity which works with local groups of teachers to explore ways of introducing a development perspective to the curriculum. The course was set up in response to the growing awareness among primary teachers of the importance of children being aware of, and sensitive to, the world outside their immediate neighbourhood and the need for creative thinking on teaching and methodology. It was designed to:

- stimulate creative work on what it is appropriate to teach primary children about distant places;
- produce classroom materials for 9–11-year-olds about Kenya and Tanzania;
- bring teachers together from two parts of England (Birmingham and Hertfordshire) to share their experiences;
- provide an opportunity for personal and professional development.

The course was widely advertised and attracted a great deal of interest. A group of five teachers from each area was selected; with two leaders, this made a total of 12 in the group.

The course fell into three phases: the preparation before the visit; the visit itself; and the synthesis and reflection on the learning stimulated by the visit. In this final stage the teachers worked on developing materials for a wider audience. These classroom materials, *New Journeys* (McFarlane and Osler, 1991), were published two years after the visit.

# PRELIMINARY VISIT

The course was organized and facilitated jointly by two leaders. They had previously worked together running in-service; both had travelled in the South, staying with families or friends; one of the leaders had participated in a previous study visit run by DEC and had also travelled in Kenya and Tanzania; this was a key factor in choosing the location for the visit.

The leaders set up the study visit by making a short preparatory visit four months in advance. They only spent ten days because of other work commitments, and therefore decided to organize only the Kenya part of the visit. This was to be where the teachers would stay first; the infrastructure in Kenya made travelling and communication easier than in Tanzania. The Tanzania visit was set up by the leaders immediately beforehand, while the teachers were in their second week, staying in different parts of Kenya. This had some limitations but was the only realistic possibility given the circumstances; a slightly longer preparatory visit would have been ideal. This preliminary visit was vital to the success of the main visit for a number of reasons.

It would have been difficult to set up accommodation and meetings when a group as large as 12 first arrives in a place. It was important to many of the group that they knew where they would be staying and the kinds of people and places they would be visiting, at least in the first week or so. A number of teachers felt quite insecure about the visit and were reassured to some degree by the information gathered in the preliminary visit. It was important that the teachers felt confident about some of these practicalities, as the visit was set up as an open-ended learning experience, and other aspects would only unfold when they were in East Africa. The preliminary visit allowed the leaders to set up contacts which the teachers could follow up on their arrival. Making contacts is time-consuming and it was important that, at least in the early stages, the group had some fruitful contacts who were expecting them. Between the preliminary visit and the arrival of the whole group, arrangements were confirmed by letter and deposits paid on accommodation.

The teachers had met together before the preliminary visit and were able to talk to the leaders about the kinds of issues they would like to explore in East Africa and the organizations they would like to visit. This helped the leaders to set up initial meetings which might be of broad interest to the group.

However, more often than not, the opportunities for visits were linked with key contact people. In this particular study visit, the main contacts were people working in development agencies, such as Oxfam, and Kenyans involved in mainstream church-based community development. This was influenced by the leaders' backgrounds in the field of development education and by a range of personal contacts. The choice of initial contacts heavily influenced the shape of the visit; the visit would have been very different if the contacts had been expatriates, European hotel owners or families in the Sikh community.

The initial visit enabled the leaders to ask advice from Kenyans about sensitive issues such as appropriate behaviour in different situations. Two or three Kenyans were very frank about their expectations about how the teachers should behave and the kinds of ways they should prepare themselves. This advice was shared with the group and influenced the planning of the preparation phase of the course.

The group was to be split for a week and would stay in three venues in Kenya. The leaders were able to visit each place and negotiate a partnership with the 'hosts'. Several of the hosting organizations had particular require-ments about who should come to them. For instance, one organization requested that their visitors should be comfortable about staying in a Catholic community, attending mass and so on. They specifically asked for people who would be flexible, open-minded and able to 'rough it' if necessary.

This raised dilemmas for the leaders about whether they should allocate placements or allow the teachers to choose where to stay and with whom. After much debate, they decided to place people. Although this caused some conflict with some of the group it was felt to be the best way of taking the Kenyans' requests seriously.

## PREPARATION

The group was selected to include both experienced and inexperienced teachers, and experienced and totally inexperienced travellers. This was a conscious choice and as time unfolded people in the group were able to support and learn from each other. However, given the diverse strengths and weaknesses of the group, the preliminary visit raised some difficult issues about appropriate preparation. As a result, the preparation weekends covered a wide range of material including sharing classroom practice, practicalities about the visit, discussion on development issues and reading East African novels. The preparation stage of the course is documented and analysed fully elsewhere (Osler, 1992).

## THE VISIT

The group spent four weeks in Kenya and Tanzania; the time was structured as a course. They met regularly to share how they were feeling, their reactions, and what they were learning. Although there were many informal conversations between group members about what they were experiencing, these meetings allowed for more structured reflection.

The first few days were spent acclimatizing in Nairobi. The group were encouraged to wander around the city in pairs without cameras, to 'soak in' the atmosphere. Visits to development agencies such as Oxfam, KENGO (a Kenyan environmental NGO) and Undugu (a local organization working in the shanty town areas of the city) gave insights into urban development programmes. These visits also offered an insight into how national and international agencies viewed the situation in Kenya as a whole.

The second stage of the visit involved dividing into smaller groups and spending a week in different parts of Kenya. One group, for example, stayed in a small town and another joined a project working with the urban poor. During this period the group, however briefly, experienced the daily lives of the communities in which they were staying.

At the end of this time everyone travelled to Arusha, a large town in northern Tanzania. Here the group undertook similar activities to those in Nairobi. Two days were set aside for a meeting and reflection on what had taken place so far. The last few days of the visit were spent relaxing in Dar es Salaam and Zanzibar, preparing for the journey home.

## THE FOLLOW-UP

On returning to England, the group met for five weekends over a period of eighteen months. In the time between these weekends, they tried out ideas in the classroom, tested photographs and ran courses to share their experiences with others. The meetings were structured to enable the group to reflect on their learning and the implications for teaching. They decided that it was worth sharing some of the practical classroom ideas with other teachers through a set of colour photographs and a teachers' handbook, *New Journeys*. The task of developing ideas and writing materials focused the group's attention and sharpened discussions.

# QUALITIES OF THE COURSE

The model of this visit/course was based on other study visit in-service courses run by DEC; these have been documented by Harber (1986, 1987). It appears significantly different from many others which involve teachers or others travelling for short periods of time to the 'Third World' on study tours or exchanges. Often study tours involve large groups moving around together, following an itinerary, planned well in advance. The focus is usually on the time spent in the place visited with little emphasis on preparing for the visit or on reflection, during the visit or afterwards. This study visit in-service course was designed with a greater emphasis on experiencing and reflecting. A number of features are central.

The course offered a structured context to experience and reflect on individually and as a group. While many teachers travel, few have the opportunity to pause for reflection and to hear other people's perceptions and experiences. Reflection was a vital element of the course. Sometimes it took the form of people writing entries in their 'public' diary; people agreed at the beginning of the course to write a diary at significant points of the course which they would later be willing to share.

It also meant meeting together to talk about what they were learning and experiencing. This was vital to the whole process; for example, there was some resistance to using a whole day in Tanzania for talking about how what the teachers had learned might influence their teaching back home, but the thinking that came out of this meeting shaped the direction of the rest of the project. Undertaking that kind of thinking while in East Africa sharpened the group's minds far more than it would have done at home.

The course was designed as a process which unfolded as it progressed, building on what had gone before. Although there was a general plan at the beginning, the leaders used the participants' views and experiences to shape the course. This is similar to the 'user involvement' model (Clay et al., 1990) which allows members some opportunities to feed into the course, but not adopt complete control. The 'self-advocacy' model of in-service explored in the same article allows participants more of a voice and a wider say about the direction of the course. This was a central tension in the planning and running of the course, as arguably the model the leaders used frustrated some of the teachers from time to time; however, a self-advocacy model might have been less challenging.

The course involved teachers meeting in their own time, over a period of two and a half years. This included weekends, after-school meetings and a month away in East Africa. The sheer amount of time involved allowed people to work intensively through ideas, test them out, reflect with others. The initial commitment was to meet for four weekends. In the event, the teachers chose to come to three further weekends.

The course was designed to challenge how children learn about 'Third World' countries and therefore it was important that the visit was to

226

somewhere in the South. A number of factors influenced the choice of places to visit: English was widely spoken in both Kenya and Tanzania; they were neighbouring countries which had followed very different development policies since independence; and they were relatively inexpensive to travel to.

The course was designed to expose a group of teachers to life in two other countries and not as a fact-finding mission. It was set up in this way for several reasons:

- A group of teachers visiting for a month would be ill-qualified to collect information about two places about which they knew very little.
- This kind of detailed information is widely documented in journals and books.
- It is best communicated from the perspectives of Kenyans and Tanzanians.

The teachers could, however, experience something of these two places, listen to the views of people in East Africa and reflect on these experiences in the light of teaching children here about them. With hindsight it would have been useful to discuss these issues explicitly as a group in the early stages of the course. As it was, there were different interpretations within the group about how far they were experiencing life in Kenya and Tanzania and how far they were finding out information. This was not as polarized as the experience identified by Harber (1986: 136) in his evaluation of a similar study visit for geography teachers. To some degree this interpretation also reflected the teaching philosophies of different group members.

One of the central elements of the course was to look at society in Kenya and Tanzania rather than to concentrate on visiting schools. The teachers visited health centres, environmental and agricultural organizations, women's projects and community groups. It was often assumed, both in East Africa and in England, that they would be mainly interested in visiting schools. Although the few visits to schools were interesting, the wider perspectives on society confirmed their choice.

One of the outcomes of this decision was that the group did not address development issues as effectively as it might have done. As part of the preparation the group were encouraged to read material on development issues but, because this reading was not followed up by group discussions, it resulted in some superficial judgements. This also raised issues about how far the teachers saw their role as political and what form this should take in the classroom.

The fact that the course was organized by a small educational charity had a significant effect on the style, on funding and on the teachers' commitment. The project was run on a 'shoestring' budget, covering the bills and some of the costs of the leader employed by the DEC; the teachers and the other leader met in their own time. Had there been financial remuneration for this the cost of the course would have been prohibitive. Equally, it would probably have changed the nature of the course and the quality and enthusiasm of the commitment of the teachers. The voluntary time offered by the teachers and leaders made the course cost-effective, in terms of actual revenue needed.

Other outcomes included the flexibility which voluntary sector organizations have; teachers had the freedom to think about issues outside the formal structure of the local education authority (LEA). Although the course did receive some financial support from the LEAs involved and the teachers had the support of their headteachers, it was not seen as a priority for the LEAs or the schools involved. Each teacher, therefore, was involved through his or her interest in the challenge of the course; this led to a very committed and self-motivated group.

## MEMBERSHIP OF THE GROUP

Teachers from Hertfordshire and Birmingham were invited to apply for the course by letter. Each applicant was interviewed and the final group selected using a wide range of criteria; for example, people who would be open-minded and flexible about the experience; those who would be able to cope with a month away in an unknown place without home comforts; those who could work as a team. The leaders were also looking for a balance of experiences and perspectives. The group came from different educational standpoints; for example, one successful applicant wrote:

> I firmly believe in child-centred education and in the value of building upon children's direct experience . . . Children need to understand basic concepts such as similarity and difference, co-operation and interdependence, change or causation to arrive at a true picture of their own country or any other. Just to learn content, i.e. what food, climate, clothes, houses, etc. are like in another country, may not accurately convey how that country is, how it is developing and what has caused those changes.

Another saw her role differently:

> My role, were I to succeed on this course, would be to channel children's enthusiasm by bringing them factual information and moreover understanding of the issues which I believe first-hand experience can alone promote.

These different standpoints illustrate the spectrum of perspectives within the group. The course sought to accommodate such different standpoints in order to encourage real debate about development education in the classroom. These views sometimes caused tension within the group, but when this was brought into the open it offered more creative opportunities than if the group had been more homogeneous.

The group consisted of ten women and two men; this reflects the applications, and to a large extent, the population of primary teachers in England. Unlike a previous study visit to The Gambia (Harber, 1986: 139), in which there were nine men and two women, the group found it easy to gain access to Kenyan and Tanzanian women. Issues about the gender balance of the group are explored further by Osler (1992).

One of the strengths of the group was the variety of personal and professional experiences of the group members, who taught in both rural and urban schools and in predominantly white and culturally diverse communities. It is worth stressing how the experience of the study visit was enriched by the contributions and perspectives of the three black group members, who in different ways gave the group access to people and viewpoints they might otherwise have missed. Each of the black women experienced East Africa differently from their white colleagues and to some extent from each other. They were able to offer each other mutual support, especially when their white colleagues were unable to appreciate their different perspectives.

One of the group was a Sikh woman who had lived in Kenya until she was eight and for whom this was a first return visit. She had access to the Sikh community in Nairobi, because of relatives who lived there; however, she also found that when she was alone she had easier access to the Asian community in the places she stayed. She reminded people that Kenya and Tanzania were multicultural societies facing some of the tensions about economic power and discrimination found in England.

Another group member was Ghanaian. She wrote:

As a West African I would like to know a little more about another part of Africa, the life style of the people, languages, education system and development. This will help me to draw a comparison to help children and staff here gain a wider picture of the richness and complexity of the different countries in Africa.

This woman was particularly knowledgeable about the political background to life in these countries and was able to offer insights from her own wide experience.

The third participant, of mixed European–Asian descent, found many East Africans curious about her background. This sometimes led quickly into some interesting discussion on intercultural issues; for example, the position of the Asian community and the Swahili coastal culture.

It is interesting to note that since the return to England, many of the group have moved on in their professional life; five have had promotion, two have left teaching and one has moved into a new area of education. This suggests that the kinds of people who apply for this style of in-service course are continually looking for challenges in their personal and professional lives.

These experiences confirmed the leaders' initial ideas that it is important, as far as possible, to select a balanced group. The qualities of flexibility and open-mindedness are vital, although difficult to identify. They were surprised how people reacted when they were away from home and how difficult it would have been in advance to predict which group members had the internal reserves and security to make the most of the visit. Some people found it difficult to be away from home and to be placed in a new role making a number of emotional and practical demands on them.

# VALUE FOR CURRICULUM DEVELOPMENT

The study visit and the course together were designed not only for the personal and professional development of the teachers involved but with a wider purpose. From the outset there was a commitment to devising approaches and materials which could be used by teachers who had not had the opportunity to be involved in the course. These were shared in the form of *New Journeys*, a teachers' handbook and colour photopack. The task of sharing the experience through materials also helped to justify the cost of the course. Harber (1987) explores a similar kind of outcome from another study visit.

This task was a strong motivating factor for the group. Equally, the study visit acted as a shared experience which bonded the group together. For example, on returning to England, many of the group found it difficult to explain what they had experienced to family, friends and colleagues. For many it was a relief to meet as a group again where there was a shared understanding. As the group had relied on each other in East Africa, they continued to rely on each other in a different way on their return. This resulted in a strong group commitment which gave the teachers the energy and impetus to work creatively on curriculum possibilities.

The task of how to share thinking with a wider audience focused the teachers' discussions and gave a real purpose for meeting. The process of writing materials helped clarify thoughts and ideas. It meant that the group had to argue out points and challenge each other, continually reminding each other of what they had experienced and what might or might not be practical in the classroom. The element of identifying a task which involved disseminating some of the learning was therefore very important to the design of the whole course.

However, in this course there were tensions between the in-service and the curriculum development. The most effective material which came out of the project was developed when the teachers were able to translate what they had learned from East Africa into imaginative classroom practice. Difficulties arose when the two failed to connect, for example when teachers built on their previous classroom practice without making reference to what they had learnt in East Africa, or when they translated an oversimplified understanding, for example about colonial history, or interdependence, into classroom practice.

# OUTCOMES

Evaluation took place throughout the course and influenced how it developed. At the end of the course, the teachers were invited to evaluate the course as a whole, including the visit. The length of the course allowed the teachers to cover a wide range of material:

It was just the beginning; lots of new questions have been raised, much more than I had imagined.

It gave me a valuable insight into the danger of judging people and situations too rapidly.

This visit raised many questions for me which I did not expect in terms of life style, spirituality, faith in human relationships, etc. I found it challenging, hard to come to any conclusions, and inspiring.

The visit exposed the teachers to life in another part of the world, however briefly. They had access to people, organizations and situations normally out of reach of travellers. This direct experience challenged many of their ideas about the 'Third World' and development issues. One of the unquantifiable outcomes of a study visit is the sustained interest which the group have developed about the places they visited and about the issues which they have encountered. This is especially interesting when it is noted that the leaders felt that this element was not addressed wholly successfully in the course.

The course also included a strong emphasis on classroom practice, methodology and content. On many occasions the teachers talked about what they had been doing in the classroom and bounced ideas off each other. In the final evaluation of the course, group members wrote:

Sharing teaching approaches has been extremely valuable.

The course has heightened my awareness of what I am teaching about and what I am teaching for.

Several of the group were challenged by the notion of teaching about other places. In the preparation stage, one teacher argued strongly that it was not appropriate to teach children about other places except through broad concepts such as change or media awareness. The course challenged her thinking about the place knowledge might play in children's learning and how this might be appropriately introduced.

Other members of the group began to see the importance of teaching about issues and the complexity of them; they realized that because of the complexity and the danger of content overload, skills for approaching this were important; for example, skills at recognizing bias, acknowledging that there would be diverse experiences in any one place, and so on.

It is interesting to note that the course leaders had also hoped that as well as personal and professional development, there would be changes in the schools in which the group worked. This was of limited success with little concrete evidence of change. Some of the teachers hoped their involvement in the project would change staff attitudes, while one or two shared their experiences more formally through school-based in-service. Arguably, for this to happen more effectively, more structured attention needs to be paid to this aspect and more concrete support offered. For instance, the group might have designed a standard one-hour in-service session to run in their own schools.

One of the aims of the course was to share ideas with a wider audience. *New Journeys*, the photopack and teachers' handbook produced by the group, offers ideas for teaching about distant places, using the examples of Kenya and Tanzania. The style of the publication reflects the ethos of the whole course. It seeks to offer starting points, practical classroom strategies and support for teachers, without being prescriptive. It is designed to be used in many different ways and to inspire teachers' own ideas. The materials therefore encourage the continuation of the process of creative thinking started by the course.

# CONCLUSION

The model of a study visit in-service course explored in this chapter builds on the idea that a group visit to another place can offer a valuable focus for learning. In this case a study visit enabled a group of teachers to learn from each other and from the people whom they met whilst in East Africa. They learned about themselves, about development and some of the implications for education. As an element of an in-service course, a study visit can provide a stimulus for creative work. When a study visit is planned and structured carefully it can offer a personal focus and group reflection which can have a major impact on people's lives.

# REFERENCES

Clay, J., Cole, M. and Hill, D. (1990), 'Black achievement in initial teacher education – how do we proceed into the 1990s?' *Multicultural Teaching*, **8** (3), 31–5.

Harber, C. (1986), 'Development education in context: an evaluation of the West Midlands–West Africa project', *International Journal of Educational Development*, **6** (2), 133–41.

Harber, C. (1987), 'The West Midlands–West Africa project: a teacher-led inservice course', *British Journal of Inservice Education*, **13** (2), 86–90.

McFarlane, C. and Osler, A. (eds) (1991), *New Journeys: Teaching about Other Places. Learning from Kenya and Tanzania*, Birmingham: Development Education Centre.

Osler, A. (1992) 'New journeys in development education: preparing teachers for a study visit', *Educational Review*, **44** (1), 59–72.

# CHAPTER 14

# Development Education in France: The Role of Unesco Clubs

*André Zweyacker*

## DEFINITIONS OF DEVELOPMENT

When we use the term 'development education' before an audience of non-specialists – or even specialists – we are inevitably asked what we mean by development or development education.

Clearly, there is no single answer. By a not uncommon paradox, attempts have been made to express the concept by referring to its opposite: for more than 40 years, descriptive criteria and analysis have been applied to the concept of underdevelopment. This has not, however, produced a really satisfactory answer to questions concerning the nature of development.

The term 'development', originally borrowed from physiology, was quickly taken up by economists, often in conjunction with 'growth'. This opened the way to all sorts of quantified measurements used by organizations such as the World Bank. The truth of the matter is that the concept of development is multidimensional, since it covers simultaneously the economic, demographic, social and cultural aspects of present-day societies. Its scope is collective, in that it concerns the whole of society within a given territory, but it also has an individual side since it involves the personal fulfilment of each member of the community.

Development is thus an essentially dynamic and evolving concept that cannot be understood in purely quantitive and economic terms as it also incorporates an increasing number of qualitative, especially cultural, factors: this is what we call the 'cultural dimension of development'. The failure to take this dimension into account has been the downfall of many development projects.

Development is governed not only by the internal structures of society but also by a series of interrelationships and interdependence perceived at the global level, so that to study the so-called developing countries in isolation is not enough; what is needed is a dialectical approach that marries the local and the more distant, the familiar and the different, without forgetting a re-examination of one's own development. As development is an unfinished process, we cannot speak of developed counties; for the countries of the North, it would be more accurate to use the term 'industrialized countries'.

When we interpret it as a process, we can point to a few definitions: 'development is the taking of responsibility by a group of human beings for the transformation of economic, political, social and cultural living conditions'. According to the economist Carfentan, development is 'the capacity to control change while safeguarding the essence of one's identity: a society is under-developed when it is incapable of reacting positively to the major changes taking place around it'.

# DEVELOPMENT AND HUMAN RIGHTS

It is also potentially useful to regard development as one of the goals of a society's efforts: the transformation into reality, for each and every individual within a society, community or state, of human rights as they are universally defined. This is of course an idealistic vision, but it reminds us that the source and the goal of development are the human race and that means and ends should not be confused.

The implication is that all the rights of the human person must be taken into account, their indivisibility asserted. Thus, in questions of development, we must pay attention not only to economic and social rights – entitlements in regard to the state – but also to civil and political rights. In the 1960s, shortly after the arrival on the scene of many newly independent states, it was thought that the really important factor was economic growth and that the very idea of democracy could be regarded as a luxury. Experience has shown that totalitarian forms of government were no better at resolving economic problems and frequently entailed a very heavy human, social and financial cost. The fact that the essential agents of development are humans themselves, provided they are in a position to play that role and enjoy their rights in a climate of freedom, had been forgotten.

It is also important to take into account aspirations towards new rights which, in the name of solidarity, refer explicitly to the right of development, to a healthy environment, to the common heritage of humankind, and to peace.

Development and environment are becoming more and more closely associated. People are becoming increasingly aware of the importance of environmental issues within the concept of development. The linking of development and environment creates some new problems as well as ways forward; the environment raises practical problems for development, while development provides an overall frame of reference for environmental concerns.

# DEVELOPMENT EDUCATION

Development education thus means taking into account all aspects of development in a global context. This of course does not rule out studies based on a range of geographical or social scales but it does mean that attention should not be focused on developing countries alone, as tends to happen when the emphasis is on stimulating awareness of Third World issues.

In this context, what objectives may be assigned to development education?

## Knowledge objectives

- Knowledge, on different geographical and political scales, of development in action, of examples of development and its impact on the environment, and of various societies and peoples confronted with the problems of development.
- An understanding of the relations which exist between political, geopolitical, demographic, economic, social and cultural factors applied to organized societies, of the global network of interdependence, of the mechanisms of international economic relations that create imbalances and inequalities, and of the role of the international community and all those involved in international co-operation and solidarity.

It is easy to see the signal importance of information and documentation for the attainment of such objectives. Materials of all kinds are necessary, from a variety of sources, viewpoints and protagonists, on the basis of which comparative studies, critical appraisals and assessments of progress can be made which contribute to a dynamic body of up-to-date knowledge.

## Attitudinal objectives

- The fostering of cultural enrichment through an understanding of other ways of life and thought, and so a way forward to international understanding in a spirit of tolerance that rejects prejudice, racism and ethnocentric attitudes.

## Behavioural objectives

- Encouragement of initiative and responsibility.
- Encouragment of the planning and carrying through of projects: exchange schemes, especially those for young people; playing host to representatives from Third World countries, immigrant workers, students and personalities; co-operation with known and recognized partners; projects to promote solidarity through the initiation of, or involvement in, short-term or more long-term actions in Third World countries as well as projects in favour of minorities, refugees and the dispossessed in industrialized countries.

# UNESCO CLUBS AND DEVELOPMENT EDUCATION

## Unesco Clubs

Let us start with a brief reminder of the nature and objectives of Unesco Clubs. It was at the end of the 1940s that the Director-General of Unesco, Torres Bodet, proposed the creation of Unesco Clubs with the purpose of helping to promote in the general public and through public opinion, independently of official or governmental bodies, the ideals of the organization and its programmes.

These clubs for study and international relations bear the Unesco emblem but are independent of the organization. Unesco Clubs gradually increased in number, on the initiative of various personalities but chiefly teachers, until they reached the present-day figure of about 3,800 clubs in nearly 100 countries of the world. They are grouped into a World Federation of Unesco Associations, Centres and Clubs. Many of them are in schools and universities, but there also exist clubs and associations in cities and rural areas. They vary greatly, depending on the place, the local situation and the activities they offer.

The interest expressed by Unesco Clubs in development questions goes back a long way. For some of them it dates from the years of decolonization and independence; it quickly took the form of what was called at the time 'aid for the Third World' and mainly involved information on the nature of aid, which immediately led to questions such as what aid? for whom? and how?

Unesco Clubs' primary objective of dispensing development education springs from the very ideals they stand for, derived in turn from Unesco's constitution, which states that

> a peace based exclusively upon the political and economic arrangements of governments would not be a peace which could secure the unanimous, lasting and sincere support of the peoples of the world, and that the peace must therefore be founded, if it is not to fail, upon the intellectual and moral solidarity of mankind.

This ideal finds a natural outlet in the international relations maintained by the clubs. The responsiveness to international affairs and civic duties is promoted by a network of nationally and internationally co-ordinated clubs and associations, a network which transcends North–South and East–West divisions and is the starting-point for active co-operation.

Unesco's fields of competence lie at the very heart of development issues:

- education, the *sine qua non* of development, together with the right to education and literacy;
- science and technology and their effects;
- culture, which lies at the very centre of the development process, including a knowledge of the world's cultures and of their individual characteristics;
- communication, including the right to and means of communication.

This varied and complementary set of themes runs through all development issues in which clubs are able to participate through numerous programmes. Let us mention just two:

- One programme aims at *literacy for all* by the year 2000: numerous clubs have embarked on local or regional projects in support of this.
- Another concerns the World Decade for Cultural Development (1988–1997). This considers development as a series of actions to further the general welfare of populations, rooted in their own cultures and carried out with their direct participation. The Decade provides for the implementation of integrated development projects at community level, with particularly close attention being paid to the components and cultural impacts of economic and social development, in order to respond more effectively to the needs and aspirations of the populations concerned and to secure their active participation.

Possible themes for study include:

- scientific progress and cultural development;
- the preservation and enhancement of the cultural heritage;
- the creative evolution of cultures;
- culture as something that involves everyone;
- the fostering of creativity.

These themes represent opportunities for the promotion of international cultural co-operation and dialogue between cultures, and are without doubt among the main objectives of Unesco Club activities in which young people play a major role.

## Young people and development

With its theoretical and practical experience in development education in both formal and non-formal contexts, the French Federation of Unesco Clubs has tried to gain a better understanding of how young people perceive the Third World, and to gauge the positive or negative effects of such images through club activities or educational projects, gatherings of young people on this theme, teacher training courses and contacts with other instititutions in France and certain countries of the South.

Bernard Lecointe, one of the people who has co-ordinated activities of this kind, has analysed the question with considerable insight:

> The Third World, they know all about that. There flashes through the minds of young people an astonishing jumble of information amassed by chance from entreaties by the media, fleeting images, powerful yet blurred perceptions, vague recollections – a documentary on the advancing desert, a racist slogan on a wall, appeals just before Christmas to save 'them', the price of petrol dropping at the pump, a leaflet about a

four-star hotel in the Seychelles, a joke about cannibals, shanty towns or the local slum area, a scrap of song by Balavoine . . .

All this information, sometimes sought out but usually absorbed higgledy-piggledy, shapes the successive pieces of a jigsaw that young people use as a base for their opinions about the Third World. Most of the time, it triggers moral reactions and keeps myths alive: the Third World is seen as backwardness, inferiority, famine, infringements of human rights and corruption – and so they talk about the problems of the Third World; or they see it as exotic and think that 'black is beautiful'.

The information itself becomes blurred for the benefit of the media, which proposes – or imposes – its own reading of Third World realities. The message is coded for adults; without the key to that code, which can only come from constructive thinking on the subject, the young are simply putty in the hands of the media, and the marks run deep. Etched in the memory of each one of us is the unbearable distress of those bodies emptied of life, of those lives without hope. When dealing with a human calamity such as famine, the media shift the emphasis from information to sensationalism, from facts to their reverbation in people's hearts, revolt and the determination to take action. Such an approach to Third World issues is of course necessary since an emergency, by definition, brooks no delay and demands a rapid response and immediate commitment; but its undesirable side-effects in education quickly become apparent.

## ISSUES AND PROBLEMS OF DEVELOPMENT EDUCATION

As we have just seen, the difficulties spring from the subject itself, which creates mental images derived from a variety of sources, often bearing little relation to real life.

Development is unclassifiable in terms of models with clearly defined, constant and universally applicable criteria. The changing nature of development situations in the field has dented many of our certainties based on theories, ideologies and generalizations. When tested against the facts, many of the solutions proposed have proved to be totally inadequate. Today, we hardly dare any longer speak of clearly signposted and well-trodden paths to development. It is becoming increasingly hazardous to lay down rules that fit situations, to identify the scientific content of the information transmitted and to give an accurate account of the complexity of the factors involved.

The analysts' actual concepts have changed; not that this means it is now necessary to stop all general studies on the imbalances affecting the world, on the inegalitarian mechanisms of international economic relations, on the terms of trade or on the dissemination of information and communication. But it is necessary to treat them as relative, to reintegrate them into a framework of observations that are more precise, more concrete and more geographically specific and that take account of the diversity of situations.

Hence the importance of linking information as closely as possible to action, of understanding before taking action so as to avoid possible misadventures. It is an area which often plays on individual sensitivity. Poverty and injustice stimulate in young people a determination to take action which may not, in practice, be in keeping with the educational objectives for the project. This makes it essential to calm the legitimate impatience of the young. Getting to know their opposite numbers and their needs through pen-friend schemes and exchanges takes time but is a prerequisite for the success of the undertaking, which must be regarded as a long-term activity.

Projects need direction but the complexities of local situations and conflicts of interest should not be glossed over in favour of an image which, because it is over-simplified, does not reflect reality. When a theoretical image like this is set against the facts, the resulting reaction may induce an even more powerful negative image of the Third World, exactly the opposite of what is intended. Hence the importance of intellectual and emotional preparation for any action of partnership, exchange or solidarity.

Such action must be based on partnership both at home and in the Third World. An ambitious project is dependent on strong professional expertise; what is required is thorough knowledge of the area concerned, of the particular constraints and advantages and of the cultural environment. These conditions will enable appropriate exchanges that will create a momentum towards development. It is important not to be discouraged by difficulties; the aim is simply to add lucidity to a conscious commitment.

Faced with grave deterioration on a massive scale of the situation in many Third World countries, humanitarian action is absolutely vital but can be no more than a palliative. International co-operation is embodied in a multiplicity of acts of solidarity, offering comfort to the South, which no longer feels like the hidden face of the world. Solidarity also enables the North to engage in critical examination of its own development, with its increasing wastefulness, exclusion, marginalization and unemployment, leading to a developing awareness of the need to construct international relations on a new basis. It is doubtless here that the principal challenge of development education lies.

## SOME EXAMPLES OF UNESCO CLUBS IN ACTION

Not all clubs, particularly those in industrialized countries, have the opportunity or facilities to undertake projects in the field, apart from those focused on their own environment, on immigrant populations or on refugees seeking asylum. Nevertheless they can still participate in development education, through efforts to heighten awareness and to provide information and training for their members, especially the younger ones, as well as for a broader public.

In the North, partly thanks to Unesco publications, certain themes such as education, the natural and cultural heritage, the dialogue of cultures and communication problems are studied in the clubs. Members carry out research and investigations and give slide shows and video displays. Conferences and round tables attended by leading personalities, people directly involved in, or with experience of, development, are also organized on such subjects as technology and development, Third World debt or the terms of trade. There are in fact a wide range of activities centred on the problems of development. Training courses and workshops for young people from a variety of backgrounds are run in liaison with schools not only for the purpose of disseminating information but also for the preparation of development projects.

## Exchange and co-operation

It often happens that, thanks to the worldwide network of Unesco Clubs, a partnership is established between clubs from the North and clubs from the South, or between schools or universities in which the clubs are active. Twinning arrangements are set up, leading to all sorts of exchanges: exchanges of information or of visits contribute to a better understanding of the cultural environment. The importance of cultural exchanges or of exchanges of persons is fully accepted. Stimulating for the South, they help in the North, through first-hand contact with different social environments, to change the images in people's minds and to create a climate of understanding and receptiveness to the world at large.

Partnerships often engender co-operation projects. Among many examples may be mentioned participation in the construction of a women's centre at Fouankuy in Burkina Faso, of a library at Savalou in Benin and of a school in Bombay; the sending of schoolbooks to Benin and Togo; and co-operation in technical and vocational education.

Established on the initiative of Unesco, a Joint-Action Programme has been running for many years. It comprises a number of development projects submitted and set in motion by Third World countries and partly financed thanks to the participation of Unesco Clubs and Associations in industrialized countries, which are thus able to make contact and establish links with those responsible for the projects.

Examples include the establishment of an orphanage in Bolivia, improvements to the water and electricity supply systems in the Dominican Republic, a kindergarten in India, equipment for a school for the deaf in Nepal and funding for the publication of textbooks for literacy courses for rural women in Jordan.

One major Unesco project is aimed at eliminating illiteracy by the year 2000. In 1990, International Literacy Year gave this ambitious project a fresh start. The clubs in developing countries have mobilized for literacy campaigns: in Ecuador, where the clubs have extensive experience in this field; in the countries of Latin America in general and in the Caribbean; in various countries of Africa (e.g. literacy and anti-drug campaigns in Sierra Leone); and in India (health campaigns by the club at Nagpur). Here is an eyewitness report about a centre opening at N'Djamena in Chad:

> In a small hall were gathered men and women, old and young, soldiers in uniform and government employees. They seemed to get on very well with each other and I was reminded of the spirit fostered by the Unesco Clubs, a spirit of peace, equality, tolerance and mutual understanding. I heard that year the club had 500 learners in seven classes.

This kind of work is not confined to the clubs in developing countries: the Japanese Federation of Clubs has established a major programme of literacy-promoting activities in Japan itself for disadvantaged population groups and refugees (from Cambodia, for example) and in the Asia region together with the Clubs and Federation of Asia.

## Expression of solidarity

On the initiative of African federations in Togo, Benin, Mali and Burkina Faso, tree-planting camps are organized each year. These camps attract young people from various countries of Africa as well as from the industrialized countries. The Burkina Federation of Unesco Clubs organizes a tree-planting camp every year. 'The Sahel', it is said, 'is fighting against a merciless nature and desertification caused by drought and the undisciplined activities of human beings. In this struggle, trees and tree-planting are effective weapons against infertility.' In 1987, for example, 415 young participants from six countries (Benin, the Ivory Coast, France, Mali, Togo and Burkina Faso) gathered at a site in Ziniare; in addition to the planting of 6,250 trees, various cultural activities gave each participant an opportunity to discover aspects of each other's culture. This scheme involved development education, environmental education, South–South and North–South co-operation and intercultural approaches in a very enriching context.

Another interesting and original example is the creation of an experimental practical training centre at Bakel in eastern Senegal. The French Federation of Unesco Clubs, after more than ten years of exchanges and co-operation with the region of Bakel in the Sahelian part of Senegal bordering on Mauritania and Mali, joined forces with a local group to launch the idea of setting up a centre to provide practical training in Bakel. The initial objectives of this centre, which is open to the whole region (eastern Senegal, Mali and Mauritania), include the following:

- practical training for young people unable to pursue formal education, so that they can take their place in the local economy;
- the promotion of new techniques in craftwork and agriculture, in response to the challenge of drought and needs arising from changing practices;
- enhancement of the local cultural heritage;
- assistance towards the reintegration of emigrants.

The project forms part of Unesco's Joint-Action Programme. A convention has been signed between the French Federation of Unesco Clubs, the Senegalese Secretariat of State for Human Development and BREDA (Unesco's Regional Office for Africa) for building the centre. The substantial funds required come from a variety of sources: Unesco Clubs in France, Germany, Japan and the Netherlands; the French Ministry of Co-operation; and Unesco.

A five-hectare site has been allotted to the association in charge of the experimental centre (known as the CEFP), which took over ownership of the basic facilities in 1991. Once the buildings were finished, the centre came into operation. The association uses it for a wide range of activities relating to agriculture, crafts and trades, literacy and home economics. The centre is also used by outside organizations such as the GRDR (group for research and rural development) and the World Bank.

Initially, the centre concentrated on short courses in areas such as iron-forging, market gardening, cultivation with draught animals and dyeing. In 1991 it was restructured and has become a centre for exchanges and practical training. The role of the association has been strengthened and other organizations present in the area have joined as partners. A permanent technical staff has been appointed to implement the programmes of activities, which are defined each year. The staff includes a 'Volontaire du Progrès' from France. The association's General Assembly is attended by representatives of the village associations in the sub-region which benefit directly from the services provided by the centre.

The contracting partners are:

- the French Association des Volontaires du Progrès, through the assignment of a voluntary worker;
- the French Federation of Unesco Clubs, the non-governmental organization (NGO) that initiated the project, which handles the search for funding and assists the centre through its development education activities;
- the GRDR, which works in the field and provides the centre with technical back-up.

The centre can also be used by other bodies involved in development in the region.

Although its programme has four main functions (practical training, exchanges, demonstration workshops, documentation and services), emphasis is on training and the promotion of exchanges.

Courses are organized both at the centre and in the villages: 20 seminars lasting from three to ten days on market gardening out of season and in winter, cultivation of fruit-trees, farming, animal hygiene, maintenance of machinery, planting, stabilized earth construction, management of group undertakings, construction of anti-erosion devices and the fight against desertification. All in all, more than 2,700 trainee days were organized between July 1990 and September 1991.

While it cannot be denied that there have been some hold–ups and omissions, the venture has been generally successful owing to the commitment of both North and South, the quality of exchanges, local competence and outside funding.

The centre is now a tool in the hands of an association which itself groups together the representatives of user associations and enjoys the active support of NGOs and local partners. Its impact, hindered for a time by the tension between Senegal and Mauritania, is proving beneficial throughout the region. The French Unesco Clubs which initiated the project are continuing to provide support and encouragement and make frequent visits. For them it is a constant subject of discussion that is enriched by a concrete and ever-changing input.

All these activities and actions place the notion of exchange – of an exchange that induces reciprocity – at the very heart of the objectives of development education. Development education, together with its natural counterpart, environmental education, is one of the keys to understanding an otherwise unintelligible world.

To help make this world more like a world of justice, dignity and solidarity – that, it seems to me, is the moral purpose of development education.

# SOME EXAMPLES OF UNESCO CLUB ACTIVITIES IN SCHOOLS

## Promoting general awareness

### Exhibition on the island of Mauritius

The 'Association Fruits de la Passion' and the 'Échanges et Passion' Unesco Club in Toulon organized an exhibition devoted to the island of Mauritius with a view to stimulating the awareness of pupils about the problems of poor countries prior to possible action on the spot. The exhibition arose out of a lengthy correspondence with a lower secondary school in that country. This led to the idea of collecting books and games for pupils in Mauritius.

### Slide show on Africa

Under a scheme of cultural exchanges with Mali, the Unesco Club at Les Muriers, a lower secondary school in Cannes, organized a slide show on Africa at the school with the help of the CDI (local tax office), the municipal library and the CIDJ (information and documentation centre for young people). This was followed by a reading of tales by Amadou Komba, a writer from Mali, a showing of the film *Yaaba* and a visit to an exhibition on early African art.

This effort to promote knowledge about another continent has given members of the club the desire to take things further, in particular by producing a puppet show in collaboration with Togo and staging a tale from Mali called 'Tidjan'. It will not be long before this club becomes involved in action in Mali itself.

## Booklet: 'Portraits of Ethiopian schoolchildren'

The Unesco Club of the SES (special education section) in the Descartes lower secondary school in Blanc-Mesnil (Seine-Saint-Denis *département*) focused its sense of solidarity on Ethiopia. In 1988 it designed a booklet of some 50 pages made up of photos, drawings, reports and stories. The sale of the booklet, produced by the pupils with the help of professionals, aided club members to finance part of the cost of hosting five Ethiopian schoolchildren in France in May 1991, before they themselves set off for Ethiopia.

# North–South partnership in education

## The construction of a brick press in Ethiopia

In addition to producing a booklet on Ethiopia, the Unesco Club of the Descartes school embarked in 1987 on the construction of a brick press for an Ethiopian village near Chanka, the aim being to prevent the felling of trees. The project was followed up by the construction of a school in Addis Ababa. This educational action programme, called 'Tools for Ethiopia', was backed by a successful fund-raising campaign based on pledges of support. It attracted wide press coverage.

## A school with eyes on Africa

Pupils in the third and fourth years of the SES of the Descartes school have started a humanitarian aid project now being imitated by a number of similar schools in Seine-Saint-Denis. After the 1993 Easter holidays they planned to knock on doors all over the town, collecting tools for a village in Ethiopia.

Our factsheet on the hospital at Chanka shows how the problem of building materials was solved by opting for bricks of compressed earth moulded by means of hand-operated presses.

One of these presses has been made by pupils in the third and fourth years of the SES at the Descartes school and at the Debussy lower secondary school at Aulnay-sous-Bois, both near Paris. A PAE (educational action programme) of FF 5,000 has been granted by the Seine-Saint-Denis education authorities. The idea came from Dr Joel La Corre, who practises at Blanc-Mesnil, and plans were drawn up by José Condeço. The Saint-Exupéry nursery school in Sevran raised money to help pay for transport costs to Ethiopia by selling newspapers. Annie Prieur, a teacher at the Descartes school, states:

> Besides its educational value it is essentially a token gesture as we do not pretend that making this device will solve one of the major problems of Ethiopia, but we do hope to serve as a link in the chain of solidarity, and so help that country in its difficulties.

The operation is being run in co-operation with Secours Populaire, an organization which, after setting up a health centre in Chanka, is expanding its development assistance activities by building a hospital. Secours Populaire will provide technical support and has offered transportation and storage facilities for the device.

'Next year,' a teacher told us, 'it is hoped that two or three pupils will be able to travel to Ethiopia with the convoy, with the help of Unesco. What is more we are going to set up a Unesco Club, so that pupils there can become involved.'

## Exchanges with an agricultural lycée in the Ivory Coast

In 1982, the Unesco Club of the Charles Baltet agricultural *lycée* at Saint-Pouange (Aube) began participating in a scheme for co-operation between agricultural training schools and the village of Bogregnoa in the Republic of Côte d'Ivoire (the Ivory Coast). It has resulted in the construction of a dispensary, the planting of trees for fuel and the development of an area for market gardening.

In 1990 a group of students from the Bingerville agricultural *lycée* was invited to France to give a further boost to the already flourishing exchanges: later, a group of French students went to the Ivory Coast to complete the market gardening scheme. This visit included both cultural and technical activities.

## Twinning arrangements and technical training in Cameroon

The Unesco Club of the Leonardo da Vinci Lycée in Auxonne (Côte d'Or) set up a twinning scheme with a school at Garoua in Cameroon in 1990, after a long period of letter-writing between pupils.

This exchange has both cultural and technical aims: to help the Cameroon *lycée* with technical training, to develop some technological projects and to boost cultural exchange between the two countries. Two missions took place in 1990: in April French pupils went to Cameroon and in May some young people from Cameroon visited France, the purpose being to see what was happening on the spot and to give everyone a taste of different cultures.

## A pump for Burkina Faso

Members of the Third World Club at Magny-Cours (Nièvre) have been in touch with Burkina Faso for many years. In 1988, a group of pupils went there to install a solar electric fence around the garden of the rural school of Tinakoff, to fit out a third classroom and to establish a small herd to supply milk and meat. In 1990 four pupils paid another visit to Tinakoff to install a water-pump and check the condition of the equipment already installed.

This project has had financial support from the Ministry of Agriculture, the Secretariat for Youth and Sport, and various sponsors.

## A women's centre at Fouankuy in Burkina Faso

Since 1989 the Unesco Club of the general *lycée* at Chelles (Seine-et-Marne) has been engaged on a 'partnership project' under the educational action programme for the construction of an amenity/health centre in the village of Fouankuy in Burkina Faso. The project began with efforts to stimulate awareness through exhibitions on Burkina Faso, the sponsoring of children in Fouankuy, the collection of schoolbooks and other materials, and twinning arrangements.

Backed by the Burkina Federation of Unesco Associations and Clubs, by the Ministry of Co-operation and by the rectorate of Créteil, this solidarity project has been running now for several years. In 1990 those involved in the Fouankuy project participated in Burkina Faso's tree-planting campaign and finished building the amenity centre.

For the third consecutive year, pupils in the Unesco Club at the *lycée* in Chelles, in partnership with the town's college of Europe, visited Fouankuy in the summer to finish building the health centre. The seven pupils stopped in Yako, where five of them joined a tree-planting camp. The other two pupils carried on to Fouankuy, a village some 250 km from the capital, Ougadougou, where they were warmly welcomed. The villagers were looking forward to receiving medicine, clothes, schoolbooks and materials they brought with them. In this village, which had no medical facilities at all, the team set up a makeshift dispensary without a doctor to provide health care for the population, which was suffering, in particular, from an epidemic of conjunctivitis.

After being joined by the pupils in Yako, the team continued work on the health centre, under the responsibility of Mem Bicaba. Only the roof now remains to be done, but the centre will not operate effectively until a proper medical unit is established in the village to carry on the work and to train local health personnel. The project report concludes:

> It is still too soon to gauge the impact on pupils of this third camp, which has been so rich in all forms of exchange, but there seems to be a strong desire to continue with this African experiment. Fouankuy 1990 was an Adventure in Medicine for all concerned. Now we must finish the centre.

## School twinning arrangement with Benin

The Collège des 4 Arpents at Lagny (Seine-et-Marne) has been running an educational partnership with the Koutongbe lower secondary school in Benin since 1988. It was during a visit to the country and contacts with the staff, in 1989, that the Benin school's needs for textbooks and teaching supplies were identified. The Unesco Club immediately became involved in the project. Besides sending books collected from schools in the Paris region, the French side prepared a kit for the study of electrical wiring and built a pigsty in Koutongbe while continuing to keep the public in France informed by means of exhibitions and video displays.

Funds were raised within the *collège* by holding theatrical evenings and lotto parties, and outside help from local companies and various ministries facilitated the setting up of this educational action programme. Co-operation with NGOs based in France and Benin proved essential because of their knowledge of the local area. In 1989 the first exchanges between pupils took place at a work camp in Benin and then, in 1990, pupils from Benin visited France.

The aims of this North–South partnership are to improve teaching in a developing country by giving more importance to technical education, by learning about solidarity and by drawing attention to the existence of a shared language and to the many exchanges that take place between French-speaking countries. The educational action programme and its effects are alerting people to the problems of development by drawing attention to needs, the difficulties of ensuring that consignments reach their destination, and health problems.

In 1984 the Unesco Club at Ballancourt (Côte d'Or) had a meeting with the Savalou lower secondary school/*lycée* in Benin. In this African country, every school has its Unesco Club. Little by little, other Unesco Clubs, such as the Lycée Bergson in Paris and the Regional Council of Unesco Clubs of Paris/Île-de-France, are starting to support local initiatives.

In 1985 Savalou spelt out its needs: a library for the school and the renovation and equipment of the hospital. A partnership contract was drawn up between the schools which resulted in the equipping of the library in 1987 and renovation work being carried out on the hospital in 1989. Since then, a mission has gone to the town each year to ensure that the joint action plan is proceeding smoothly. This visit provides an opportunity to bring objectives into line with real needs and see that the equipment is being used properly.

The project was established with the support of several partners, including the Ministry of Co-operation, the Secretariat of State for Youth and Sport, the local authorities, private companies in the region and various associations.

## Cultural exchanges

### Burkina Faso

The Bernard Palissy Lycée in Agen (Lot-et-Garonne) and its Unesco Club introduced a development education programme in 1985 as part of the *lycée* curriculum for geography and civic instruction.

In 1985–6 they took part in the Voluntary Co-operation Forum entitled 'When pupils award grants'. The grant offered was used to buy a pump for the village of Tintane in Mauritania.

In 1986–7 the *lycée* organized a theatrical evening and a carnival in the town, the profits from which were used to fund a soil improvement and conservation project around the Koumbri Dam in Burkina Faso.

In 1988–9 the pupils in the Unesco Club carried out a PAE, 'A grain mill for Silla', in Burkina Faso. The project was awarded the Raoul Follereau prize of the Fondation de France worth FF20,000. As part of this project, the pupils used a radiotelephone to question those in charge of the Silla project, Médecins du Monde and SOS Sahel International France.

In 1989–90 a video film on 'Customs and future outlook in Burkina Faso' and a poster were produced by members of the Palissy Unesco Club, who also organized a PAE called 'A tree for the Sahel'. This was followed up by a fund-raising operation among Agen shopkeepers to finance the purchase of millet in the south of Burkina Faso. Arrangements went ahead to set up a twinning scheme with the Yamwaya Lycée in Ouahigouya, which included a consignment of books and, after an assessment of needs, the setting up of a documentation centre and a classroom for practical work. In the summer of 1990, 13 pupils and three teachers from the *lycées* at Palissy and Chelles visited Silla at their own expense to take part in a tree-planting campaign.

Recently, a PAE on French-speaking countries enabled pupils of the *lycée* to produce a book of stories and tales from the Sahel, gathered in the course of their visit in the summer of 1990. They also took part in the African Week held as a curtain-raiser to the NGO Forum in Agen.

## Tunisia

In June 1990 the Association Levons l'Encre, a pen-club at Les Lochères school in Dijon (Côte d'Or), organized a trip to Hammam-Sousse in Tunisia to enable pupils in the final year of primary education to meet their pen-friends at the Sahloul school.

This trip followed two years of joint work on subjects such as Tunisian folk tales, olive trees, dromedaries and traditional cooking. The activities also included a production on traditional ways of life in Tunisia, a 'Tunisia' exhibition in October 1990 and the hosting of Tunisian pen-friends in November 1990.

This cultural exchange was made possible by grants from the Ministry of National Education, by local authorities and by private sponsorship.

## India

The Unesco Club of the Lycée Condorcet in Montreuil (Seine-Saint-Denis) sponsored a child living in a shanty town on the outskirts of Delhi in India to make it possible for the child to attend school in the normal way. This project led the club to organize an information campaign on that country at the school and, in February 1990, a trip to India.

The information campaign was focused on India, a developing country, and at the same time served to prepare for the trip. The display was arranged by professionals and teachers and covered a variety of themes, including the culture and civilization of India, an introduction to art, a workshop on Indian writing, history and geography, and Indian literature.

Twenty pupils and three accompanying adults went on the trip, whose aims were to give practical expression to their knowledge of the culture and languages of India by living with Indian families and visiting sites on Unesco's World Heritage list, establishing contact with the humanitarian organization that operates in the shanty town of Nand Nagari where the club's sponsored child lives and, as part of the Year of France in India, giving an opportunity to young French pupils from a disadvantaged suburb wanting to know about the outside world.

# CHAPTER 15

# Education for Equality: Countering Racism in the Primary Curriculum

*Adrian Blackledge*

In proposing a new curriculum for equality it is important to recognize the common aims and objectives of anti-racist education and development education. Development education sets out to enable people to understand and participate in changes in their own lives, their community and their world. Anti-racist education is an essential and integral part of this process, with its emphasis on skills of critical questioning, conflict resolution and social justice at local, national and international levels. Lynch (1989) identifies the common ground as concern with values, conflict, justice, creative citizenship and democracy. He calls for an educational approach which addresses cultural diversity and the achievements of human justice. A curriculum for development education must have at its heart anti-racist education; such curriculum reform must be strong on discussion, persuasion, participation and justification.

This chapter provides a survey of the success or otherwise of government, local education authority and school policies in the United Kingdom designed to prepare students to live in an increasingly multicultural society. It emphasizes the common goals of development education and anti-racism, and in this context offers a philosophy and practice of education which teaches equality and justice, and considers a case-study of a year 5 (age 9–10 years) class in a large, inner–city primary school adopting this approach over two terms.

## GOVERNMENT RESPONSE TO DIVERSITY

The increase in Britain's cultural diversity has led to a series of different educational responses. The initial government response to the immigration in the 1950s of large numbers of people from the Caribbean and South Asia was to ignore them. The assumption was that if everyone was equal before the law, then black immigrants would grow to be just like the white people, and they would become invisible in a tolerant society. This strategy of making no policy was, the government hoped, helping the immigrants by not favouring them.

By 1958, however, racial tension had become apparent in British cities, and the educational response was to offer reception centres to children arriving in the United Kingdom with little or no comprehension of English. At this time the government also initiated the policy of 'bussing' immigrant children to different areas if their numbers exceeded 33 per cent of a school's population. The rationale for this response was that if there were not too many black faces in one place, they would not be a problem. This *assimilationist* approach sought to compensate for children's linguistic difficulties, while disturbing the education of the indigenous population as little as possible.

In the early 1960s educationalists began to take more account of the cultural and historical factors associated with various immigrant groups. The view developed that if teachers knew about the life style, religion and culture of their pupils then they could make allowances for their differences. But this approach, which became known as one of *integration*, still insisted that the key to success was the rapid acquisition of spoken English and socialization into English culture:

> the emphasis was still on integrating minorities with the host society and culture in order to create a culturally homogenous society.
>
> (Cohen and Cohen, 1986)

It was up to minority groups to change, not the majority society. The emphasis was almost exclusively on ethnic minority students as immigrants from other countries, rather than as part of British society. Any problems they had were seen as their own linguistic or cultural deficiencies, since they were being given the opportunity to integrate into British culture.

From the late 1960s to the early 1990s, with the emergence of second and third generations of black students in British schools and a realization that existing education policies had failed to address their needs, a new range of strategies was required. Rather than appearing in discrete stages they overlapped, and can all be found in various forms in British schools today. *Multicultural education* appeared in at least two distinct stages; *anti-racism* in schools emerged as a radical alternative, while *interculturalism*, *global studies* and *development education* all pitched their hats into the ring as the essential philosophies to prepare children for a multicultural society. I will provide an overview of the rationale and relative successes of recent policy and practice before going on to propose a strategy for the future, and to consider the work of a class of children in a Birmingham primary school.

## SCHOOLS' RESPONSE TO DIVERSITY

During the early 1970s an approach to multicultural education developed which was based on teaching about immigrants' countries of origin. Materials included songs, ethnic art and exotic costumes. Much of this kind of work was found in multiracial schools, and has been characterized as the 'saris, steel bands and samosas approach' (Macdonald, 1989), which came to be seen as tokenistic, and barely affected the curriculum in any genuine way. Many schools still exercise this kind of 'multiculturalism', for example celebrating a Diwali assembly while operating an ethnocentric curriculum. This kind of multicultural education was based on the idea that the poor performance and alienation in school of black children could be cured by improving their self-image. Stone (1981) has questioned the notion of low black self-image, while Parekh has rejected the theory that there is any single cause of the under-achievement of black children, describing such simple conclusions as 'the fallacy of the single factor' (Parekh, 1986). There was a real danger that, rather than promoting a positive view of different groups, Caribbean and South Asian cultures would be generalized as exotic, quaint and static. Lynch points out that there was no attempt to change the curriculum for all children, and that the effect of this kind of tokenistic multicultural curriculum 'may have been to strengthen the "them" and "us" perception of both or all groups' (Lynch, 1989). The emphasis was on difference to the exclusion of similarity, and social distinctions 'were sharply accentuated by mostly well-intentioned but often disastrously misguided policies and practices' (Lynch, 1989).

A platform for those who sought to extend multicultural education to the wider curriculum came with the publication, in 1985, of the Swann Report, which recommended that all cultures should be valued equally in society, and that this message should be taught in schools:

> We believe that education has a central role to play in preparing all pupils for life in today's multicultural society, by ensuring that the degree of ignorance which still perists about ethnic minority groups is not allowed to remain uncorrected and that all teachers, pupils and thus the future citizens of society are much more adequately informed about the range of cultures and lifestyles which are now part of this country.
>
> (DES, 1985)

The report insisted that in all schools, including all-white schools, the whole curriculum should be permeated with learning about cultural diversity. Attempts were made to introduce curriculum reform. For example, in some primary schools, particularly in multiracial areas, there was an explosion of interest in world religions, in cross-curricular work about South Asian and Caribbean families and homes, and in ethnic musical instruments. Largely white authorities responded by writing policies for multicultural education, but the level of commitment to their genuine implementation remains unclear. Massey (1991) suggests that many local authorities failed to present multi-cultural education as good practice relevant to all pupils, and failed to provide co-ordinated in-service training for teachers. Massey warns against the danger of 'expecting policies and initiatives themselves to function as change agents' (1991). The gap between policy and practice has dogged recent developments in multicultural education. Willey noted that:

In predominantly all–white schools, pluralist aims have made virtually no impact at all. In multi-racial schools developments have often been pre-occupied with cultural differences.

(Willey, 1984)

The realities of black–white relations in society remained little affected. In terms of employment opportunities, housing and the prevalent attitudes of a majority of the white community, black people still found themselves subjected to discrimination.

The Swann Report provided a useful lever with which to open up the curriculum to an approach emphasizing cultural diversity. Parekh (1986) is forthright in his argument for a move away from the monocultural curriculum, which 'damages and impoverishes all children, black and white'. Parekh adds a word of warning, however, counselling against narrowness and dogma in teaching about cultures, advising sensitivity and sympathy, allowing cultures, religions or societies to speak for themselves. It may be because schools have not always heeded this advice that curriculuar multicultural education has been criticized from both radical and conservative quarters.

# CULTURE IN EDUCATION

The report of the Macdonald Inquiry (1989) questioned the central tenet of multicultural education by arguing that the notion of valuing 'other cultures' was misplaced. Culture was, said Macdonald, not the neat package of food, dress, music and language that was being conscientiously taught in thousands of schools across the country, but included

the work patterns and life styles of people and how they deal with employers, landlords, schools, families and so on, in a society which is divided into hierarchies according to such factors as race, sex, class, age and geography.

(Macdonald et al., 1989)

Macdonald also questioned Swann's assumption that if people understood each other's cultures, then racial conflict would gradually disappear. This formed part of a sustained critique of multicultural education by those who felt that for all its respect of other cultures, discussion of black people's place in British society was being deliberately ignored. Willey argued that 'multicultural policies have uniformly failed to address the central influence of racism' (1984). Cohen and Cohen protested that the cultural pluralist position

fails to confront what is regarded as the cardinal influence on the life situations of ethnic minority groups in Britain, that is racism.

(Cohen and Cohen, 1986)

# RACISM IN SCHOOLS

Multicultural education, by avoiding the racist structure of society, left racism not merely untouched but strengthened. It was now possible for policy-makers, having dealt with the problem, to feel that they no longer owned responsibility for the needs of black people. The complacency created promoted the view that black children were provided with a positive self-image, while their white peers had become more hospitable. There was a call for an approach to education for cultural diversity that was more rigorous in questioning the power structures of society and the place of black people within them. Massey (1991) and Swann (1985) noted widespread evidence of racism in schools, while Banks (1986) found that from their early years when they first come to school some children have 'anti-democratic attitudes' which tend to harden if steps are not taken to make them more democratic.

The New Right, in particular Flew (1987), regard anti-racist education as revolutionary, arguing that racism is a natural human condition, and educational underachievement is due to black pupils' cultural deficiencies. Jeffcoate (1979) opens the door to this point of view, stating that to exclude racist attitudes from the classroom is an infringement of freedom to speech, and that to deny racists the opportunity to express themselves is anti-democratic. These criticisms are based on the notion that institutional racism does not exist, and therefore does not need to be challenged. Lynch (1989) notes that the failure of anti-racist education to draw on the traditions of prejudice reduction through development education left practitioners exposed to this kind of offensive.

Perhaps more importantly, there is little evidence that parents were consulted in the rapid development of anti-racist policies. The Council of British Pakistanis spoke for two thousand members in expressing reservations that lack of consultation with the community could build up

> a stereotype of the underprivileged 'Paki' . . . it is possible that this stereotype will be accepted while the message is ignored.

> (1984)

A telling and coherent critique of anti-racist education is provided by the Committee of Inquiry into Racism and Racial Violence in Manchester schools, which was set up after the murder at Burnage High School of Ahmed Iqbal Ullah in September 1986. While defending anti-racism as a principle, the report criticizes anti-racist policies as practised since 1981 on several fronts. The report suggests that anti-racist practice was often symbolic rather than real, and was therefore meaningless. The report insists that an anti-racist curriculum must involve the whole community:

> It has become ever more evident to us that anti-racism in symbolic gestures is meaningless and can clearly reinforce racism. If the school does not involve the total community, teachers, ancillary staff, students and

parents, both black and white, in the efforts to tackle racism in school, the whole exercise will end in failure.

(Macdonald et al., 1989)

At Burnage High School this failure finally had tragic consequences. The report says that anti-racist policies in the 1980s characterized black students as victims, and white students as racists. These policies led to white students feeling under attack, and bore little relation to black students' experiences or needs. Anti-racist education, said Macdonald, had been 'an unmitigated disaster', because it oversimplified a complex set of human relations, and slotted them into a black versus white pigeon-hole.

This brings us to a position when tokenistic multiculturalism has been discredited as patronizing; where curriculum multiculturalism has failed to address issues of equality; and where anti-racist education has been practised in an over-simplistic way which bore little or no relation to the needs of black or white students. What, then, for the future of anti-racism/multiculturalism? If the radical critique is pursued to its logical conclusion, then the school, as a reflection of the social structure, is not the place in which to help bring about equality. Such pessimism, however, is misplaced. If education alone cannot make structural changes in society, then it can at least promote social criticism and critical thought. It is this philosophy of education for equality that we must carry forward as the central tenet of curricular reform to challenge racism in the 1990s and beyond.

# TOWARDS EDUCATION FOR EQUALITY

Carrington and Troyna (1988) emphasize that planning to reform the curriculum must involve the community: 'The active involvement of parents in the development of initiatives . . . seems to us to be the most appropriate way forward.' The Burnage Report, which bemoans the lack of a successful model of multicultural education for the future, nevertheless approves of good practice in which students are making decisions and exploring relationships, equality, gender and race, while developing critical questioning skills alongside self-confidence (Macdonald et al., 1989). Massey (1991) provides further impetus to the notion of a multicultural curriculum as a process for growth, one which focuses on critical awareness and respect for others; which exposes children to a variety of value systems, encouraging them to 'explore them, question them and develop their own responses to them'. Here is the basis of curriculum reform which pulls together the best of educational practice of recent years in its emphasis on learning skills for equality and democracy.

# EDUCATION FOR DEMOCRACY

What of the content and pedagogical method of such an approach? In a recommendation which has sometimes been overlooked, the Swann Report advocated political education as a means of countering and overcoming racism at both institutional and individual levels:

> Effective political education should also lead youngsters to consider fundamental issues such as social justice and equality and this should in turn cause them to reflect on the origins and mechanism of racism and prejudice at an individual level.

(DES, 1985)

Education for equality has a major part to play in providing a curriculum to counter racism. The content of a curriculum designed to teach skills for democracy and equality must go beyond a traditional 'environmental studies' approach. There must be an explicit commitment to subject matter which enables children to confront inequality and to learn skills of critical questioning. Singh (1988) points out that teachers cannot take an entirely value-free position, as their commitment is towards both educational and moral values. Therefore the content they make available should offer opportunities to consider democracy and justice. The Macdonald Inquiry was impressed by work in Manchester schools which enabled young people to develop a project about the boxer Len Johnson. Issues of women's rights, racism, the Irish question, class – all these were explored by the students, who developed skills in history, geography, humanities, drama, art, language. In a creative project which emphasized the student's interests and involved decision-making, the committee said:

> we clearly have before us the essential elements of good educational practice . . . We see it very much as an example of good practice and as a model of anti-racist practice for the future.

(Macdonald et al., 1989)

# CURRICULUM CONTENT

Duncan (1988) also insists on a meticulous approach to curriculum planning. If the Crimean War is the topic, then Mary Seacole is as much (if not more) the heroine as Florence Nightingale; Martin Luther King, Gandhi, Nelson Mandela are essential figures in twentieth-century history: 'black pupils need black heroines and heroes to model themselves on' (Duncan, 1988). I would go further and suggest that black heroines and heroes are heroines and heroes to all children in all schools. Duncan gives examples of relatively recent school reference books which seek to deny the history of African people. He abhors the ethnocentric curriculum, and insists that since the planned curriculum is powerful in the formation of attitudes, it must be free of racism in what it omits and what it includes: 'In short, an anti-racist multicultural approach to the curriculum is vital' (Duncan, 1988). Massey (1991) supports this view, reminding us that a multicultural curriculum is not one which simply passes on 'lumps of a variety of cultures'.

Care must be taken, then, to ensure that curriculum content emphasizes equality and provokes a questioning attitude. However, there must be more to curriculum reform than its content. Teaching methods as well as content selection must be attended to if good practice is to be established. Massey (1991) argues for a wide range of co-operative and collaborative learning techniques. Lynch points to research which shows significant correlations between co-operative learning and academic achievement, insisting that the latter is a prerequisite for any successful reform, and that 'Equality and excellence can be pursued at the same time and in the same curriculum' (1989). The point is salient: if we are proposing a curriculum for equality which does not push children to the limits of their potential, then we are failing them. It is a criticism which has been levelled at anti-racist/multicultural approaches in the past, whether justly or not. It must be inadmissible in future.

If we are proposing a curriculum for racial equality, then, it is essential to plan carefully and ensure that themes include opportunities for critical questioning, reference to social justice, involvement in the community, attention to global concerns, and consideration of similarities and differences between peoples of the world, all within a co-operative and collaborative learning context. Carrington and Troyna (1988) look to anti-racist education as a constituent of a more broadly based programme of political education, which 'celebrates negotiation rather than imposition; co-operation and collaboration in preference to competitive individualism'. Children must be taught to be critical, questioning, active participants in society, and catalysts for change. Although many teachers are sceptical about the possibilities of such an approach within the constraints of the recently introduced National Curriculum in the United Kingdom, I will offer a case study of a year 5 class (9 –10 years old) whose learning largely arose from a curriculum for equality, but which also met the criteria of government legislation.

## CASE STUDY

The class in question consisted of 30 mixed-ability children. Most of the children were of Mirpuri-speaking Pakistani descent, while a smaller number were from Sylheti-speaking Bangladeshi families; others included children of Malaysian and Afro-Caribbean families. The school had previously adopted a 'multicultural/anti-racist policy'. This spoke of creating an anti-racist environment in which children's languages and home cultures were valued, and children were taught to ask critical questions. The school was in the process of updating this with an 'equal opportunities policy statement'. There were a number of different levels of commitment to a curriculum for equality evident in the school. The work of the class in question therefore did not necessarily exemplify a whole-school approach to racial equality policies, but rather represented a stage in their development. The school favoured a cross-curricular, thematic approach, and was at this time very much concerned to fulfil government requirements to meet statutory curriculum guidelines. The prescribed school themes for year 5 were pollution and conservation (autumn term) and hidden messages (spring term). The 'pollution' topic got under way with the children and teacher together establishing existing knowledge about the theme, and developing starting-points for investigation. Although the aims of the thematic work were to provide learning opportunities in a range of curriculum areas, particularly science, technology and geography, emphasis would also be on encouraging children to ask critical questions about their environment, and to begin to take responsibility for the development of their local community. If they could discover something of the democratic processes affecting changes to their area, their learning would encompass education for social justice and racial equality.

The class walked around the local area, making note of and classifying observed pollution. At a local supermarket, recently closed down, the children found asbestos dumped in split bags in the car-park. They took photographs, and sent the evidence, with carefully worded letters, to the Environmental Health Department. Notes of noise pollution, air pollution, water pollution on canals and erosion of buildings beside the motorway led to research work on acid rain and letters to environmental organizations.

In the classroom groups of children recycled paper and researched the effects of deforestation. A piece of waste land was noticed close to the school. The children made a detailed survey of the land, and discovered that it was very polluted. They decided that the area should be improved, and used to serve the community. The children worked collaboratively, in mixed-ability groups, to provide comprehensive proposals for the best use of the waste ground. Discussion was dynamic, and occasionally heated. Negotiation, persuasion and compromise were very much in evidence. Ideas were imaginative and interesting; for example one group proposed to build a new mosque where Pakistanis, Bengalis and Malaysians could pray and learn together. Other proposals included a wildlife park, a swimming pool and an adventure playground.

Small groups of children went to the homes of parents and other local residents; children interviewed the residents, mainly women, in their home language, with mini tape-recorder to hand, asking them what they thought of current proposals for the development of the piece of land. Here parents were not merely asked to passively support the children's development work, but became an essential and active part of the project. Children returned to school, played back their interviews, and interpreted and summarized their findings. There was discussion of whether the parents had previously been asked their views on this matter. Already these children were learning about local development issues, and the place of the community in planning decisions.

The children had written to the local Resident's Association and learned that the piece of land was to be used by the local professional football club as a coach park. Children designed questionnaires for parents, asking whether they had been consulted, then invited to the classroom members of the Residents'Association and the City Council Planning Committee. A councillor duly attended and inspected the children's models and plans of their proposals most carefully, and answered their questions with concern, saying that he supported them, but that a majority of councillors on the committee had approved the football club's planning application. He also answered questions about the local democratic process, and the proportions of black and women councillors sitting in the City Council.

A great deal of preparation was required of the children in the formation of appropriate questions, and in the presentation of printed proposals. A visit to the council chamber was arranged, and the children wrote letters to the chairman of the football club. Other forms of lobby were played out in enthusiatic and committed drama sessions. During these sessions the children were able to develop skills of debate and questioning in a dynamic but unthreatening context. A group of the children also noticed that there was a competition for schools involved in community environmental projects, sponsored by a morning television station. They wrote for details, refined their proposal, edited and presented it on word-processor, and entered.

Although the children's project did not immediately effect a change, they learned a great deal about power, local consultation and the democratic process. The skills they used for finding out, interpreting and presenting information were learned effectively because their motivation was high. If criteria for developing a curriculum for equality include learning about social justice, democracy, decision-making and critical questioning, then these children were working through such a curriculum. Their growth as individuals and as a class was notable, and the academic standards achieved in, for example, interviewing adults in the community, and presenting professional-looking proposals to the city council and national television, were remarkable.

Singh (1988) suggests that a crucial stage of children's development is 'the inculcation of sound critical thinking'. There is no doubt that these children developed a critical attitude to their environment, and to the democratic process which shapes their community. They took greater strides forward because they were involved in a project they believed in: for equality, social justice and the improvement of their local environment.

The topic of 'Hidden Messages' was more classroom based, and was largely concerned with gender issues. Using photo-resource packs, in conjunction with world studies materials, children developed awareness of assumptions about women and work, women in the home, women in history, and the presentation of women and girls in children's literature. Once again most of the work was carried out collaboratively, while opportunities were always available for the most able children to extend their skills.

Initially the children considered photographs of women in traditional and non-traditional roles, added captions, debated and discussed questions arising, and wrote stories from the perspective of women in a variety of situations. It was important that children were allowed the time and space to talk to each other, and to adults in the classroom, about their opinions and assumptions, without predetermined dogma demanding that they conform to its views. Children read and researched, and wrote and illustrated information books about Rosa Parks, Winnie Mandela, Millicent Garrett Fawcett and Dora Russell. This collaborative work led to groups pursuing work on the suffrage movement and the civil rights movement in the USA.

There was once more a high level of commitment in extended drama sessions, when children and teacher in role-play made decisions about how to bring about equality of employment for women. These sessions engendered such enthusiasm in children and teacher that they would often last for a whole afternoon. Issues of bias in advertising were considered, using a range of media including magazines and television. Two of the children decided to devise a questionnaire to discover from teachers reasons why, in their opinion, there were only two male staff in a team of 25 in the school. There was consideration of women's roles in other cultures, especially drawing on the children's and families' knowledge of society in Malaysia, Pakistan and Bangladesh. Positive images of women in Britain were looked at, and letters sent to women MPs. Children considered gender bias in reading schemes and in traditional folk-tales and fairy-stories; they wrote their own, non-sexist versions of both, once more working collaboratively in groups.

If this topic did not involve the children in actively altering their environment, or engaging explicitly with racism throughout, it certainly led them to ask critical questions, to consider the justice of the status quo, to challenge the place of women in society, and to respect those who take a non-traditional role. In the careful planning of the theme, curriculum content was selected which would enable children to develop critical thinking; the variety of pedagogical models employed allowed them to work collaboratively, while demanding the highest academic standards.

No effort was made to force children to adopt rigid principles, though they were certainly aware of their teacher's commitment to equality of opportunity. It was far more important that the children learned how to think and evaluate than that they learned what to think. Skelton (1988) notes that the principles of co-operation, democracy and egalitarianism which are central to anti-sexism form the basis of the learning experiences provided for children in the primary classroom. In establishing in children an open, questioning attitude rather than an immutable dogma, the project laid the foundations of skills for discussion, debate, persuasion and co-operation.

There is little doubt that this class, over two terms, developed skills in language, science, geography, history, drama and technology to a higher level than they would have if they had been less committed to their work; that is, if it had been less meaningful to them. However, this is a subjective assessment, and Massey (1991) warns against a less than rigorous evaluation. He argues that schools should build race equality issues into their assessment policies, using 'performance indicators' which are developed in conjunction with headteachers, advisers and parents. He also reminds us that National Curriculum assessment and testing must not be allowed to inhibit education for equality.

Blyth (1989) suggests that thematic work can have a built-in assessment procedure, and that skills, concepts and attitudes can be appraised by asking children, for example, to 'submit a serious proposal for the development of a patch of waste land'. Assessment of the child and evaluation of the curriculum must be rigorous, and must be integrated within planning. Teachers will need to make judgements about the value and effectiveness of the reforming curriculum, the strategies they adopt and the outcomes of classroom work for equality. Equity and excellence must be pursued together, with neither falling behind in favour of the other.

The junior class I taught were taking steps along this road, and there is no reason why the same approach cannot be modified to suit the needs of early years or secondary students; nor should significant modification be required for children in mainly white schools. If we can reject dogma and tokenism, then a curriculum can be created which emphasizes social justice, cultural pluralism and the global environment; in short, we will have strengthened the framework of development education by the introduction of skills for democracy and equality, and the growth of sensitive attitudes necessary to identify and challenge injustice.

# REFERENCES

Banks, J. (1986), 'Multicultural education and its critics', in Modgil, S. et al., *Multicultural Education: The Interminable Debate*, 221–31, Lewes: Falmer.

Blyth, A. (1989), 'Process, content and assessment in primary humanities', in Cambell and Little, *Humanities in the Primary School*, Lewes: Falmer.

Carrington, B. and Troyna, B. (1988), *Children and Controversial Issues*, Lewes: Falmer.

Council of British Pakistanis (1984), 'Voices from the other side', *Multicultural Teaching*, **11** (2).

Cohen, L. and Cohen, A. (1986), *Multicultural Education*, London: Harper & Row.

Department of Education and Science (1985), *Education for All*, The Report of the Committee of Inquiry into the Education of Children from Ethnic Minority Groups (The Swann Report), London: HMSO.

Duncan, C. (1988), *Pastoral Care: An Antiracist/Multicultural Perspective*, London: Blackwell.

Flew, A. (1987), *Power to the Parents*, London: Sherwood Press.

Jeffcoate, R. (1979), *Positive Image: Towards a Multiracial Curriculum*, London: Writers and Readers.

Lynch, J. (1989) *Multicultural Education in a Global Society*, Lewes: Falmer.

Macdonald, I. et al. (1989), *Murder in the Playground*, London: Longsight.

Massey, I. (1991), *More Than Skin Deep*, Sevenoaks: Hodder & Stoughton.

Parekh, B. (1986), 'The concept of multicultural education', in Modgil, S. et al., *Multicultural Education: The Interminable Debate*, 19 – 31, Lewes: Falmer.

Singh, B. (1988), 'The teaching of controversial issues: the problems of the neutral chair approach', in Carrington, B. and Troyna, B., *Children and Controversial Issues*, Lewes: Falmer.

Skelton, C. (1988), 'Demolishing "The House That Jack Built": anti-sexist initiatives in the primary school', in Carrington, B. and Troyna, B., *Children and Controversial Issues*, Lewes: Falmer.

Stone, M. (1981), *The Education of the Black Child in Britain: The Myth of Multi-racial Education*, London: Fontana.

Willey, R. (1984), *Race, Equality and Schools*, London: Methuen.

# CHAPTER 16

# Two Approaches to Development Education in Finland: The Baltic Sea Project and Education in Human Rights

*Liisa Jääskeläinen and Solveig Lindberg*

This chapter addresses two approaches to development education in Finland, the Baltic Sea Project and Education in Human Rights. The general co-ordinator of the Baltic Sea Project, Liisa Jääskeläinen, highlights some key issues in this regional project, designed to create an international network between schools. The Baltic Sea Project focuses on environmental issues, sustainable development, and education for international understanding. The second Finnish initiative, a project on Education in Human Rights, was introduced to all schools in 1988. It is described here by Solveig Lindberg, from the perspective of a teacher in a participating school.

## THE BALTIC SEA PROJECT

The Baltic Sea Project is primarily an attempt to focus attention on the need for improved environmental education in the Baltic coastal states. The countries bordering on the Baltic share many environmental problems, one of which is pollution of the Baltic Sea. These problems can only be solved by co-operation among those countries, which have different languages, cultures, habits, traditions and technical standards. In attempting to solve the environmental problems, education is one of the key factors. The Baltic Sea Project (BSP) had therefore initiated co-operation among schools in all the countries around the Baltic. These include Denmark, Estonia, Finland, Germany, Latvia, Lithuania, Poland, Russia and Sweden.

Today, some 200 schools are active in the BSP. Most are secondary schools situated on the Baltic coast. In many schools, the BSP has been organized as a cross-curricular initiative; most often the work has concentrated on science. The working language is English.

## Aims of the BSP

The BSP will work to create a new kind of co-operative practice between educators from countries having similar environmental problems, who are prepared to educate students to contribute to solving environmental problems. The project aims at developing school-specific, national and international models for action by the following means:

1  To increase the awareness of the students about the environmental problems in the Baltic Sea area and to give them an understanding of the scientific, social and cultural aspects of the interdependence between humankind and nature.

2  To develop the ability of the students to study changes in the environment.

3  To encourage students to participate in developing a sustainable future.

The project has sought to achieve its goals by:

- building a network of schools, teachers and other educational institutions;
- creating and developing common programmes for environmental education and international education;
- organizing joint activities and events;
- publishing the BSP newsletter (ASP/INISTE, 1990–2) and other relevant information.

## Organizational framework of the BSP

For the purpose of promoting international understanding, Unesco established an Associated Schools Project (ASP) in 1953. The aims, concepts and main contents of international education are defined in the 1974 Recommendation concerning Education for International Understanding, Co-operation and Peace, and Respect for Human Rights and Fundamental Freedoms. The recommendation includes environmental education within international education.

The International Environmental Education Programme (IEEP), launched by Unesco jointly with the United Nations Environment Programme (UNEP) in 1975, was in 1990–1 in its seventh biennial phase. The Unesco General Conference and UNEP's Governing Council have emphasized the supreme importance of environmental education.

In 1984 Unesco established an International Network for Information in Science and Technology Education (INISTE) to promote exchanges of information and co-operation between member states in the field of science and technology education. In many cases INISTE is supported by national networks.

All the Baltic coastal states take part in the Associated Schools Project and the INISTE network. The ASP schools and the INISTE are an interesting and challenging pair. What value would science and technology education have if it did not further sustainable development? How could sustainable development be effectively furthered without the contribution of science and technology education?

In 1988 Unesco invited ten Member States from different parts of the world to participate in an inter-regional project (IRP), to ensure an improved multiplier effect of results obtained through the Associated Schools Project. The participating member states are Argentina, Australia, Bulgaria, Chad, Finland, Germany, the Republic of Korea, Thailand, Trinidad and Tobago, and Tunisia. Launching BSP as a pilot project for the IRP was Finland's special contribution to the IRP. The IRP network formed the inter-regional institutional framework for the BSP during its formative stages.

## Global perspectives and the BSP

Our local, national and regional policies must adapt rapidly to global requirements and global policies. At all levels human activities must adjust to the global situation through radical changes in the use of energy and natural resources, in international relations and trade, and in life styles.

Despite all our good intentions, our methods of building communities, producing artefacts and allocating energy have become the cause of widespread destruction to the living surface of our planet. Our fragile planetary home is suffering from the greenhouse effect, decreasing ozone in the upper atmosphere, the acidification and pollution of soil, the pollution of the marine environment, the exhaustion of natural resources, the daily disappearance of species of plants and animals, and gross inequality between human beings. The problems are caused by humans and they can only be changed by humans.

In December 1987, the General Assembly of the United Nations accepted a resolution concerning the implementation of sustainable development, contained in a report from the World Commission on Environment and Development called *Our Common Future*. The resolution urged the governments of Member States and UN special agencies to embark upon action to ensure that promotion for sustainable development begins to be furthered in the activities of authorities, plans of operations and budgeting.

Sensitizing human minds to the need to reach a state of sustainable development is the critical challenge to international education and science and technology education in ASP and INISTE schools.

# History and background of the BSP

The BSP's ethical and organizational roots were provided by the international community and can be traced in various ways. For the formulators of the BSP the following events have been significant.

## 1948

UN Universal Declaration of Human Rights.

## 1953

In 1953 the Unesco Associated Schools Project (ASP) was launched with 33 secondary schools from 15 states dedicated to practising the ideals and principles of international understanding and peace.

## 1972

Recommendation No. 96 of the first United Nations Conference on the Human Environment in Stockholm proposed the preparation of an international programme relating to environmental education both in school and out of school, having an *interdisciplinary* approach and embracing all levels of education.

## 1974

Also as a follow-up to the UN Conference in Stockholm, in March 1974, the seven Baltic States signed the Convention on the Protection of the Marine Environment of the Baltic Sea Area, also called the Helsinki Convention.

In November 1974 the 18th session of the General Conference of Unesco adopted the Recommendation concerning Education for International Understanding, Co-operation and Peace, and Education relating to Human Rights and Fundamental Freedoms.

## 1975

In January 1975 the International Environmental Education Programme (IEEP) was launched jointly by Unesco and UNEP and was followed by an international workshop on environmental education held in Belgrade and organized by Unesco.

## 1977

A regional meeting of experts on environmental education in Europe was held in Helsinki with 29 member states attending. The 'working group for environmental education at the pre-school, primary and secondary levels' pointed out that there were some major constraints to the development of environmental education in schools and cited the following:

- Schools are subject matter orientated, and environmental education is interdisciplinary.
- Schools tend to avoid values education, and environmental education emphasizes valuing processes.
- Schools tend to avoid social issues and controversy, and environmental education emphasizes schools' and community problem solving.

- The school programme is already crowded and some administrators and teachers view environmental education as yet another subject area.

The educators of the 1990s are invited to evalute how much school practice has changed since this meeting.

In October 1977 the first Inter-governmental Conference in Environmental Education was held at Tbilisi in the Georgian SSR. This conference was the culmination of the first phase of the International Environmental Education Programme (IEEP).

## 1980

The Helsinki Convention came into force and the governing body of the convention, the Baltic Marine Environment Protection Commission (the Helsinki Commission), was established.

# Launching the BSP in 1988

In December 1988 Unesco convened an International Consultation of the Associated Schools Project in Bangkok (with ten member states participating), to launch an inter-regional project (IRP) aimed at ensuring a greater multiplier effect of the results of the ASP. At the Bangkok consultation it became evident that a whole series of ASP regional and sub-regional environmental projects should be launched. The consultation concluded that Finland could co-ordinate schools with projects concerning the pollution of the Baltic Sea; that Bulgaria could co-ordinate schools with projects to help solve the pollution of the Danube; that the Federal Republic of Germany with Chad and Tunisia could co-ordinate schools around the problem of the growth of the Sahara; and the ASP schools in Asia would start a project around ecological problems caused by deforestation, flooding, drought and soil erosion.

## 1989

In April 1989, the Finnish National Commission for Unesco convened the International Consultation in Helsinki concerning an environmental education project on the Baltic Sea. The consultation on the Baltic Sea Project (BSP) was attended by 17 representatives of the National Commissions for Unesco from all the Baltic States, with Norway as an observer. In the opening address the Chairman of the Finnish National Commission for Unesco, Mr Erkki Aho, pointed out that in the BSP, a component of education for international understanding can be derived from Unesco's Associated Schools Project (ASP), while Unesco's International Network for Information in Science and Technology Education (INISTE) could provide the elements of science.

The Norwegian National Commission for Unesco organized a regional environmental education workshop for European ASP teachers at Lillehammer in May 1989. The Lillehammer Workshop examined different aspects of the ASP and produced the following interpretation of the aims of environmental education:

1  To reinforce children's innate love of nature;

2  To encourage an ethic of respect and responsibility for the environment;

3  To give knowledge and develop attitudes and abilities that will enable students to participate actively in protecting and improving the environment;

4  To develop a lifelong commitment to environmental protection;

5  To promote a holistic understanding of all sides of environmental problems at the global and local levels as a basis of solving them: 'think globally – act locally';

6  To stimulate new patterns of behaviour and life styles that are consistent with equitable and ecologically sound management of world resources;

7  To increase awareness of regional environmental problems and the necessity for solidarity and co-operation among all European countries to solve them;

8  To promote a responsible role of Europe in the world community in solving global environmental problems. In Lillehammer it was also decided to write a handbook on environmental education for European teachers.

In August 1989 the second Nordic Conference on Science and Technology Education was held at Heinolain, Finland. Among the issues discussed was the need to realize environmental science projects that would help implement the Baltic Sea Project (and the North Sea Project).

Also in 1989 two especially important Unesco Declarations were agreed. From the Ivory Coast, the International Congress on Peace in the Minds of Men produced the Yamoussoukro Declaration and from Canada, the Conference on Survival in the 21st Century produced the Vancouver Declaration. The Vancouver Declaration highlights four key issues facing humankind:

• an accelerating increase in population growth over the past 150 years from 1 billion to over 5 billion with a current doubling time of 30–40 years;
• a comparable increase in the use of fossil fuels leading to global pollution, climate and sea–level change;
• an accelerating destruction of the habitat of life, initiating a massive and irreversible episode of mass extinction in the biosphere – the basis of the earth's ecosystem;
• an unimaginable expenditure of resources and human ingenuity on war and on the preparation for war.

The Declaration traces the origins of the problem and suggests some alternative visions for our planet, rooted in a variety of cultures:

Such visions change the conception of man in nature and call for a radical transformation of models of development; the elimination of poverty, ignorance and misery; the end of the arms race; introduction of new learning processes, systems and mental attitudes; implementation of better forms of redistribution to ensure social equity; a new design for living based on a reduction of waste; respect for biodiversity; socio-economic diversity, and cultural diversity that transcends outmoded concepts of sovereignty.

(Unesco, 1989)

The Vancouver Declaration points out that 'time is short – every delay in establishing a world eco-cultural peace will only increase the cost of survival'.

## Educational approach and joint programmes of the BSP

The educational approach of the project has been guided by four general principles:

1   To achieve a balance between a holistic view and individual subject studies;

2   To change the role of the student from passive recipient to active constructor. To change the role of the teacher from supervisor to guide in a learning process;

3   To use networks to provide participants with opportunties to learn and pass on new ideas;

4   To use international co-operation as an inherent element of school work.

The joint programmes have focused on water quality (Coastwatch BSP), the Baltic Sea Schools' Research Campaign with HELCOM, and the users of the Baltic Sea (Baltic Sea 2000).

## International contacts

The success of the BSP can be measured partly through the international contacts that have been established; these have varied a great deal and include the exchange of correspondence, exchanging exhibits and videos, and exchange visits between participating schools. During these visits the students usually study a local environmental problem together. International co-operation has been consolidated through events such as an international BSP youth camp in Kiel, Germany in 1991 and an international workshop for teachers and students in Kotka, Finland in 1992.

The project plans to publish a BSP teacher's guide and to initiate a research campaign during the 1993–4 school year, concluding with an International BSP Conference in Karlskrona, Sweden in September 1994.

# EDUCATION IN HUMAN RIGHTS

In 1987 the Finnish National Board of General Education collaborated with the United Nations Association and Unesco in a pilot project on human rights education in 11 schools. In 1988 the project on education in human rights was extended to all Finnish schools to mark the 40th anniversary of the Universal Declaration of Human Rights. The aims of the project were to enable students to:

1  understand what human rights are;
2  use human rights as a criterion in daily life, judgement of news, world events, development issues (Osler, 1988: 24–5).

This section describes how one school began to explore the meaning of education in human rights.

## School context

Katedralskolan in Turku is a school which prides itself on having roots in the oldest school in Finland, the cathedral school of the Middle Ages. It is an upper secondary school leading to the matriculation examination. It has about 180 pupils and some 20 teachers, which is fairly typical of Finnish upper secondary schools. It is a school for the Swedish-speaking minority in Turku. Finland is a bilingual country and although only about 6 per cent of the population speak Swedish as their mother tongue, this minority has the same linguistic rights as the majority. This allows Swedish-speaking children schools of their own.

Working in a minority school in Turku gives us certain benefits. We work under the same conditions as the majority schools, but since the Swedish minority in Turku is very small, we all live in close contact with the Finnish-speaking population. Most of our pupils are therefore more or less bilingual. Thus our pupils have access to two cultures, which, although similar, still show certain variations.

## International approach

Perhaps this awareness of language and culture is one of the reasons why it has been very easy to interest our pupils and teachers in international contacts. Ever since the Katedralskolan of today came into being as an upper secondary school in 1976 we have aimed at giving the pupils an international outlook and a feeling of international responsiblity. It was therefore quite natural that we were eager to become a Unesco school and that we were very happy when we were accepted.

Becoming a Unesco school has influenced the atmosphere in the school a great deal. We are grateful to Unesco and the Finnish Board of Education for the help and inspiration we have received. It has also meant getting a partner school in Hungary. We are in close contact with the Hungarians and we have had some unforgettable exchanges of pupils with them. Now we also have a partner school in Kenya. This school works on an afforestation programme, to which we give some annual financial help.

## Learning through projects

In 1978 one of our teachers went to a course on project work at schools. This resulted in our first project, where all the pupils and teachers worked together on the theme 'Mass Media'. Although we were quite inexperienced, the project was a success and we decided to continue and develop project work. In the years to come we had one project on 'Latin America', another on 'The Theatre through the Ages' and one on 'Africa'. In the spring of 1988 some Finnish schools were asked if they were willing to work out a programme to celebrate the 40th anniversary of the Declaration of Human Rights. Katedralskolan was one of these schools. The staff decided that, if the pupils were willing to do so, we would participate with a project week on 'Human Rights'.

## Planning for education in human rights

In the spring we called a meeting of the whole school. The idea of having such a project week in the autumn was first suggested and then we were all asked to write down everything we knew about human rights. Most of us very quickly noticed that there was room for improvement. After some ten minutes we were asked to form groups of six and come up with suggestions about what we would like to know about the subject. The suggestions were then discussed for some minutes and we agreed to do a project on this theme.

It was also agreed that we would deal with human rights in Finland. We did not want to depend on books and reports from other countries, we wanted to meet people in our own surroundings. We also wanted to show that human rights is something that concerns all people, no matter where we live. We also decided to use five days at the end of October for the project.

The next big meeting was held about one month before the project was to take place. We then recalled what we had decided in the spring, drew up some outlines and elected a committee to take care of the more detailed planning. The committee consisted of three teachers and three pupils, one from each age group. This committee met three or four times before the project started.

# Human Rights project week

About two weeks before the project was due to begin we put up a huge sheet of paper on a wall. The pupils and teachers were asked to write down everything they could think of concerning human rights, possible and impossible ideas, and suggestions. This sheet of paper hung on the wall for about a week. The working committee then sorted out the suggestions and made up some 30 proposals for group work. Some examples:

*Ethnic minorities*

1 Lapps;

2 Jews;

3 Turkish immigrants;

4 Gypsies;

5 Evacuees from Karelia, the part of Finland that was lost after World War II;

6 Today's refugees: (a) Chileans; (b) Vietnamese;

7 The Swedish minority in Finland.

*Non-ethnic groups:*

1 Men/women;

2 City people/country people;

3 People with disabilities;

4 Old people;

5 Conscientious objectors;

6 Sexual minorities;

7 Juvenile offenders;

8 Discharged prisoners;

9 Hidden immigrants (foreign people working in Finland as individuals, and foreigners married to Finns);

10 The Declaration of Human Rights (background, history, situation today);

11  Documentation group (video recording and written report of the project).

# Group work

Now another big sheet of paper was hung on a wall with all the topics of the group work. The pupils were asked to put their names under the topic they wanted to work with. After some discussion it was decided that the teachers should form a group of their own. The rules were:

1  There should be both boys and girls in all groups.

2  There should be people from all age groups.

3  Best friends were encouraged not to work in the same group.

4  The pupils were asked to choose an alternative, in case they could not be placed in the group of their first choice.

When this sheet was taken down, the working committee met again and made the final division into the groups. Two teachers promised to be responsible for all the material needed, paper, crayons, material for the overhead projectors, video tapes, and cassettes.

The project week then began with a meeting where the participants were given information and could ask questions about things they felt uncertain about. We agreed to work between 8.30 a.m. and 2.30 p.m. regardless of normal schedules. Three days should be used for group work and two days for reporting to the whole school. Suggestions for the reports were given and the pupils were informed that all groups should have to give a report. No group could get up and read a written report, though. Video tapes, music, cassettes, journals, paintings and drama were suggested.

Most of the groups worked very hard and many of them used a lot more time than the agreed six hours a day. They went out into the city and interviewed people in the streets. They visited libraries and newspapers, old people's homes, the prison, the police, and they went to see social workers and refugees.

# The rights of people with disabilities

One group had chosen to investigate the situation of people with disabilities. During the first day they planned their work, decided to use video for their report and planned what they should record and how to do it. The next day they went to the library and collected facts on various handicaps, and compiled what they had learnt into an introduction to their film.

On the third day they went out into town with a video camera. One girl simulated blindness with dark glasses and a white stick. The rest of the group mingled with the people in the street. The 'blind' girl then tried to cross the street but seemed not to be able to do so. The first time no one came to help her, so she had to be rescued by a group member. The second time she did not have to wait very long. Most people just stared at her, but a friendly alcoholic came up to her and not only helped her across the street, but also offered to walk with her to the place she was going.

Another girl went out into town in a wheelchair and tried out various difficult situations, like using a public call-box, for instance. Everything was recorded on video and shown during the reporting. A group member commented on their work: 'I don't think that we know what it is like to be born blind or to sit in a wheelchair, but at least we have an idea about what it feels like. And personally I have learned from this.'

## Evaluation

For two days we watched and listened to the group reports. Some of them were very good, some gave rise to a very lively discussion afterwards, some touched us deeply, some shocked us when we realized how little we had known before. And, of course, some reports showed that the group had not taken their work as seriously as they should have done. But is there a school where all the pupils do their very best every day? It was also quite evident that the two or three lazy groups were ashamed when they saw the results of the others.

The last item on the programme was an assessment of the whole project in the form of a discussion with all the participants. Some themes gave rise to a heated discussion and new ideas came up. We all agreed that we had learned a lot, that we had enjoyed the week and that the feeling of togetherness had increased during the project.

## Guidance for planning projects

Some points that we found important if a school wants to go in for such projects:

1  All normal teaching should stop. The pupils and the staff should concentrate on the project only.

2  It should be the pupils' project in the first place. They should be responsible and they should not have the feeling of being watched over and manipulated by the teachers.

3 It should not be over-organized, so that the participants are tired and scared of it before it starts. The creativity of the participants should not be limited by too many rules and strict timetables.

4 Teachers and pupils should work together as equal members of the groups.

This autumn we will have a new project week. This time it will be on the myths of the world, the origin of humankind and the world. We hope that it will be a project where we can use a lot of art, music and drama. We hope that it will give us a chance to stop and think about life and we hope that we will find how many things there are that unite us, the peoples of the world.

# REFERENCES

## Baltic Sea Project

ASP/INISTE (1990/1992), *The Baltic Sea Project Newsletter*, 3 vols, Helsinki: Associated Schools Project and International Network for Information in Science and Technology Education.

Unesco (1989), *Vancouver Declaration on Survival in the 21st Century*, Unesco.

## Education in human rights

Osler, A. (1988), *Development Education in Secondary Schools*, Report of European Teachers' Seminar at Bolu-Abant, Turkey, September 1987, Strasbourg: Council of Europe.

# Index

and ethnic minorities 37, 42
Sivard, R. L. 12
Skelton, C. 259
Skills: cross-curricular 168;
development of in primary
schools 201–2
Small-group work 202
South, the 53–4; development
models of 65–7, 68; images
of in geography textbooks
75–6, 80–3; media portrayal
of 114–21; see also 'Third
World'
Spain, environmental
education 103–4
Speaker's Commission on
Citizenship 27
Starkey, H. 23, 44, 45, 97
Stereotyping: of ethnic
minorities 37–8; in
geography textbooks 80; in
modern language teaching
92, 95, 99, 109
Stobart, Maitland 23
Stone, M. 39, 251
Sutherland, M. 177
Swann Report (1985) 39–40,
41, 251, 252, 253, 255
Sweden: cross-curricular
projects 5–6, 153–65; human
rights education 25–6;
National Curriculum 153–4,
165

Tanzania, study visit to 6,
222–32
Taylor, P. J. 68
Teachers: and INSET 143–5;
and media education 121,
126–30, 131; in partnership
with NGOs 4, 5, 58–9: and
geography 73–4; primary
school in Ireland 203, 205;
primary school in Kenya
214, 215–16; study visit to
Kenya and Tanzania 6,
222–32
Teaching, quality of 178
Textbooks: geography 4,
74–86; stereotypes in 92
Thant, U 12
Thelin, Bengt 25–6
Themework: in Irish primary
schools 198–201; see also
Whole-school themework
'Third World': and
development education 235;

geography textbooks on
74–6; human rights and
democracy 14–15;
limitations of term 53;
relations with Europe 34;
young people's images of
237–8; see also South, the
Third World Centres 14
Thomas, O. G. 116
Toh Swee-Hin 67, 68
Tomlinson, Sally 43
Tourist brochures, used in
modern language teaching
97–9
Townley, C. 1, 51, 68
Troyna, B. 38, 254, 256
Tunisia, cultural exchanges
with France 248
Tunstall, J. 115
Twinning arrangements, and
French Unesco Clubs 245,
246–7

Underdevelopment 65, 67–8,
75, 233
Unesco: Associated Schools
Project (ASP) 263, 264, 265;
and human rights education
in Finland 269, 270;
International Network for
Information in Science and
Technology (INISTE) 264;
recommendation (1974)
17–18; Vancouver
Declaration (1989) 267–8
Unesco Clubs 6, 233–48:
activities in schools 243–8;
cultural exchanges 247–8;
Joint-Action programme
240, 242; literacy campaigns
240–1; objectives of 236–7;
tree-planting camps 246
United Kingdom (Britain):
Asylum Bill (1991) 43; and
citizenship rights 43; ethnic
minorities in 37; human
rights education 26–8;
International Human Rights
Day (1981) 21–2; and
multicultural education 36;
origin and growth of
development education
12–14; Race Relations Act
(1976) 37; racism 35; see also
National Curriculum
United Nations (UN): concept

of 'right to development'
20–1; and Danish peace
education 188; definition of
development education 1,
51, 68–9; Universal
Declaration of Human
Rights 11–12, 44; see also
Unesco
Universal Declaration of
Human Rights 11–12, 44,
173
User involvement model 226

van der Gaag, N. 115, 116,
118, 119
Vancouver Declaration (1989)
267–8
Vietnam war 13, 14, 17
Voluntary Committee on
Overseas Aid and
Development 14
Voluntary organizations 56

Wahlstrom, Per-Ake 14
Ward, Barbara 19
Watching the World 125–6, 131
Waugh, D. 80, 83, 85
Webster, J. R. 213
Whole-school themework 5,
135–49; and assemblies 139,
142; choosing a theme
139–40; and displays 145–6;
factsheets for 141–2; global
approach to 138–9; and
INSET 143–5; in Ireland 200
Wiles, P. 113, 115, 120
Willey, R. 251–2
Williams, J. 38
Women, and development
education 2
World Bank 242
World Conference of Teaching
Professions (WCOTP) 2
World Decade for Cultural
Development (1988–1997)
237
World Development
Movement 14
'World in Action' (television
documentary series) 115
World Studies Project 8–13, 15,
19
Worldaware (formerly Centre
for World Development
Education) 14
Worldview 78–9, 81, 82, 85
Wright, D. 74–5, 80